The Practical Guide to Aging

The Practical Guide to Aging

What *Everyone* Needs to Know

Editor
Christine K. Cassel, M.D.

Developmental Editor
George A. Vallasi

New York University Press
New York and London

Library of Congress Cataloging-in-Publication Data
The practical guide to aging: what everyone needs to know / edited
by Christine K. Cassel : developmental editor, George A. Vallasi
    p.   cm.
  Includes bibliographical references and index.
  ISBN 0-8147-1515-X
  1. Aged–United States–Life skills guides. 2. Aged–United
States–Family relationships. 3. Aged–United States–Social
conditions.   I. Cassel, Christine K. II. Vallasi, George A.
HQ1064.U5P676 1997
646.7′9′0973–DC21   97-21571
                                                  CIP

While every attempt has been made to make all the information in this book as accurate and up-to-date as possible, conditions, medications, and human knowledge change. Before making a final decision on any substantive matter covered in this book, you should seek the advice of an appropriate professional.

The opinions and suggestions contained in this book are solely those of the individual authors and do not necessarily reflect those of their affiliated organizations, which are given for identification purposes only.

New York University Press books are printed on acid-free paper, and their binding materials are chosen for their strength and durability.

Contents

vi   Contents

Grow old along with me!
The best is yet to be . . .

Robert Browning *Rabbi Ben Ezra* (1855)

George A. Vallasi is Vice President of Chernow Editorial Services, Inc. and specializes in the development of reference and resource materials. He conceived of and developed the *Encyclopedia of Artificial Intelligence* and was coeditor of the *Columbia Encyclopedia*, 5th ed., the *Concise Columbia Encyclopedia*, 2d ed., and the *Reader's Adviser,* 13th ed. For these projects, he coordinated the selection of subjects to be included, wrote customized software, and designed a number of solutions to problems involving desktop publishing, bibliographic verification, and author-generated word-processing files. He is now developing a series of resource projects for the mass market and is exploring new ways to use computers to disseminate information. When time permits, he enjoys cooking for friends and listening to classical and big band jazz music.

Acknowledgments

There are a number of people who, during the time this book was being planned, written, and edited, contributed generously of their time and talents. They have been of great impact and the writers and editors feel it is a better book for their help. Although not every suggestion was incorporated, every voice did make us rethink, reevaluate, and refine our work in some way. We wish to thank Jerry H. Gurwitz, M.D., of the Meyers Primary Care Institute, University of Massachusetts Medical Center and the Fallon Healthcare System of Worcester, Massachusetts, for his timely advice; Paula Rochon, M.D., of the Bay Crest Centre for Geriatric Care in North York, Ontario, for her review of the material on pharmaceutical treatments; Scott Weiner, R.Ph., of New York, for his help with pharmaceutical labels; Heyward Ehrlich, Ph.D., of Rutgers University, for always taking the role of our intended reader and telling us what he would like to learn; Carol L. Kandall, M.D., Ph.D., of New Haven, for her careful reading of several chapters and her recommendations; M. Cindy Hounsell, Executive Director of WISER, Women's Institute for a Secure Retirement, Washington DC, for her assistance with retirement planning; Nathan Bluestein and the late Blanche Chernow, whose problems suggested the need for this book; Colin Jones, former Director of New York University Press, for committing to this project; his successor, Niko Pfund, for his enduring patience during several delays; and my partner, Barbara Chernow, Ph.D., of Chernow Editorial Services, for her continual support, understanding, prodding, and indefatigable forbearance.

Christine K. Cassel, M.D., is Chairman of the Department of Geriatrics and Human Development and Professor of Geriatrics and Medicine at the Mount Sinai Medical Center. Before that she was Professor of Medicine and Public Policy Studies, Chief of the Section of General Internal Medicine, Director of the Center on Aging, Health, and Society, Director of the Center for Health Policy Research, Director of the Robert Wood Johnson Clinical Scholars Program, and George M. Eisenberg Professor in Geriatrics at the University of Chicago. She is a past president of the American College of Physicians, Physicians for Social Responsibility, and the Society for Health and Human Values and is chair of the American Board of Internal Medicine and Vice Chairman of the Board of the Greenwall Foundation. She is a member of the Institute of Medicine of the National Academy of Sciences and the Association of American Physicians and has been appointed to the President's Advisory Commission on Consumer Protection and Quality in the Health Care Industry. Her more than 100 journal papers display expertise in aging, health policy, bioethics, the social impact of genetics, and demographic and epidemiological forecasting. Among her books are the textbooks *Geriatric Medicine*, *Ethical Dimensions in the Health Profession*, and *Approaching Death: Improving Care at the End of Life*. She has served as a consultant to the Veteran's Administration, the Institute of Medicine, the Health Care Financing Administration, the National Institute on Aging, the Agency for Health Care Policy and Research, and the United States Congress. She lives in New York City with her husband, a public health physician.

Introduction

Christine K. Cassel

In the United States and other developed countries we take it for granted that most people can expect to live well into old age. Not only do we take it for granted, we may dread it, and joke about how we wish we could avoid aging. We rarely, if ever, stop to realize that this expectation of a full life span is a recent miracle of the twentieth century. In the year 1900 average life expectancy in the United States was 47. Most children died in infancy or in childhood of infectious diseases, many women died in childbirth, and in general premature death was a familiar part of life for all families. Life expectancy in this country has almost doubled in this century, and US longevity is exceeded by at least 15 other countries around the world. This remarkable accomplishment is unprecedented in the history of the human race, and has occurred in a relatively short period of time. No wonder we do not have obvious solutions to the challenges of the aging society—challenges ranging from the family and community to the state and federal level, challenges including medical care, education, transportation, work, housing, financial planning, intergenerational relationships, and spiritual life—to name a few.

The advances in life expectancy are due in part to better living conditions, in part to the advances in health behaviors, and in part to advances in medical care. If we are to truly appreciate these extended lives and added years we must understand the dimensions in all three of these areas in which individuals can help to make the quality of life better for themselves as they care for aging parents and to improve the likelihood that their own aging years will be happy, productive, and meaningful ones.

Until relatively recently, most Americans did not like to think about aging. We considered ourselves a youth-oriented society characterized by "the Pepsi generation." That is changing now, however. The first baby boomers have now turned fifty and are beginning to encounter aging in their own parents and in themselves. Most people in their fifties and many even in their sixties now are faced with issues related to aging parents. This too is a new reality made possible by improved health status, but it has raised many important issues with which society has not dealt before, and many important challenges for individuals and their families, for which there has not been clear guidance. These include the formation of wills, advance directives, and health care decision-making.

President Clinton began wearing a hearing aid in 1997 at the age of fifty-one because he was having trouble distinguishing conversation in crowded rooms. This is a manifestation of presbycusis, a condition probably exacerbated by exposure to loud noises (he acknowledges enjoying rock music). More research needs to be done on ways to treat hearing impairment related to aging but there is no doubt that it is a very common disorder. Americans are caught up in debates about prevention of aging by taking Vitamin E or DHEA, but too often ignore obvious ways to protect important functions we all need as we age. As young people we take hearing, vision, and strong bones for granted. We focus more on health risks where mortality risk is high—such as heart disease and cancer. This is good, but not enough. We will all live longer as we postpone death from heart disease or cancer, but those added years will not be good ones unless we sustain function and quality of life as much as possible.

Care of one's hearing, vision, and physical activity to maintain bone and muscle strength are easy and important measures to improve the likelihood of successful aging. However, we do not have total control over our health as we age. For example, we do not really know how to prevent Alzheimer's disease—but we are learning more every day. Aging-related disabilities have carried a stigma, causing people to avoid discussing issues such as dementia, falls, or urinary incontinence. Without seeking help, people may suffer unnecessarily with conditions that can be ameliorated or even reversed with good medical care. Many social analysts believe that now that the baby boomers are beginning to experience aging for themselves, the stigma may be lessened and people may begin to have more interest in health promotion, social policy related to aging, and intergenerational interactions.

This book is a guidebook for all of us who are at the brink of this aging society, at every age. It gives practical information to help people understand the medical issues that they and their family members face as well as many other important dimensions. One of the most important lessons we teach young physicians about the aging process is how health depends on many things other than medicine as we age. Many chapters of this book demonstrate that truth most vividly.

This book came about as a partnership of many people, the chapter authors, the developmental editor, George Vallasi, and the Chernow Editorial Services staff. I owe them all gratitude for their hard work and thoughtful suggestions.

The Practical Guide
to Aging

Cathryn A. J. Devons, M.D., M.P.H., is a geriatrician at The Mount Sinai Medical Center in New York City, where she is an Assistant Professor at the Medical School and is an attending physician in the Coffee Geriatric Practice. She is also the director of medical student training for the geriatrics department of Mount Sinai and the geriatric consultant for the Phelps Memorial Hospital Center in Sleepy Hollow, New York. An avid lover of the outdoors, she enjoys running (two New York City marathons), skiing, and rollerblading. She lives in New York City with her physician husband, the director of clinical research in cardiovascular drugs for a major pharmaceutical company, and their dog, Lexi.

Better Aging Starts with You

Cathryn A. J. Devons

Since 1900, the proportion of the United States population older than 65 years of age has grown from 4% to more than 12%. More than 30 million Americans are over the age of 65, and and this number is rapidly growing. With the aging of the baby boomers and their children, projections indicate that by the year 2030, 22% of Americans will be older than age 65. In fact, the fastest growing subgroup of the elderly is the "oldest old," those over 85 years of age.

As a result, older people are developing a new attitude. Growing older is not an end to a productive life, but the beginning of a new style of living. They are not only concerned with living longer, but with remaining active, productive, and independent. Although aging inevitably brings about changes, it should not necessarily lead to a diminished ability to enjoy life.

To remain healthier for a longer period of time, older people are practicing preventive medicine and participating in health education programs. Not that long ago, it might have seemed paradoxical to discuss health promotion and disease prevention in the elderly. But, the increase in life expectancy and the knowledge that many of the changes traditionally associated with aging are more reversible than previously thought, have made prevention an important theme in geriatric medicine today.

"Normal" vs. Successful Aging

One characteristic of the aging population is the great variation in the physical and mental well-being of its members.

3

In fact, as people age, they become less, not more, alike. Many body changes that are considered "normal" were traditionally regarded as irreversible. These include changes in vision, hearing, blood pressure, heart function, and bone density. Now, however, people recognize that the way in which one changes physically and mentally is influenced by many factors, including genetics (heredity), environment, personal habits, diet, and psychological makeup. Thus, many of these "normal" changes can be modified by adjustments in behavior patterns.

The willingness to make these adjustments is part of "successful aging," a concept promoted by John Rowe, a renowned geriatrician who is president of the Mount Sinai Medical Center in New York. By not accepting all bodily changes as normal, one can learn to "age more successfully." For example, the "usual changes" that occur in the heart, such as coronary artery disease, can be minimized or even avoided by a low-fat diet and exercise. Other examples of turning "normal aging" into "successful aging" include taking calcium and exercising to prevent osteoporosis, having cataract surgery to improve vision, and avoiding sun exposure to prevent skin cancer.

By practicing preventive medicine, older persons can focus on aging in the most successful way possible for them as individuals.

The Importance of Preventive Medicine

In many cases, prevention should begin long before the age of 65. Life-style changes, such as a healthy diet and exercise, cannot begin too soon in a person's life, but it is never too late to start. Even after age 65, preventive medicine can significantly improve a person's quality of life.

What are the greatest health threats to the older population? What preventive steps can be taken to reduce the risks and minimize impact of such diseases? Statistics show that heart disease, stroke, and cancer together account for three quarters of all deaths in the over-65 population. Of the chronic diseases that affect older persons and inhibit their lifestyles, arthritis, hypertension, heart disease, memory loss, and vision and hearing impairment rank among the most common. By following the preventive positive health measures outlined in this chapter and other parts of this book, a number of diseases can be avoided, and people with chronic conditions, can work to reverse them or at least keep them from worsening.

Primary Prevention

The first line of defense is always to identify and reverse risk factors that may predispose a person to developing an illness. Sometimes such primary prevention requires a physician's care or instruction, but people can also practice many preventive techniques themselves.

The best example of primary prevention involving a physician's care is the prevention of infections by use of vaccinations, a practice that has been most successful with children. In fact, the eradication of many infectious diseases of childhood through vaccination programs is one of the triumphs of American medicine. Unfortunately, this record of accomplishment has not yet been matched in the case of older adults. However, all elderly people should take advantage of the three most widely recommended vaccinations: influenza, pneumovax, and diphtheria/tetanus.

Influenza and pneumococcal infections (a common cause of pneumonia) are significant causes of illness and even death among the elderly. Effective and safe vaccines against both types of infections have been developed, and should be used more widely than they are.

Each year three virus strains are selected for inclusion in the influenza vaccine. Because the vaccine is not live, you cannot acquire the infection from the vaccine. The only contraindication (reason not to receive it) is an allergy to eggs. All elderly persons, others at high risk, and health care workers should receive an annual vaccination in the fall.

The pneumococcal vaccine, called pneumovax, protects the body from 23 types of pneumococcus infections. Because of the devastating consequences of pneumonia in the elderly and the chronically ill, this vaccination is a particularly important preventive measure. We do not know exactly how long the vaccination is effective, but currently recommend that all older persons receive the vaccine once after reaching age 65. There is no known danger in receiving the vaccination twice, and for some people, a doctor may recommend a repeat vaccination after ten years.

Finally, it is important to continue to receive a diphtheria/tetanus booster every ten years.

Individuals may practice primary prevention themselves by maintaining a health lifestyle, which can help avoid many illnesses. It is important to keep your weight at a healthy level and eat low-fat, low-salt, and high-fiber foods. Keep as active as possible, following a program of planned physical exercise at least three times a week. Minimize the risk of skin cancer by staying out of direct sunlight and using protective lotions. When necessary, recognize the need to adapt to certain changes, such as slower reflexes. Be careful when driving—know your limits and always wear a seatbelt. Similarly, be sure your home is safety proofed, with adequate lighting and a bathroom equipped with handrails and other safety features. Minimize alcohol use, stop smoking, and remember that safe sex is important at any age!

Secondary Prevention

Secondary prevention consists of treating an existing condition or disease so that a more serious condition does not develop. For example, proper treatment of hypertension can reduce the risk that the patient will later suffer a stroke. Thus, early diagnosis of existing problems is necessary for effective secondary prevention. An annual physical examination and personal awareness are your best tools in achieving this goal.

Probably the most important example of secondary prevention is the early detection of cancer, before the lesion site has a chance to grow or metastasize (spread to other sites in the body). Cancer is the second leading cause of death in the elderly; 50% of persons who die from cancer are elderly. Several criteria are used to determine which cancers are most amenable to screening. Generally, these cancers are fairly prevalent, can be detected by a simply screening test, have an impact of the patient's quality of life, and have a known course of treatment. All the cancers that geriatricians routinely screen for have a very high cure rate if detected early.

The American Cancer Society offers the following recommendations for screening examinations for persons over age 65. To screen for breast cancer, all women should perform monthly self-examination of their breasts, have a yearly physical examination by a physician, and have an annual mammogram. After age 65, cervical cancer should be screened for annually with a Papanicolaou (Pap) smear until three or more are negative. At that point, based on personal history, a physician may decide screening is no longer necessary. However, women should still have an annual pelvic examination. All men should receive an annual digital rectal examination, as well as a blood test for PSA (prostate specific antigen). All older persons should be screened for colon cancer by having a an annual rectal examination by a physician, checking the stool for occult (not visible) blood, and having a sig-

The Checkup Checklist

The frequency of tests described below can vary according to the individual's medical problems and family history. This chart is meant to be a general guideline only and not a substitute for the particular recommendations of an individual's physician.

Self-examination (Ask your physician to train you in these tests)

- **Skin.** Look for growths, change in size or color of existing moles, and discolored portions of skin. Monthly.

- **Mouth.** Look for growths, irritated sites, and discoloration. Monthly.

- **Breasts.** Feel for unusual lumps. Monthly.

- **Testes.** Feel for unusual lumps. Monthly.

Physician examination

- **Eye examination.** Should include screening for glaucoma, cataract, and retinal degeneration. Annually

- **Cholesterol screening.** Frequency depends on the individual's history.

- **Hearing evaluation.** As needed.

- **Screening for hypertension.** A blood pressure reading should be taken every time you visit your physician.

- **Rectal examination and stool guaiac test.** These two brief exams for colon and rectal cancer should be performed annually.

- **Flexible sigmoidoscopy.** Every 3–5 years.

- **Pap test.** Annually, may stop after 3 or more negative tests after age 65 at discretion of physician.

- **Pelvic examination.** Annually.

- **Mammogram.** Annually.

- **Manual breast exam.** Annually.

- **Rectal examination of prostate and blood test of prostate specific antigen (PSA).** Annually.

Dental checkup

- **See your dentist annually.** Even if all the natural teeth are gone, denture fit should be checked.

moidoscopy every 3 to 5 years. Other parts of the body that should be carefully examined during every annual physical examination include the lymph nodes, the skin, and the mouth.

Changes in Body Appearance and Composition

The first perceived signs of aging usually include loss of strength and stamina, farsightedness, hearing loss, baldness in men, and menopause in women. Changes in some facial dimensions result from continued bone growth in the skull and the lengthening of the nose and ears.

In addition, people may find they are shorter—a normal height loss. The amount varies from person to person depending on heredity and the presence of osteoporosis. Some loss of height is natural, as is a slight bending of the back in advanced age, but this change can be minimized by taking calcium and vitamin D, taking estrogen if indicated, exercising, and treating osteoporosis when it occurs.

Another visible change can occur in body weight. Although people frequently gain weight during middle age, weight generally declines in later life. The composition of the body also changes, with a decrease in muscle mass and an increase in fat. These changes can be modified by eating sensibly and continuing to get regular exercise.

Other changes in the composition of our bodies cannot be seen with the naked eye, such as changes in the molecules that make up our cells, which affect all of our organs and tissues. For example, as our immune system begins to work less effectively, we become more susceptible to illness. Because the immune system sometimes fails to recognize our bodies as our own, a greater number of autoimmune diseases are seen with advancing age.

The Senses

Of all the senses, good hearing and vision are the most important for maintaining independence in old age. Because some of these problems appear gradually, people often accept the change as part of the aging process. However, many vision and hearing losses can be corrected or minimized with external aids, medication, laser treatment, or surgery. Because sensory losses can cause isolation, create a barrier to communication, and place a tremendous burden on an older person, annual vision and hearing examinations are recommended. For a more detailed discussion of serious vision and hearing impairments, see the chapter, "Medical Problems of the Elderly."

Vision

As a person ages, normal changes in the eye can result in visual impairments—some more severe than others, some more preventable than others. These changes include reduced flexibility of the lens, cataracts, macular degeneration, diabetic retinopathy, and glaucoma.

For example, as a person ages, the lens of the eye becomes thicker and heavier. This reduced flexibility, which results in a loss of accomodative ability, can cause problems with near vision. It is a determining factor in presbyopia, which literally means "old eyes." Presbyopia is the reason why older people need to hold reading material farther and farther away. More than 90% of people over the age of 75 become affected by presbyopia.

A second normal change that has adverse consequences is cataract formation. Cataracts occur when the eye's lens becomes clouded, obscuring vision (the name suggests the physical result, vision appears as seen through a waterfall or cataract). Protecting the eyes when in bright sunlight can help in preventing this condition. Cataracts, however, can be treated effectively by surgical removal and lens implantation.

Macular degeneration is a common cause of partial vision loss in older persons that causes a loss of central vision. Affected persons have to rely on peripheral or side vision. The cause is traced to changes in the tissue of the retina, which is responsible for transmitting visual images to the brain. New evidence suggests a link between macular degeneration and cigarette smoking. In some cases, laser treatment may result in some improvement in vision, but in most cases visual loss is permanent. This is a disorder that needs an aggressive approach to research.

Diabetic retinopathy, which is caused by changes in and destruction of tiny blood vessels in the retina, is a complication of long-standing diabetes. Laser photocoagulation has been proven useful in preserving sight, thus making an annual check-up with an ophthalmologist a necessity for all diabetics.

Glaucoma is characterized by increased pressure inside the eye, with resultant visual field losses. People with glaucoma lose peripheral vision, or the ability to see things from the side. For reasons that are not well understood, African Americans are particularly at risk for developing glaucoma. Screening for the condition is extremely important as if it is left untreated, it can lead to irreversible blindness. Several medication eye drops are available that can effectively lower this increased pressure.

Hearing

About a quarter of people over the age of 65, and half of those over age 80, have impaired hearing. Persons who have had prolonged exposure to loud noise or who have had many ear infections are more susceptible to hearing difficulties in later life. Some people who are suffering from hearing loss may have a buildup of ear wax, or cerumen, which is exacerbating the problem. Ears should be examined and cleaned of excess cerumen prior to audiologic testing.

Presbycusis, which is a decreased ability to hear at higher frequencies, is the most common form of hearing loss among the elderly. Devices that amplify sound are the most effective way to correct prebycusis, particularly with recent improvements in hearing aid technology. For persons who do not want a hearing aid, assistive listening devices that amplify sounds into headphones are relatively inexpensive and can be very useful for amplifying conversations and listening to television, plays, and concerts. Televisions are now equipped with a "closed caption" feature and there are also devices that can be installed in a telephone to amplify the conversation.

Taste and Smell

The senses of taste and smell work closely with one another. Indeed, it is often difficult to distinguish between the two. Most studies indicate that olfaction, or the ability to smell, does decline with age. The primary causes are respiratory infections, head trauma, and nasal congestion. Studies of age differences in taste sensitivity also reveal some age-associated decline, but this loss is thought to be minimal. Although elderly persons are more likely than younger persons to have isolated areas of loss of taste, the overall ability to taste is largely preserved. The number of taste buds does not decline and most complaints of loss of taste are actually the result of an impaired ability to smell.

If the senses of taste and smell do become diminished, the older person should pay particular attention to maintaining good nutrition, as appetite may also be impaired. One also has to be careful about the loss of ability to detect spoiled food, leaking gas, and smoke. Thus, carbon monoxide and smoke detectors in the home are a necessity.

Teeth and Gums

Proper hygiene of the teeth and mouth are essential for many human functions, including the ability to speak, chew food, and even smile. A few generations ago, nearly all older people eventually lost most of their teeth. But improvements in dental care offer a greater chance for tooth preservation. The most common oral problems, dental caries (cavities) and periodontal (gum) disease, can be avoided with appropriate preventive programs. Among the measures·that should become part of your routine are the use of a soft-bristle toothbrush, flossing, antiplaque rinses to reduce gingivitis and other oral infections, and fluoride treatments, even if started in adulthood, to prevent tooth decay. In addition, a professional dental hygienist should clean your teeth every six months.

The Skin

For many people, wrinkled skin heralds the onset of aging. The epidermis and the dermis, the two outermost layers of the skin, become thinner, and the separation between them diminishes. In addition, the amount of collagen, which is a protein found in the dermis, decreases, as does the number of elastin fibers, which provide elasticity. There is also a loss of fat under the skin. As a result, the skin develops a tissue-paperlike appearance. By pinching older skin gently on the back of the hand, one can see that it takes a longer time than previously to return to normal. These changes give the skin a wrinkled look and make it more susceptible to such injuries as bruising and tearing. A lifetime of unprotected sun exposure can accelerate these normal changes. In addition, cigarette smoking exacerbates facial wrinkles.

Delayed Skin Healing

As people age, wounds take longer to heal, and the strength of the healing skin is reduced until recovery is complete. The factors that affect healing time include a decline in the immune and neurologic systems, which delays inflammation after exposure to an irritant. This slower response time may cause excess harm to the skin after exposure to a toxic substance. Aging may also result in impaired nerve function, which can diminish sensitivity to pain and result in a longer reaction time. As a result, burns are more serious in older people.

Dry Skin

Dry skin, called xerosis, along with the resultant itching of the skin known as pruritus, is one of the most common problems older people experience with their skin. With all people, skin is driest in the colder, less humid months of winter. However, this problem is more prevalent in the elderly because of the decrease in normal secretions of skin glands and the effects of poor blood circulation. Dry skin can cause flaking, redness, and rashes. Treatment includes avoiding hot water and harsh soaps, using of moisturizers and humidifiers, and drinking plenty of liquids.

Benign Skin Growths

With advanced age, the number and kind of benign skin growths increases. Most commonly, these include noncancerous growths and "age or liver spots." Seborrheic keratoses are wartlike raised lesions with a "stuck on" appearance and cherry angiomas are bright red, small spots. It is not usually recommended that these types of lesions be removed.

Skin Cancer

Skin cancer is the most frequent form of cancer among Caucasian people. Generally painless, it can cause serious illness if neglected. The most common type of skin cancer, basal cell cancer, looks like a clear, waxy nodule. Squamous cell cancer looks more like rough, scaly skin, and often grows in sun-damaged areas. The most serious, and often life threatening, form of skin cancer is malignant melanoma. This skin cancer appears like a dark mole. The warning signs of skin cancer include a rapidly growing, new or large mole or skin growth, with irregular borders or different colors, or possibly with bleeding or ulceration. Consult your physician if you observe any questionable changes in your skin.

Prevention

The best prevention for accelerated signs of aging skin and skin cancers is avoidance of ultraviolet radiation. This includes proper clothing in sunshine, such as the use of hats, avoidance of the midday sun, and the regular use of a sunscreen with an SPF of 15 or more. Regular skin self-examination and examination by a physician are also advisable.

Changes in Temperature Regulation

Advancing age is associated with a progressively diminished capacity to regulate body temperature. This is caused by the loss of fat beneath the skin, which usually acts to insulate the body, and a less effective circulatory system. This explains why elderly people tend to become colder more quickly than younger people. Medical conditions, such as diabetes, hypothyroidism, or Parkinson's disease can further impair the body's ability to regulate temperature.

Hypothermia

Older people are at an increased risk for accidental hypothermia, which occurs when the body's temperature falls below 95 degrees. Even a relatively short exposure to cold or damp conditions can cause this condition in an elderly person. For example, accidental hypothermia can result when a frail person falls into a deep sleep because of alcohol consumption or the use of sleeping medications. It can also occur if a frail person falls asleep next to an air conditioner. Because the consequences can be very serious, and may affect the heart, hypothermia is considered a medical emergency.

Hyperthermia

Hyperthermia is also a serious risk to an older person's health. Unlike younger people, who experience hyperthermia as a result of overexertion in the heat, older persons frequently do not sense a rise in the temperature around them. Because older people have fewer sweat glands, which normally work to keep the body cool, and can neither recognize nor respond to heat as well as younger people, the elderly are at an increased risk for heat stroke. As with accidental hypothermia, alcohol and sedatives increase this risk. Immediate medical treatment to bring the body temperature down must be sought if hyperthermia occurs.

Changes in Sleep Patterns

Older persons are often plagued by sleeping problems, including trouble falling asleep and frequent awakenings that prevent them from receiving a good night's rest. A common misconception is that elderly people need less sleep than younger persons. In truth, many elderly people complain that a lack of sleep at night makes them tired during the day. The result is frequent napping. Studies of the elderly have shown that despite spending more time in bed, total sleep time decreases. At approximately age 50, the amount of deep sleep also begins to decline.

Although common among the elderly, sleep problems should not be accepted as a normal part of aging. A number of approaches can help alleviate the problem.

Among the least desirable is the use of over-the-counter sleeping medications or prescription sleeping pills. In general,

Recommendations for Improving Your Sleep

- **Establish a sleeping routine.** Try to go to bed and get up at regular times.

- **Make sure your sleeping area is conducive to sleeping.** The bed should be comfortable, the room dark, the temperature neither too hot nor cold, and excess noise eliminated as much as possible.

- **Make yourself comfortable.** Wear loose pajamas or a nightgown — do not fall asleep with clothes on.

- **Eat and drink sensibly before bedtime.** Avoid big, heavy meals before bedtime. A light bedtime snack or warm milk may prevent middle-of-the-night cravings. Do not drink caffeine-containing drinks (e.g., coffee, tea, cola) in the evening. A single alcoholic drink may help relax you, but more may have the opposite effect (as well as cause other problems).

- **Avoid waking in the night to urinate.** Do not drink a lot of fluids in the evening. Empty your bladder before retiring. If you take diuretic medications (water pills), ask your doctor if you can take them in the morning. If you suffer from incontinence, discuss it with your physician.

- **Use the bed only for sleeping and sex.** If you like to relax by reading or watching television before bedtime, do it in another room.

- **Avoid excessive napping.** This can disturb the sleep-wake cycle, and make sleeping at night harder.

- **Try to get regular exercise.** It is good for your overall health, and will help you to feel sleepier at night.

- **If illness hinders sleep, consult your physician.** Pains, indigestion, or shortness of breath that either prevents you from falling asleep or wakes you up from sleep need medical attention.

- **If anxiety or depression hinder sleep, consult your physician.** These are medical problems that should be treated.

- **Avoid long-term use of sleeping medications.** Before starting any sleep medication, even one sold without a prescription, consult your physician. These medications, either on their own or through interacting adversely with your other medications, can have unpleasant or possibly even dangerous side effects. In general, avoid these medications, or at least use them sparingly!

sleeping pills should be avoided when possible. Although these medications are sometimes appropriate for short periods of time, they have many side effects, including daytime drowsiness, dry mouth, urinary retention, increased risk of falls, and the possibility of developing a chemical dependency. All such medications should be discussed with your doctor prior to use.

As with other problems, a better approach is to identify the underlying cause. Problems in falling asleep may be caused by anxiety or worry, or may be symptomatic of depression. Many depressed people wake early in the morning and are then unable to fall back to sleep. If you experience these problems, consult with your physician.

Changes in the Digestive System

The digestive system encompasses the entire route that food travels from the mouth to the rectum. Normally the digestive tract does not change too much as we age. However, several problems seem to affect older persons more than younger individuals.

Heartburn

Among the most common digestive problems is heartburn, which can occur when the sphincter (a sort of valve) that separates the esophagus from the stomach becomes too relaxed. It is also often associated with a hiatal hernia, a very common, usually asymptomatic, condition found among older persons. With a hiatal hernia, the top portion of the stomach slides up into the chest. As a result, the contents of the stomach, including acid, are able to regurgitate, or "reflux," up the esophagus. This can be one cause of a burning sensation in the chest. Another cause can be medications, such as potassium and tetracycline, which can cause heartburn if not taken with enough water.

Heartburn is usually diagnosed with an "upper GI series" (X-ray) or upper endoscopy. The problem can usually be treated by avoiding lying down immediately after eating, elevating the head of the bed, and avoiding certain foods such as caffeine, alcohol, and chocolate. A variety of antiacid medications also are available, but because chest pains can be symptomatic of more serious conditions (such as heart disease), one is cautioned against self-diagnosis and treatment.

Diverticulosis

Diverticuli are small, pocketlike projections that commonly occur in the large intestines of older persons. Although diverticuli appear in almost all older people in Western countries, it is largely unheard of in Third World nations. Diverticuli are thought to be the result of eating a low-fiber, low-residue diet. Usually this change in the configuration of the bowels does not cause any symptoms, but if the diverticuli become infected, diverticulitis results. This condition, which causes abdominal pain and fever, is treated with antibiotics. However, a severe infection which perforates the intestines, may require surgery. To prevent infection, it is prudent to avoid small seeds such as sesame and poppy seeds, which can become lodged in a diverticulum and can cause irritation. A high-fiber diet and bulking agents, such as psyllium, are also recommended to regulate bowel movement.

Constipation

Constipation is one of the most common complaints expressed by older persons visiting the doctor. This slowing of the bowels is caused by a loss of muscle tone that is associated with aging. It is often an annoying, uncomfortable chronic problem, which is aggravated by constipating medications and a low-fiber diet.

If you experience frequent constipation, especially if your bowel habits have changed; noticed a change in color or shape of stools; or have bloody or black stools, consult a physician.

In such cases, a medical examination is necessary to eliminate medical diseases, colon polyps, or cancer. The doctor's will request information on the history of the problem before conducting a rectal examination, testing for occult blood in the stool, and possibly performing a direct sigmoidoscopic or colonoscopic visualization of the intestines.

To treat constipation, the physician will first eliminate or adjust the dosages of any aggravating medications. Next, the patient will be asked to increase fiber intake, by consuming such foods as bran, psyllium (found in such products as Metamucil), raw vegetables, and fruit, remain physically active, and drink plenty of fluids. If these measures still do not provide effective relief, stool softeners, such as senna and docusate, may be used, but the regular use of other laxatives is not advised, as chronic use may damage the intestines.

Nutrition and Aging

It is simply the truth—"You are what you eat." We all know that the food we eat affects our health and well-being, but this becomes particularly true as people age. The role of good nutrition in the prevention of chronic diseases such as heart disease, hypertension, diabetes, and osteoporosis is well established. It is also likely that a healthy diet helps reduce the risk for developing other diseases such as cancer. Although the diseases mentioned below are discussed in detail in the chapter, "Medical Problems of the Elderly," use the guidelines below as the basis for creating a healthier diet.

Cholesterol, Salt, and the Prevention of Atherosclerosis

Cardiovascular disease is the leading cause of death among the elderly in the United States. Atherosclerosis, the major cause of cardiovascular disease, is an accumulation of cholesterol deposits around the arteries. If these deposits form on the blood vessels that surround the heart the patient is diagnosed with coronary artery disease.

Many factors increase a person's risk for cardiovascular disease. Some, such as advanced age, male gender, and genetics (family history) cannot be changed. Other risk factors, however, can be reduced by modifying your behavior. These include obesity, elevated cholesterol levels, smoking, lack of exercise, stress, high blood pressure, and diabetes. There are cardiac benefits at all ages to weight loss, exercise, and freedom from smoking, and it is never too late to begin living a healthier lifestyle.

Because cholesterol intake can play a significant role in coronary artery disease, measurement of cholesterol levels in blood is generally part of a routine check-up. For most patients, but especially for those with heart disease or other risk factors, the desired total cholesterol level is less than 200 mg/dl. A reading from 200 to 240 mg/dl is borderline high, and above 240 mg/dl is high. If the blood is taken after an overnight fast, the laboratory can also measure the components of the total cholesterol. High-density lipoprotein (HDL) cholesterol, which is considered protective, should be greater than 35 mg/dl. With HDL cholesterol, the higher, the better. Aerobic exercise — exercise that uses more oxygen and exercises your heart as well as your muscles — can help increase your HDL cholesterol. Low-density lipoprotein (LDL) cholesterol is the component that causes atherosclerosis; it should ideally measure less than 130, but, in any case, should not exceed 160. A low-fat diet can help decrease your LDL cholesterol.

People who already follow a sensible, well-balanced diet, it is not necessary to change in your later years to a very restrictive fat-free diet. However, if you suffer from obesity, high cholesterol, heart disease, or have other high risk factors for heart disease, dietary modification is highly desirable. Although a certain amount of fat in the diet is necessary, fat should not constitute more than 30% of the calories consumed. "Saturated fats" contain the highest amount of cholesterol and are considered the most dangerous for the heart.

Therefore, learn which foods are high in saturated fats and minimize their role in your diet. Become a product label reader to help guide your food selections. In establishing a healthy diet, try to avoid butter, cheeses, chocolate, coconut, egg yolk, lard, fatty meats, and vegetable shortening. Additional tips for for cutting down on fat and cholesterol are to broil rather than fry foods, use polyunsaturated margarine, use low-fat or skim milk and low or no-fat cheeses, trim fat from meat and avoid the skin, and avoid organ meats and marbled meats, such as sausages and salami.

Salt intake should also be minimized, preferably to fewer than 2 grams daily, especially in persons with high blood pressure. If you crave the taste of salt, speak with your physician about the appropriateness of a salt substitute.

Calcium, Vitamin D, and the Prevention of Osteoporosis

Osteoporosis is a bone disease that affects approximately 25 million Americans, 80% of whom are women. The bones in our bodies are constantly turning over and being remodeled. When the body loses more bone than it makes, the bones become thin and the risk of breakage increases. The risk of osteoporosis increases with age, particularly for women who have reached menopause.

Because the consequences of hip fractures and compression fractures in the spine can be devastating for the elderly, preventive measures should be taken. Although there are medical treatments available, such as estrogen therapy for women and new medications for slowing down bone loss, they cannot reverse bone thinning after it has occurred.

The most effective preventive measures are the recurring themes of a healthy diet and exercise. To maximize peak bone mass or to reduce the risk of further bone loss, the body needs adequate amounts of calcium in the diet. For elderly persons, the average daily calcium intake should be between 1500 and 1800 mg. Most people do not consume enough foods rich in calcium to obtain the daily minimum. In fact, it is difficult—even with a healthy diet—to receive sufficient calcium from foods alone. For example, although one glass of milk, 8 oz of calcium fortified orange juice, a cup and a half of broccoli, and 6 oz of salmon are all foods high in

The Food Guide Pyramid

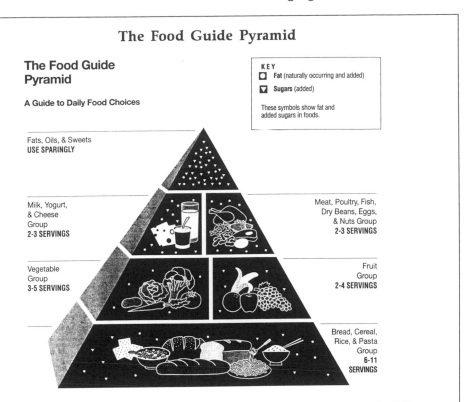

The Food Guide Pyramid

A Guide to Daily Food Choices

KEY
☐ Fat (naturally occurring and added)
▼ Sugars (added)

These symbols show fat and added sugars in foods.

Fats, Oils, & Sweets
USE SPARINGLY

Milk, Yogurt, & Cheese Group
2-3 SERVINGS

Meat, Poultry, Fish, Dry Beans, Eggs, & Nuts Group
2-3 SERVINGS

Vegetable Group
3-5 SERVINGS

Fruit Group
2-4 SERVINGS

Bread, Cereal, Rice, & Pasta Group
6-11 SERVINGS

This simple diagram illustrates the number of servings of different food types you should eat on an average day for a nutritious diet as recommended by the Human Nutrition Information Service of the U.S. Department of Agriculture. Please note the word average; it would be too difficult (and too monotonous) to have a perfectly balanced menu every day, but every three or four days' worth of meals should average out to these recommendations.

calcium, each contains only 300 mg of calcium. As a result, the average American takes in only 500 mg of calcium in his or her daily diet.

Therefore, older people, who have no contraindications such as kidney stones, should take calcium supplements to prevent or slow down osteoporosis. The most popular form of calcium is calcium carbonate, which is also the main ingredient of many antacids. Some people, however, find calcium citrate easier to tolerate because it causes less constipation and stomach upset. In either case, the recommended dose is 600 mg twice a day. Remember that taking the supplement with meals and with a sufficient amount of vitamin D helps the body absorb the calium. Many calcium supplements are al-

What Makes a *Serving?*

Bread, Cereals, Rice, and Pasta

1 slice of bread
1/2 cup cooked rice, or cooked cereal
1 oz of ready-to eat cereal

Vegetables

1 cup chopped raw or cooked vegetables
1 cup leafy raw vegetables

Fruits

1 piece of fruit or melon wedge
3/4 cup juice
1/2 cup canned fruit

Milk, Yogurt, and Cheese

1 cup yogurt or milk
1 1/2–2 oz cheese

Meat, Poultry, Fish, Dry Beans, Eggs, and Nuts

2 1/2–3 oz of cooked lean meat, poultry, or fish
1/2 cup of cooked beans, 1 egg, or 2 tbs of
    peanut butter = 1/3 serving

Fats, Oils, and Sweets

Use as sparingly as possible.

These are the Food Guide Pyramid definitions for a *serving*—a dietary measurement unit. However, it is not expected that you will always consume just one serving of each food in any meal. For example, a single *portion* of pasta might equal 2–3 servings.

ready enriched with vitamin D or you can add a multivitamin with 400 IU of vitamin D to your daily nutrition program.

The second important preventive measure is regular, "weight-bearing" exercise. Walking at least three times a week is a good start. How far you walk depends on your physical condition; if you are able, an hour each time is desirable. Walking and other forms of exercise help to slow down loss of bone and also build muscle mass, which improves balance and builds a protective cushion in case of a fall.

Enjoying a Healthful Diet

Changing to a better, more nutritious diet is difficult for some people. They use the wrong approach and frequently fail, falling back on old dietary habits. Starting from their established diet, they remove everything not recommended in the new diet, and what is left—the lowest common denominator—is what they try to use. No wonder they fail. If you plan a diet change, do not just subtract, but add as well. Here are a few tips:

- Accommodate your favorite foods in your new diet. Either find new recipes that provide a more healthful approach or, by cutting back severly on fat, oil, meat, whole milk, and other recommended low-usage foods, have a splurge once in a while. Treat your diet as you would a weekly budget—having more or less of some things each day, but achieving a balanced goal by week's end. With such planning, you will not have to cheat.

- Put in new flavors to take the place of flavors you are taking out. Use more herbs, lemon, garlic, and onions.

- Learn some new cooking methods that help retain the flavor and nutritional elements of basic foods. Steam vegetables—never boil them. Sauté foods, not fry them. Roast vegetables (peppers, onions, tomatoes, corn) to intensify the flavor. Use the *en papillote* technique (cooking in paper) for simple, nutritious cooking with great flavor, unusual presentation, and easy cleanup.

- If you have trouble switching to low-fat versions of some staples, do it in stages—wean yourself. If skim milk is not palatable for you, try two-percent milk. When you get used to it, move down to one-percent, and then skim. Mix low-fat cream cheese with the regular kind.

The Role of Diet in Cancer Prevention

More than half of all diagnosed cancers occur in elderly persons. In the last few decades, the role of nutrition in cancer prevention has grown in importance. Unfortunately, the impact of diet is difficult to study; there are many complicating factors and the results of any particular diet may take a life to time to manifest themselves. Still, even though the exact mechanisms are not understood, certain foods do seem to reduce the risk of cancer. For example, evidence shows that consuming fruits and vegetables offers some protection. The reverse definitely seems true—people who consume low amounts of fruit and vegetables have higher rates of cancer. More specifically, the antioxidants, beta-carotene, and vitamins C and E have been studied as a means of cancer prevention. Beta-carotene, in particular, seems to play a protective role against lung cancer. In addition, antioxident-rich foods are also high in fiber and low in saturated fats. For these reasons, the National Research Council recommends an average daily intake of five servings of fruits and vegetables.

Vitamin B_{12}

Vitamin B_{12} deficiency is a cause of anemia that becomes more common with advanced age. The problem is not inadequate intake, but rather the body's inability to absorb sufficient amounts of the vitamin, usually because of problems in the gastrointestinal tract. If the level of vitamin B_{12} becomes low, the person may develop a condition called pernicious anemia. In addition, the deficiency may also cause weakness, neurological problems, and memory loss. When a physician is evaluating a patient for memory loss, a blood test of the B_{12} level is generally obtained. Although some people receive B_{12} injections just to "feel better," there is no medical evidence to support this treatment. Vitamin B_{12} should be given only to people with a demonstrated deficiency in the blood.

Sexuality and Aging

Even though normal age-related changes occur in both men and women, sexual interest and activity are normal at any age. Problems should be addressed as they arise, but do not assume that sexual satisfaction is only for the young.

Changes in the Male Reproductive System

The medical profession has long studied the possibility that aging men go through changes that could be collected under the heading "male menopause." Whether or not this term is used, changes seem to or do occur, but much more gradually than in women. For example, aging men will experience a slight drop in testosterone levels, but this is not significantly different from changes found in normal middle-aged men. In this context, at least, changes in men are not analogous to menopause in women.

In fact, one study found that three quarters of men over age 70 reported being sexually active, but most men remained concerned about the natural changes in sexual function that do take place with aging. In general, the system simply slows down. Erections may take longer to achieve, be less firm than desired, and end more quickly. Ejaculation may take longer, the volume may be less, and the force somewhat diminished. But, even with these changes, it is possible and natural to continue to enjoy sexual activity.

A more serious problem is impotence—the inability to obtain an erection sufficient for sexual intercourse on a regular basis. Impotence affects an estimated 10 to 20 million American men and should not be regarded as a normal part of aging. In some cases, acute or chronic illnesses and specific medications may affect one's sexual performance. For example, diabetes, especially when poorly controlled, and vascular (blood vessel) diseases, are common medical conditions than can cause impotence. If, however, no reversible medical cause can be found, other treatment options should be discussed with a physician. These include medications, injections, external vacuum devices, implants, and revascularization procedures.

While many human organs and tissues shrink with age, the prostate almost invariable enlarges. The prostate is the male organ responsible for making the seminal fluid that mixes with the sperm produced in the testes. The prostate is a circular organ, wrapping itself around the urethra (the tube that carries urine) at the base of the bladder. Approximately 10% of 40-year-old men have some enlargement of the prostate, compared to 80% of 80-year-old men. When the gland enlarges, it can partially or completely block the passage of urine from the body. This can result in urinary dribbling or a weakened stream. Prostate exams should be part of a regular physical, as medications are now available that can reduce the size of the prostate. There are also relatively simple surgeries which can be used to reduce the size of the prostate. In addition, further tests may be suggested so that your physician can determine if the enlarged prostate contains cancer cells. If so, a full set of diagnostic tests should be arranged with a urologist.

Menopause and Other Changes in Women

Menopause, which occurs at the average age of 50, is one of the most widely recognized normal age-related changes. It means the end of reproductive capability for women. During menopause, women experience a decrease in the amount of estrogen, the female sex hormone. By the end of menopause, no eggs are left in the ovaries. For the majority of women, menopause is accompanied by a number of uncomfortable symptoms, such as hot flashes, night sweats, palpitations, anxiety, and irritability. These symptoms are caused by a temporary imbalance in the body's ability to regulate heat as estrogen levels diminish. Generally, the symptoms last one or two years and occur infrequently. When the body adapts to the lower estrogen levels, the symptoms disappear. Unfortunately for some women, the hot flashes occur more frequently and may last for up to five years.

Even after menopause occurs, many women experience other symptoms related to the loss of estrogen. For example, the skin lining the wall of the vagina becomes thinner, and vaginal secretions may lessen. This may result in uncomfortable intercourse unless extra lubrication is used. The thinner skin, combined with muscle stretching from childbirth, may lead to a lessened ability to control urination, called stress incontinence. The loss of estrogen also puts older women at higher risk for osteoporosis, atherosclerotic heart disease, and may even be linked to the development of Alzheimer's disease.

Women who experience discomfort during sexual activity should discuss this problem with their doctor. A number of treatment options are available. One might elect to receive estrogen replacement therapy, either in the form of pills or vaginal estrogen cream. Estrogen replacement is now combined with progesterone (another female hormone). The combination greatly reduces the risk of endometrial (uterine) cancer. It is important for women who have not had a hysterectomy (removal of the uterus) to use both hormones. Estrogen replacement many also be linked to a slightly higher risk of breast cancer. It is important for women on hormone replacement therapy to be especially diligent about receiving annual Pap tests, pelvic exams, and mammograms. For those who cannot or do not wish to use estrogen, lubricants can be used to reduce irritation.

It is important to note that estrogen replacement is not just used for the symptoms of menopause. It is extremely effective in reducing the risk of osteoporosis and heart disease. The benefits and risks of hormone replacement therapy need to be carefully weighed by each woman together with her physician.

Mental Changes

Memory loss and other mental changes are perhaps the most worrisome problems associated with growing old. Loss of memory is one of the most common reasons for older persons or their families to seek the advice of a geriatrician. Many people still fear that becoming "senile" is an inevitable consequence of growing older. We now know that many people continue to have active and productive minds well in their nineties and beyond!

Still, although many people remain mentally alert with advancing years, disorders that affect mental functioning are more common as we age. If a loss of memory or mental ability causes serious concern, a medical evaluation should be obtained. Medical professionals no longer group these problems under the term "senility," but attempt instead to diagnose and treat the specific problem.

Depression

Later life can be a time of great loss — job, social status, independence, friends, and family all seem to disappear or diminish. These losses may cause stress at a time when the individual is least able to cope with it. As a result, many older people often feel empty and lonely.

Although all of us feel sad from time to time, clinical depression is an illness that can cause debilitating and potentially dangerous changes in the body. Depression is not a normal consequence of aging; it is a problem to recognize and treat.

One of the main hallmarks of depression is a loss of interest in previously enjoyed activities. This may be accompanied by a change in appetite, too much or too little sleep, poor concentration, loss of energy, and thoughts of suicide. If these problem become constant, consult with a physician. It is important to rule out any underlying medical conditions before attributing symptoms to depression.

If depression is diagnosed, both drug therapy and psychotherapy offer effective treatment options. A number of available medications work because of the link between depression and the depletion of neurotransmitters (chemicals that carry signals between nerves) in the brain. Of course, since drug therapy cannot address all of the problems associated with depression, psychotherapy may prove useful in helping people to adapt to losses and transitions in lifestyle. Family support in the form of love and understanding, concern, and acceptance is also vital for older people.

Dementia

Dementia is defined as a decline in mental ability which impacts on the ability to function normally. It is important to note that there are many causes of dementia, but perhaps the most feared is Alzheimer's disease, which is estimated to affect two to four million Americans. Estimates of the number affected are likely underestimated because people do not always seek a physician or obtain the appropriate testing. Alzheimer's disease is characterized by degenerative brain changes that can be seen only microscopically in the form of neurofibrillary tangles and senile plaques (nerve cells surrounding an amyloid core). There are also changes in neurotransmitters, which are responsible for transmitting signals in the brain.

Alzheimer's disease begins with memory loss, usually for recent events. However, unlike normal forgetfulness, the problem gradually becomes worse. In time, the ability to perform simply tasks, such as balancing a checkbook, remember dates, or travel to familiar places may be lost. There are often problems remembering words. The person also undergoes personality changes, frequently becoming uncharacteristically irritable or depressed. As the disease progresses, the person will need help with eating, dressing, and other everyday activities. During the late stages of Alzheimer's disease, the person will be unable to either walk or speak.

Remember, however, that not all people with memory loss have Alzheimer's disease and other causes may be reversible. Therefore, careful diagnosis is very important. Alzheimer's can be a difficult disease to diagnose, because no single test absolutely identifies the problem for the medical professional. Alzheimer's is a "clinical diagnosis," which is a determination made after all other causes of memory loss have been eliminated. A good medical evaluation for memory loss generally includes a complete history of the problem; a mood assessment to rule out depression; a medical history; review of medications; a comprehensive physical examination; blood tests (including blood counts, chemistry, thyroid, B_{12}/folate, and syphilis test); and either a CAT scan or an MRI of the brain. The diagnosis of Alzheimer's can not be made by CAT scan or MRI, but one can see evidence of strokes, tumors, head trauma, or normal pressure hydroencephalus.

Alzheimer's disease is extremely stressful for both the patient and the family. In addition to help from medical professionals, family members should investigate support organizations that can help with the physical, psychological, and emotional trauma this disease engenders. The Alzheimer's Association is an excellent resource for finding support services.

Functional Assessment and Geriatrics

The ability to remain independent and continue daily life routines is of major importance to the quality of life of elderly persons. Thus, the geriatrician, a physician who specializes in the care of older adults, assesses not only the patient's medical condition, but also focuses on the impact of medical, psychological, and social factors on a person's ability to function independently. In addition to a medical history, a physical examination, and laboratory tests, a geriatric assessment should also evaluate the patient's ability to perform the "activities of daily living" (referred to as "ADLs") and the "instrumental activities of daily living" (referred to as "IADLs") independently. ADLs include the ability to bathe, dress, and attend to toilet functions by oneself. IADLs relate to the ability to live in the community and perform such functions as shopping, cooking, and using the telephone.

The geriatrician will assess how the person walks, whether or not he or she needs a cane or walker, and will obtain a falls history. The older person will generally be queried about memory loss, depression, incontinence, vision, hearing, nutrition, social supports, and advance directives. Such a comprehensive assessment is time consuming. Often, the geriatrician will work with a nurse and social worker to obtain a complete picture of how effectively each patient is managing his or her life.

Do It Now

All of the recommendations in this chapter—exercise, weight loss, a balanced diet, moderate salt and alcohol consumption, no smoking, periodic self-examinations of your body, and knowing your limits—can be summed up in two rules: use, do not abuse, your body and use your head. To this I would add, it is never too early nor too late to make changes that can improve the quality of your later years. Get started now.

Martin J. Gorbien, M.D., is a geriatrician at the University of Chicago Pritzker School of Medicine, where he is an Assistant Professor of Medicine. In addition to treating patients, he is the Director of the Geriatric Medicine Fellowship Program. He has published the results of his research on the medical problems of the elderly in several professional journals and is a frequent speaker at both medical conferences and community group presentations. He is a member of the Clinical Practice Committee of the American Geriatrics Society and also serves on the editorial board of the American Hospital Association's *Discharge Planning Quarterly*, and as a reviewer for the *Journal of the American Geriatric Society* and *The Cleveland Clinic Journal of Medicine*. As a youth, he was greatly affected by his grandparents and other elders in the family. As a result, he decided to be a doctor specializing in treating the elderly. At that time, geriatrics was not a board-certified subspecialty, but it did not deter him. His first job, in preparation for his career, was working in a nursing home at the age of fifteen.

Medical Problems of the Elderly

Martin J. Gorbien

The decision to visit a physician is not always an easy one. This chapter will help you prepare for a doctor's visit and will discuss some of the common medical problems of older adults. As a geriatrician, I find one of the most common concerns expressed by patients and their families is the difficulty in finding a physician who has the time to listen and manage the many coexisting problems that a senior citizen may have. Certainly, many older adults have had the good fortune of aging gracefully and have maintained an excellent functional status that allows an active lifestyle. Others, however, may need answers regarding a number of medical conditions. Often, the physician is asked if a particular ailment is associated with "normal aging" or with a process unrelated to age. Clearly, many conditions become more common with age, but are not necessarily inevitable for all older adults.

Selecting a Physician

The task of selecting a physician can be challenging. You can start by talking with friends and family members concerning their own physicians. A personal recommendation based on someone's positive and long-standing relationship with his or her primary care physician can yield information regarding a physician's style of care, communication skills, and particular interests within the doctor's specialty. For example, many physicians specializing in either General Internal Medicine or Family Practice may have particular expertise in treating certain medical conditions, such as arthritis, heart disease, or diabetes. Certainly, individuals who have a number of medical conditions will benefit from a primary care physician who will acts as a "quarterback" or "orchestra leader." This helps to ensure that medications, preventive care (such as vaccines, mammograms, Pap smears, prostate exams, and other screening procedures), and appropriate referrals to subspecialists are well coordinated. Large medical centers, hospitals, and many types of senior centers have referral sources that can help direct persons in search of a new physician. Often, questions can be asked about the physician's practice, credentials, the hospitals to which the doctor admits patients, and the types of insurance accepted (for example, does the physician accept Medicare assignment?). Sometimes, the first visit should serve to determine if the "fit" between doctor and patient is a good one. Not infrequently, older adults seek new physicians when they relocate, develop a new or serious condition, or have questions about existing diagnoses. A number of seniors maintain dual residences, spending winters in a warm climate or extended periods of time each year with family members. In such situations, it is prudent to maintain contact with a physician in each location. Ideally, the physicians will know about each other and correspond as the need arises. Physicians who care for older adults often assist patients in this manner.

The first few visits with a new physician are certainly important. This is the time for the doctor and patient to become acquainted and negotiate a plan of care that is mutually satisfying. The doctor will need quite a bit of information at the outset, and the patient (or the patient's surrogate) is responsible for facilitating this process. By following the list of suggestions in the table, you will help ensure that the doctor will have the proper information to answer questions and make recommendations.

These guidelines can make one's visits to the physician as productive as possible. Providing thorough background information will ensure that there is sufficient time for the patient and physician to talk openly about matters of interest and concern. Selecting a physician can be challenging, but by asking the right questions, using the available community resources, and preparing for the initial visits, the chances of a successful match will be enhanced. Now, let us direct our attention to some of the common medical problems of older adults.

When First Visiting a New Doctor

- Bring all prescription and over-the-counter medications (including vitamins, minerals, and herbal medications) to the visit.

- Request (in writing) that records be sent by your former physician to the new physician. Be certain to follow up on your request.

- Request (in writing) that any hospital records regarding hospitalizations, surgeries, and tests (x-rays, lab work, cardiac testing, etc.) be forwarded to the new provider as well. Be certain to follow up on this request, as there may be a lag period.

- Jot down your medical and surgical histories, as you will be asked about conditions and procedures that may have been quite remote.

- Record your drug allergies and intolerances.

- Record any preventive care that you may have had, such as vaccines (pneumovax, tetanus booster, and flu shots), mammograms, Pap smears, prostate exams, and so on.

- If your health care has taken place at many different hospitals and medical centers, bring all those addresses to the visit.

- Be sure the doctor has a clear picture of your current lifestyle — your normal activities, your diet, what type of residence you live in, whom (if anyone) you live with, and the physical and emotional demands that you regularly face.

- Make a list of your priorities, questions, and concerns regarding your health, as this will help the physician understand how the priorities of your care can be negotiated. Good communication is the key to a successful patient–physician relationship.

- Many people find it helpful to bring a friend, spouse, or relative to the visit to act as an "advocate." This, of course, is a personal decision and can be helpful in certain situations.

Hypertension

Hypertension, or high blood pressure, is an important public health problem that affects many adults — and certainly, many older adults. Hypertension is common, asymptomatic, and dangerous. It is a major risk factor for heart attack and stroke. The good news is that generally it can be treated quite easily. Currently, many good and safe choices of treatment are available for this "silent" condition. Blood pressure readings should be taken at every doctor's visit (regardless of the doctor's specialty!), even if the purpose of the visit is in connection with another condition. In this way, the physician develops a log of blood pressure readings. Such logs are important, because hypertension should not be diagnosed based on a single instance of an elevated reading of blood pressure.

The heart is a pump made of muscle that, through a cycle of contracting and relaxing, pushes the blood under pressure through the circulatory system to all parts of the body. A blood pressure reading is a set of two numbers. One corresponds to the pressures in the arteries when the heart is pushing the blood at full contraction and, the second, when the heart is resting. Blood pressure is generally measured in millimeters of mercury (mm Hg). In older adults, the systolic (top) reading should be less than 160 mm Hg and the diastolic (bottom) reading less than 85 mm Hg. High blood pressure can be diagnosed as mild, moderate, or severe; this classification is based on the readings, as well as on the ways in which the elevated pressures have affected the heart, retina (back of the eye), kidneys, and central nervous system (e.g., if the patient has suffered a stroke). These modifying factors or coexisting conditions will determine the speed and intensity with which a physician treats the hypertension. The majority of patients (90% to 95%) have what is referred to as "essential hypertension." The most common form, it is probably inherited. In the remainder of patients, hypertension has a secondary cause that may be a renal (kidney) condition or perhaps a chemical produced in an abnormal fashion. Your physician will determine if you fall into this small and uncommon category by taking a complete history and performing a complete exam. Another "subtype" of hypertension is referred to as "isolated systolic hypertension," which is an elevation of the systolic pressure to 165 or greater, with diastolic numbers that are either normal or mildly elevated. This is probably the result of a stiffness or noncompliance of the vascular system. Although this common clinical condition was once the subject of controversy, the "SHEP" (Systolic Hypertension in the Elderly Program) study proved that this form of hypertension requires treatment to reduce the risk of heart attack and stroke.

Your doctor will ask about your family history (it is useful to know if your relatives suffer or suffered from hypertension or heart disease). A physical exam will be performed, with attention to the heart, lungs, vascular system, and retinas. Often, a urinalysis, electrocardiogram (EKG), and basic blood work (checking complete blood count, kidney function, and cholesterol) will be completed as part of the evaluation. These results, along with the actual blood pressure readings, will determine how to proceed. Your doctor may advise you to adjust your diet by restricting salt intake, losing weight, and lowering the fat content of foods consumed. All of these help to reduce hypertension in the majority of hypertension patients. In addition, both tobacco and alcohol have negative effects on blood pressure and the cardiovascular system. Physicians can help motivated patients to stop smoking and may recommend that patients cut down on, or even eliminate, the intake of alcoholic beverages. These strategies are directly or indirectly focused on reducing the risk factors for heart attack and stroke, which are the two serious complications of hypertension. You may also be encouraged to begin an exercise program to help reduce blood pressure and associated cardiac risk. The patient can assist the physician by monitoring his or her own blood pressure at home. When done accurately, this helps give the physician more frequent data on which to base a diagnosis, as well as recommend and evaluate treatments.

If changes in diet, exercise, and other aspects of one's lifestyle do not sufficiently lower blood pressure to an acceptable range, medication will be suggested. Although many people are reluctant to begin pharmacologic therapy for hypertension, so many safe and effective drugs are now available that a successful regimen can be found for everyone. Initially, the patient will take a single drug; many people can be treated with just one drug. In other cases, a second or even third drug may be suggested to lower the pressure to a safe and desirable range. The selection of the medication will be influenced by age, race, gender, concurrent medications, and coexisting medical conditions. For example, a person with coexisting congestive heart failure (fluid in the lungs) might do best with a diuretic (water pill) and/or an ACE (angiotensin converting enzyme) inhibitor, whereas an individual with coronary artery disease or angina pectoris may do better with a beta-blocker or calcium channel blocker. Each category of medication has its own risks and benefits, and the physician and patient should talk openly about these issues. Occasionally, drugs for hypertension can affect bowel and urine function, sexual function, balance, energy, appetite, and even memory! Always ask your physician about these symptoms should they occur. A patient should be advised never to stop medications without the advice of one's physician, because certain medications should not be stopped abruptly. If you are experiencing an unacceptable side effect, a new drug will probably be chosen. Your blood pressure will then be monitored while the dosage of the new drug is adjusted to your needs. Whether treatment for hypertension includes one, two, or even three drugs, make every effort to take your medication as directed, so the effectiveness of the drug can be evaluated. The future holds great promise for the treatment of hypertension; even now, a safe and effective treatment is available for each individual experiencing hypertension.

Coronary Artery Disease

Coronary artery disease (CAD) results from narrowing of the arteries that supply blood to the heart. The scope and seriousness of this problem is indicated by the fact that 72% of all cardiovascular deaths occur in people over age 65. Of these, 69% result from complications of CAD. As one ages, CAD becomes more prevalent; 50% to 60% of men will have CAD by 60 years of ago. The incidence of CAD rises from 46% in the sixth decade to 84% in the ninth decade of a person's life. However, in the last thirty years, progress in prevention and treatment has decreased the rate of deaths due to cardiovascular disease to almost 30% in people over 80 and 45% in those 65 to 70 years old. Although the idea of "prevention" in very old individuals may seem paradoxical, we know that the modification of risk factors can result in a lowering of morbidity and mortality due to coronary artery disease.

Hypertension is a major risk factor for the development of CAD. As discussed above, treatment of hypertension is safe and effective in older adults. Cigarette smoking is another important risk factor; the likelihood of death because of CAD correlates with the number of cigarettes smoked. Cigarette smoking also affects the blood vessels outside of the heart and can lead to the development of other forms of vascular (blood vessel) disease, such as peripheral vascular disease (that is, poor circulation in the extremities). Of course, there are many compelling reasons for a person to quit smoking besides CAD prevention. Primary lung diseases, such as emphysema, chronic bronchitis, and lung cancer, are some of the more common smoking-related disorders. Exciting evidence suggests that age-related changes in the body's neurochemistry may actually make it easier for older individuals to throw away their cigarettes.

The topic of cholesterol and the elderly has been widely studied and debated in medical literature. It has still not been clearly determined if lowering serum cholesterol in older adults results in a longer or higher-quality life. Because the current life expectancy is 15 years at age 65 and 6 years at 85, the decision to lower cholesterol should be handled on an individual basis. Caregivers for older adults are always concerned that the restrictions of a strict low-fat diet may prevent a person from enjoying a diet that is healthful in other ways. The restriction of fat may inadvertently result in the consumption of too few calories or too little protein or calcium. Patients with and without heart disease are sometimes shocked to hear their physicians tell them that the occasional egg or bowl of ice cream may, in fact, be just fine.

However, the issues for a 60-year-old are often quite different from those for an 85-year-old. Also, we do know that levels of the various lipids (fatty substances) found in the body are fairly accurate predictors of the development of heart disease. An individual's total cholesterol is one predictor of the development of heart disease. The low-density lipoprotein (LDL), the so called "bad" cholesterol, is a risk factor for CAD. Conversely, the high-density lipoprotein (HDL) is the protective or "good" type of cholesterol. Rigid guidelines for the management of lipids in the elderly do not yet exist, and common-sense measures regarding dietary restriction and exercise are always the first step in responding to unfavorable numbers. A patient should discuss this with his or her physician, because the decision to use medication to lower cholesterol in older people deserves thoughtful consideration of a variety of related topics. Older women will also want to discuss the relationship of estrogen replacement therapy to the prevention of coronary artery disease, which is the leading cause of death among women.

The symptoms of CAD may range from the acute heart attack (myocardial infarction) to chest pain (angina pectoris) to symptoms that may be less obvious, such as shortness of breath, vague chest tightness, or jaw pain. Your physician may label other symptoms as your "anginal equivalent." The symptoms of a heart attack may become less "classic," or more "atypical," as a person ages, and chest pain may coexist with shortness of breath, nausea, fainting, or dizziness. Thus, for the physician, obtaining and interpreting cardiac symptoms is challenging, particular with a patient who may trouble communicating as a result of Alzheimer's disease.

The evaluation of coronary artery disease is similar in young and old individuals. In older persons, however, we are always hunting for the atypical presentation of common conditions, such as CAD. The search always begins with a thorough history and physical exam. Studies for this type of heart disease will probably include an EKG, some type of stress test, and, in certain cases, a cardiac catherization (or coronary angiogram). There are a variety of stress tests that do not require a person to run on a treadmill (because of osteoarthritis or frailty). If necessary, the heart can be stressed by the use of a chemical. These newer tests have been quite important in assessing patients who may have CAD. A coronary angiogram is a more invasive test that directly visualizes the arteries of the heart and reveals information about the pumping capacity of the heart. This test, which is safe in elderly individuals, is used when more invasive treatment, such as coronary artery bypass grafting (CABG, pronounced "cabbage") surgery or coronary angioplasty (the removal of plaque from an artery) are being considered.

The treatment of symptomatic CAD usually begins with medications. Aspirin to thin the blood and nitroglycerin tablets to place under the tongue in case of an acute onset of chest pain are commonly used in conjunction with other forms of medications. The daily use (in some combination) of beta blockers, calcium channel blockers, and nitrates (forms of nitroglycerin) are among the most common drugs for CAD. Although effective in many people, they can occasionally cause side effects. Beta blockers can cause a feeling of fatigue, impotence, or mild cognitive slowing; calcium channel blockers can cause problems with constipation or swelling of the legs; and nitrates can cause a light-headed feeling or headache, which commonly subsides after the initial treatment period. These drugs can be used in combination to treat, for example, coexistent hypertension or congestive heart failure.

When medical treatment is not successful in treating the symptoms associated with CAD, your physician may offer CABG as an alternative, but only if the coronary angiogram suggests that the lesions are amenable to this type of surgery. In the very early days of bypass surgery, elderly individuals were not regularly offered this option. However, we now have very promising information regarding the safety and effectiveness of this more invasive treatment of CAD. New findings suggest that coronary bypass surgery in elderly people may have a positive effect by limiting chest pain, increasing activity, exercise tolerance, and functional status, and improving the overall quality of life. In the last few years, percutaneous transluminal coronary angioplasty (PTCA) has been used with increasing frequency to open clotted arteries in older adults. This alternative method of coronary revascularization (for patients with selected lesions) is also quite effective in preventing heart attacks and prolonging life. Medical and surgical treatment can be quite successful for individuals with CAD. In properly selected patients, the benefits of these advances in medical technology can be measured in part by the improved quality of life they provide for patients with CAD.

Falls

Many people are concerned about falling, and the ensuing injuries. Among people living in communities, one third of the individuals over 75 years of age fall each year; one half of that group are repeat fallers. Of these falls, 75% occur at home. Only 5% to 10% occur during performance of a hazardous activity. At home, low chairs, soft furniture, and dim lighting may contribute to an increased risk of falling. In nursing homes, each person falls an average of once or twice a year. Risk factors include poor balance, weak hip muscles, and taking more than four medications.

Accidents related to falls are the sixth leading cause of death in persons over 65 years of age. Although many people who fall do not sustain an injury, 5% do experience a fracture, and 10% of falls result in hip fracture. With these statistics in mind, researchers have focused more attention on the questions of falls, gait, and balance in aging individuals. Changes in gait, increased sway, and the inability to adapt to rapid changes in position are likely contributors to this age-related increase in falls. Clinicians and experts in biomechanics have begun to study these important topics in increasingly sophisticated ways.

Most all of us know someone who has had an injury related to a fall. One result—a significant "fear of falling" again—is seen in 10% to 25% of people who fall. Because of this concern, people may restrict their activities in a way that may lead to isolation. Although falling is not always

Avoiding Falls

Although there are many medical explanations for falls among elderly people, research indicates that environmental factors significantly contribute to nearly half the falls that occur in and around the home. A few changes can much improve your chances of not falling.

- **Lighting.** Is the lighting good, neither too bright nor too dim, throughout your home? Are there danger spots (e.g., inadequate lighting over stairs or near exits) that should be attended to? Would a night light in the bedroom help?

- **Floor covering.** Are all the rugs and carpets securely tacked down or backed with antiskid material? Are the kitchen and bathroom floors too slippery, especially when wet? (Another problem with floors that are too highly waxed is glare.)

- **Furniture.** Do the chairs have arm rests to help you stand up? Are the seats high enough and firm enough to make standing easy? Does every piece of furniture offer a secure handhold in case of dizziness or weakness? TV snack tables may be convient at times, but can be hazardous. In addition, they do clutter the pathway.

- **Clutter.** Is there too much furniture or is it improperly arranged? At a time when getting around may be more difficult, some attention should be given to streamlining the pathways.

- **Adaptive sensory guides.** Such subtle decorative touches as wainscoting or a decorative strip of wallpaper trim at about waist level can add an artificial horizon to a room that will help you better keep your balance. Stairway handrails should extend slightly beyond both top and bottom stairs to act as a guide in transversing these two danger steps.

- **Twilight.** For many this time of day, with its rapidly changing light and contrast levels, can be a particularly dangerous time outdoors. Try to move outdoor activities to either earlier or later in the day benefit form more even lighting conditions.

a sign that a person is experiencing a functional decline, the hip fracture is a dreaded complication of falls. This can be particularly serious in elderly women, who are more likely to experience osteoporosis. Estimates indicate that there are 200,000 hip fractures per year. Other common fractures resulting from falls occur in the humerus (upper portion of the arm), wrist, and pelvis. Falls can also result in sprains, soft tissue injuries, and occasionally head injury that may lead to a subdural hematoma (bleeding around the brain). This serious injury can cause further problems with mental status and balance and is quite easily diagnosed by a CT (computed tomography) scan of the brain.

Individuals who are hospitalized have a special set of risk factors for falls. They include:

- Increased age
- Female sex
- Abnormal mental status
- Polypharmacy (adverse interactions of several drugs)
- Wandering
- Use of restraints
- Vision deficits
- Musculoskeletal deficits
- Neurologic deficits

During each office visit or hospitalization, physicians should review each patient's medications. One purpose is to identify medications that might increase a person's risk for falls. Any medication that can lead to sedation (for example, tranquilizers, sedatives–hypnotics, and antidepressants) may have a negative impact on a person's gait and balance. Medications that lead to a common side effect called postural (or orthostatic) hypotension (a drop in blood pressure when changing from a lying to a standing position) can lead to falls. If cardiac medications or any of the others discussed earlier cause this condition, the need for the drug should be reevaluated.

Of course, a number of medical conditions that span the entire range of organ systems may increase a person's's risk for falls. The following is a partial list of such conditions.

- Stroke
- Parkinson's Disease
- Pernicious Anemia (B_{12} deficiency)
- Cervical Spondylosis (nerve damage of the cervical spine)
- Infection/Dehydration (e.g., pneumonia)
- Vision and Hearing Deficits
- Dementia (for example, Alzheimer's disease)
- Vertigo; Meniére's disease
- Neuropathy (associated, for cxample, with diabetes mellitus)

Much can be done to decrease a person's risk for falls. They include a thorough review of medications in conjunction with a comprehensive history and physical examination. The physical should pay special attention to neurologic problems. These steps will give the physician important information about a person's strength, gait, balance, and mental status. Physician and patient should discuss underlying conditions that may lead to falls—and treat them aggressively. The risks and benefits of medications that may affect gait and balance should be clarified. Many programs exist for community-dwelling individuals who would like to reduce their risk for falls. An occupational therapist can complete a home inspection by recommending a variety of comparatively minor changes that will improve safety in the home environment. For example, the occupational therapist may suggest that you discard throw rugs, enhance nonglare-lighting, adapt a washroom for one's special needs, and evaluate the height and safety of certain types of furniture. A physical therapist can evaluate an individual's strength, gait, and balance in a formal and systematic way. The result may be the development of an exercise program designed to increase muscle strength and coordination. Increasing numbers of fitness programs are designed with the older adult in mind. Even the very frail can exercise in a way that will lead to safer performance of their activities of daily living.

Osteoporosis

Osteoporosis is an age-related condition that results in the loss of bone density (without other concomitant bone disease) and leaves individuals at risk for fractures. Twenty-four million Americans have osteoporosis; 1.3 million new fractures are recorded annually. Many experts consider osteoporosis a part of normal aging, but not all individuals who live a long life will develop this condition or the symptoms related to it. Osteoporosis is far more common in women and results, in large part, from a postmenopausal decrease in estrogen, a hormone that enhances calcium absorption and affects vitamin D metabolism. Thus, a physician may recommend estrogen replacement therapy for some postmenopausal women; it has been shown to reduce the risk of fractures by up to 50%. The lifetime risk of hip fracture for white women over 65 years of age is 15%, whereas the risk is 6% and 3% for white and African-American men, respectively. Fifty percent of white and Asian women over 50 years of age have osteopenia (low bone density), which can lead to fractures. Vertebral fractures or compression fractures of the mid- or low back, which have a lifetime risk of 30%, are common as well. These may appear as asymptomatic findings on x-rays or they may result in episodes of heightened pain. Fractures of the wrist, which may occur by falling on an outstretched hand, are another common type of fracture among people with osteoporosis. Although bone density is somewhat predictive of the likelihood of fracture, there are many exceptions to this relationship.

A number of secondary causes of osteoporosis are not related to gender. These include smoking and alcohol, both of which have negative effects on bone density. In addition, immobility, even in the early stages of bedrest, can lead to noticeable demineralization. A number of malignancies, such as lymphoma and multiple myeloma, can also cause osteoporosis, as can such drugs as phenytoin (seizure medication), prednisone, and heparin. Finally, changes in hormonal status (for example, hyperparathyroidism, hyperthyroidism, and estrogen deficiency) may result in the development of osteoporosis.

Although the "typical" candidate for the development of osteoporosis is an older, petite, white, or Asian woman with an early menopause and a positive family history, many other secondary factors clearly need to be considered as risk factors.

Although a person may not become aware of his or her osteoporosis until a spontaneous fracture occurs or until skeletal deformities (for example, kyphosis, or curvature of the spine) are noticed either by x-ray or physical exam, increased educational efforts will ideally lead to earlier detection and prevention. Although treatment for osteoporosis has improved, it often can be a preventable disease. These preventive efforts, however, need to begin at a young age, or at least in midlife.

If a physician suspects that an individual has osteoporosis, the physical exam will include evaluations of specific organs (particularly the liver and kidneys), the thyroid gland, hormones, and the possibility of underlying malignancies. The physician will include a review of the patient's medications and lifestyle, including exercise and tobacco and alcohol use). If appropriate, the physician may recommend that the patient undergo a bone density test. For many women, in particular, this procedure is used to assess risk for fracture and to monitor bone loss over time. The test uses a technique known as "densitometry," which involves a small amount of x-ray exposure to the wrist. There are two types of bone tissue in our bodies, cortical, a dense type that forms the covering for the long bones, and trabecular, tissue of a more open, lacier design that is found at the center and ends of the long bones. Although the body loses both types of tissue mass in osteoporosis, relative losses of trabecular bone is generally about 50% greater. The wrist is composed of mostly trabecular bone and is a convenient place to test. The risk for fracture is calculated by comparing the patient's bone density results to those of people of the same gender, age, and race. Although this technology is constantly improving, it is not yet recommended for all women.

Current treatments for osteoporosis include recommendations for changes in lifestyle, particularly a regular exercise program and a healthful diet that includes the proper amounts of calcium (1 to 1.5 grams/day) and vitamin D (600-800 IU/day) daily. However, more controversial treatments, particular for women, involve the use of hormones. The decision to begin estrogen replacement therapy should be based on a careful evaluation of the medical benefits and risks. A women should discuss these issues with her physician, so that she understands both estrogen's cardioprotective effects and its small potential to increase the risk of breast or uterine cancer. With this in mind, the physician may recommend a second hormone, progestin, to decrease the risk of endometrial (uterine lining) cancer. Although estrogen replacement therapy reduces the risk of fracture by 50%, its most effective use is probably in the immediate postmenopausal period, when bone loss occurs most rapidly. Thus, the successful use of estrogen to minimize bone loss depends in part on a woman's age. The evidence for its positive effects is less impressive as women grow older.

Although fluoride may be used to increase bone density, its effectiveness is still unclear and side effects, such as nausea, can be troubling. A fairly new treatment is a hormone called calcitonin, which is now available in the United States as a nasal spray. Calcitonin effectively increases bone density (at least in the short run) and has the added benefit of reducing the pain that comes from osteoporosis-related fractures. Another class of drugs, the bisphosphonates, continue to show promise as an additional agent for slowly increasing bone density over time.

The prevention, diagnosis, and treatment of osteoporosis remain complex, but advances in all of these areas are significant. In particular, research into bone metabolism has resulted in new approaches to the pharmacologic treatment of established osteoporosis in older women and men.

Osteoarthritis

Osteoarthritis (OA) — the most common form of arthritis — affects 40 million Americans. A progressive disorder that affects the hands, knees, and hips, OA is distinguished by a loss of cartilage in the joints. This cartilage normally acts as a cushion. Subtypes of OA include "oligoarticular OA," which affects one or two of the large weight-bearing joints in the lower extremities. This condition, which increases with age, affects men and women equally. Erosive or generalized OA affects women more than men. Its onset occurs between the ages of 30 and 50. After reaching age 50, the condition may go into remission, leaving the individual pain free, but with some deformity. The third type of OA, which is age related, is a result of a preexisting condition, such as gout or rheumatoid arthritis.

Thus, although OA is a common condition whose prevalence increases with age, it is not (in contrast to osteoporosis) a normal consequence of aging. The joints of aging people without OA differ in a number of ways from aging people with OA. In people with OA, the cartilage shows an increase in water content, a decrease in a number of key biochemical components, and a generalized disruption of the collagen network.

The cause of OA is unknown, but many theories have been offered to explain its origin. Among the possible factors is the role of heredity, which is not well understood. Other possible factors include obesity, which may increase the stress across joints, and repetitive movements (related to an occupation or a hobby), trauma, and a history of inflammatory arthritis.

If the cause is unknown, the clinical manifestations are very familiar. They include morning stiffness, pain (as the result of tiny fractures around the joint), swelling, crepitus (creaking of the joint), and decreased range of motion. When large, weight-bearing joints, such as the hip or knee are involved, patients may also complain of instability ("the joint giving way"). When the hands are involved, deformities of the fingers may be seen in the form of nodules in the finger joints and swelling. Bony deformities can also be highly visible in degenerative disease of the knees. X-ray films will reveal narrowing of the joint space, osteophytes or "bone spurs," and bony sclerosis at the joint margins. The symptoms of OA are similar in both young and old patients. OA of the weight-bearing joints can increase one's risk for falls.

The evaluation of a patient complaining of symptoms of OA often involves x-rays, but a comparison of x-ray findings with findings in an arthroscopy (direct examination of the joint space) show that x-rays often do not correlate well with symptoms. The patient may also go for a radiograph, which provides clues regarding other forms of bone disease (for example, rheumatoid arthritis, osteopenia, or a bone lesion due to metastatic cancer), as well as for laboratory tests that help distinguish OA from rheumatoid arthritis, rheumatologic disease, and systemic conditions that may affect the joints. By examining the joint fluid, physicians can make more accurate distinctions among the various forms of inflammatory joint disease.

Because OA is a degenerative disease, its progress cannot be stopped. Therefore, treatments are designed to relieve the symptoms. A stepwise approach should be used in determining the appropriate treatment, beginning with medication, injections, and physical therapy. If these are ineffective, surgery should then be considered.

The first-line treatment for the pain and swelling associated with OA is generally acetaminophen, aspirin, or nonsteroidal anti-inflammatory agents (NSAIDs). However, the latter two classes of drugs should be used with caution, because they can have significant side effects, particularly gastrointestinal discomfort. NSAIDs, for example, can affect the kidneys, elevate blood pressure, alter the body's electrolytes, and interact negatively with other medications. When using these drugs, the dose should be modified based on the age and renal function of the specific patient. Patients using aspirin or NSAIDs should notify their physicians immediately if they experience any gastrointestinal symptoms.

A second treatment consists of injections of corticosteroids into the joint space to relieve pain. This can be effective in an arthritic joint, such as a knee, hip, shoulder, or even a disc space in the spine, but it is limited to a maximum of three treatments per year.

Another approach to relieving arthritic symptoms is physical therapy. This may involve the use of hot and cold packs, water exercises to improve mobility, and the use of muscle-strengthening, low-impact and range-of-motion exercises to improve a person's ability to function on a regular basis.

If, after these treatments, pain persists in a large joint, such as a knee, shoulder, or hip, a physician may recommend surgery. Some patients gain considerable relief after arthroscopic surgery, during which the surgeon removes devitalized cartilage and loose bodies. In the case of the knee, the surgeon may also repair damaged ligaments.

However, arthroscopic surgery is not appropriate for all patients. Some individuals will need to undergo a total joint replacement. This type of surgery is often the best option for patients with severe, symptomatic joint disease that has resulted in immobility and pain and has proven resistant to medication. In these cases, the risks of immobility often outweigh the risks of such surgery. Because of advances in joint replacement surgery, even frail individuals can tolerate the procedure and, with appropriate rehabilitation, can regain their ability to function.

Prostate Disease

Benign prostatic hypertrophy (BPH) is a common condition among aging men. At about age 45, the male hormone testosterone may cause the prostate gland to start growing. By age 50, affected individuals will begin to experience symptoms of BPH. A 50-year-old man has approximately a 25% chance of needing prostate surgery in his lifetime; 90% of 80-year-old men will have BPH.

As the enlarged prostate impinges on the posterior urethra (the opening through which urine passes), a man may experience difficulty in beginning the stream of urine, straining, irritation, decreased stream, dribbling, a sensation of incomplete voiding, nocturia (nighttime urination), or urgency (which may be accompanied by urge incontinence). A person may experience one or many of these symptoms, which can manifest themselves in varying degrees. A severely enlarge prostate can cause acute urinary retention and alterations in blood chemistry that will affect the kidneys. When the urine is stagnant, the possibility of infection increases.

As a first step, men should have an annual prostate exam. When performing the digital rectal examination, the physician will check the size, consistency, and texture of the prostate, as well as check for other abnormalities in the rectum. However, the exam is not entirely reliable, because the anterior portion of the prostate is out of the physician's reach. As a result, the physician may recommend an ultrasound imaging of the gland. This procedure provides additional detail concerning the size and texture of the prostate. If the prostate exam or the ultrasound image reveal a prostatic "nodule," the doctor will recommend a biopsy. Other tests may be ordered to see how the bladder empties (excretory urography) or to directly visualize the bladder and urinary system (cystoscopy). Other conditions sometimes mimic the symptoms of BPH; these may be considered on an individual basis.

A number of medical and surgical treatments are available for BPH. In the mild to moderate stages, your doctor may prescribe one or two common classes of drugs. Finasteride slows the progression of prostatic enlargement by decreasing, over many months, the effects of testosterone, the hormone that probably causes the prostate to grow in the first place. Another class of very medications consists of alpha adrenergic blockers, which was originally used to treat hypertension. As a result of these drugs, which are often helpful in relieving the symptoms of BPH, surgery may be avoided or postponed.

If BPH does not respond well to medication, surgery may be needed. This is not an uncommon occurrence. Although a variety of procedures are available, they share a common goal—removal of the prostatic tissues that is blocking the urethra. The most common procedure is the TURP (transurethral resection of the prostate), which is accomplished by "coring" the prostate. If the prostate is too large for this procedure, other approaches are used. Because the prostate gland produces 30% of the total fluid in an ejaculation, men are concerned about the effects of surgery on sexual activity. However, sexual potency (the ability of have erections) is generally maintained. During orgasm, a man may experience retrograde ejaculation (the ejaculate flows backward into the bladder), but this does not alter the sensation of the orgasm. In fact, a man's quality of life is often improved by the surgical correction of the symptoms resulting from BPH.

Of all prostate diseases, cancer is the most feared. Prostate cancer is the most common cancer in men over 55 years of age. It is more common among African-American men than among white men. The annual figures for the United States are 132,000 new cases and 33,000 deaths.

Treatment of prostatic cancer depends in large part on the stage at which the disease is diagnosed. The staging system runs from A to D, with controversy regarding the treatment of local (confined to the gland) disease. Because many men experience no symptoms during the early stages of the disease, when treatment would be most effective, the most effective diagnostic tool is still an annual digital rectal exam. Although some doctors may recommend also measurement of the prostate specific antigen (PSA) through a blood test, this procedure is more helpful in following progression of an established disease than as a diagnostic tool.

A minority of patients do experience some symptoms, including dysuria (difficulty voiding), increased urinary frequency, hematuria (blood in the urine), or bone pain. These symptoms, however, are quite nonspecific and may relate to a number of other conditions. Statistics reveal that 80% of men reach stage C or D before prostate cancer is discovered.

The treatment options will include will include some combination of surgery, radiation therapy, hormonal manipulation (medications and/or surgery) to decrease the effects of testosterone, and/or chemotherapy. In the early stages, when prostate cancer is confined to the gland, the disease is often curable. In the more advanced stages, new treatments can slow its progress considerable. Newer surgical techniques for prostatectomy are often successful in enabling the patient to maintain sexual potency and control over bladder function.

Hearing Loss

Age-related hearing loss, which is referred to as presbyceusis, reduces a person's ability to hear sounds produced at higher frequencies. Sometimes referred to as sensorineural hearing loss, its onset is gradual and is often noticed by others before the person with the hearing loss becomes aware of the problem. Presbyceusis often affects both ears and can be symmetrical.

Hearing loss is not an uncommon problem in older adults, affecting men more often than women. The loss occurs in 30% of people over 65 years of age, 50% of 80-year-olds, and possibly 60% of nursing home residents. People with Alzheimer's disease are likely to experience hearing loss, which only further compounds their ability to absorb and interpret information.

People who suffer from this type of hearing loss have trouble with discerning sounds. Thus, conversation in crowds or noisy locations and communications at a distance become difficult because of interference from background noise. In contrast to a younger person, whose hearing range is 30 to

20,000 cycles per second, the range in older people may be limited to 250 to 8000 cycles per second. Thus, older people will have greater trouble hearing at higher frequencies. They may also experience tinnitus, or ringing in one or both ears. To counteract these problems, people may have to speak to them with greater intensity or volume.

Although many people are reluctant to discuss hearing loss with their physicians, a primary care geriatrician generally considers the possibility in examining a patient. The physician will ask about a person's history of ear surgery and exposure to loud noises. If a hearing loss is diagnosed, the physician will first determine if the cause is a comparatively simple one, such as wax clogging the auditory canal, or the result of certain classes of medications (for example, selected antibiotics, diuretics, and NSAIDs) that may impair hearing. If the physician determines that the patient is suffering from a hearing loss, the patient will undergo audiometric testing to establish the type and degree of the loss. As a result of such tests, the patient may be encouraged to use one or two hearing aids.

Hearing aids are often successful in treating sensorineural hearing loss, particularly in patients who cannot localize sound to sufficiently understand what they hear in a noisy setting or for those who cannot hear on a "bad" side. If the hearing loss is detected early, when a person can adjust more easily to amplification of sound, hearing aids have a better success rate. The use of two hearing aids can lead to even greater satisfaction through better localization of sound. If, however, a person waits until the hearing loss is profound before seeking treatment, the reintroduction of sound through the use of aids may lead to the perception that the environment is much too noisy. Thus, as with all medical problems, early detection has a significant impact on successful treatment. People with hearing loss need to acknowledge the problem, so that treatment can be recommended and so that family and friends can adjust by speaking in a more direct and articulate fashion.

A variety of types of hearing aids are available; the cost usually begins at $500. Hearing aids that fit behind the ear are more durable and are easier to adjust and repair than aids that fit inside the ear. The latter, however, are less visible and can often improve hearing at higher frequencies. Although many people over 70 years of age use their hearing aids infrequently, proper selection should still be a priority. A recommendation by a qualified ear specialist, based on high-quality audiologic testing, can result in significant improvement in a person's quality of life.

Vision and Aging

Cataracts (a clouding of the lens of the eye) are often age related, although some may be associated with disease or drug toxicity. The symptoms of cataracts include blurred vision, problems with near or close vision, and trouble seeing in bright light because of increased glare. Eighteen percent of people between 65 and 74 years of age and 46% of people between 75 to 85 years of age will complain about vision problems that are associated with cataracts. Although some cataracts are visible to an examiner without a "slit lamp," the ophthalmologist uses a slit lamp to discover cataracts at various stages of development. Most people do not have cataract surgery until their vision problems affect their lifestyle. The surgery, which is generally an out-patient procedure, can be tolerated by very frail people. With new surgical techniques, intraocular lens are implanted, so the patient does not require glasses or contact lenses. The success rate of such surgery is excellent. Ninety-five percent of patients achieve a vision level adequate for reading and driving. Up to 50% of patients will experience a cloudiness in their vision in the three years after surgery. This results from clouding of the posterior capsule of the eye and is easily corrected with laser treatment in approximately 90% of patients.

Another vision problem for older adults can be dry eyes, which occurs as tear secretion decreases with age. Tears, which are spread across the surface of the eye by blinking, generally keep the eye moist. Without such secretions, symptoms of burning or dryness may occur. These symptoms can be also be caused or aggravated by dust, smoke, and low humidity, older people should consider altering their home environments to minimize these problems. In addition, certain medications or occasionally systemic conditions can cause dry eyes. Your doctor will evaluate all of these factors and recommend appropriate treatment. Generally, this problem is not dangerous and can be well controlled by the use of artificial tears.

Ptosis, or droopy eyelids, usually results from changes in the subcutaneous tissue and ligaments of older adults. Before recommending treatment, however, the physician should evaluate the possibility of a neurologic cause. Ptosis can sometimes interfere with vision, especially if the upper lid is involved. If the upper lid droops so much that the pupil is obstructed, surgery may be required to correct the problem. If the lower lid is involved, it may fall away from the eye. This results in excessive tearing, which should be gently blotted (not rubbed) to decrease the amount of tearing.

Macular degeneration is a more serious condition of the eye that results in loss of central vision. Its cause is not well understood and involves a complex number of clinical factors, but changes in the pigmented tissue of the retina (the back of the eye) are thought to lead to this problem. This portion of the eye is important for vitamin A metabolism, as well as for other functions of the photoreceptor cells.

Eye doctors classify macular degeneration into wet or dry. In the dry type, which accounts for approximately 80% of all cases, individuals see a blurry dark spot in the center of the visual field. The degree of vision loss is variable — only 10% of affected people will experience sufficient vision loss to be described as legally blind. No precise treatment for dry macular degeneration is available, but zinc supplements seem to slow the process and a number of low vision aids can be used successfully. Wet macular degeneration is often more severe. It occurs when layers of the retina separate from each other as a result of the development of new blood vessels. Surgery or laser treatment may be helpful for selected patients and needs to be decided on a case-by-case basis.

Conclusion

For the older adult, the first step in good medical care is the selection a primary care physician who will provide direct care, as well as coordinate care delivered by other medical and surgical specialists. The second step is to be a well-informed, well-prepared, and honest patient. You should feel comfortable enough with your primary care physician to discuss and admit to all possible problems; in turn, your physician should be patient enough to discuss and explain the risks and benefits of various treatment options.

Although any discussion of the medical problems of the elderly is selective, a number of general principles are now clear. Perhaps the most compelling is the importance of early detection in determining the most successful course of treatment. The examples of medical problems discussed in this chapter may help to provide a template for approaching any number of medical concerns.

Finally, be sure your physician, family, and friends are aware of your preferences concerning the style and intensity of medical care you desire in the event of serious illness. These discussions are best carried out during periods of good health. The ethical and legal issues involved are discussed later in this book.

Margaret A. Winker, M.D., is a board-certified internist, geriatrician, and clinical pharmacologist, who is a senior editor at the Journal of the American Medical Association. She is particularly concerned about the accurate and clear dissemination of medical progress and information beyond the medical community. She serves as Chair of the American Geriatrics Society's Public Education Committee and was a member of the advisory group convened by the Harvard School of Public Health and the International Food and Information Council Foundation to establish guidelines for journalists, researchers, and editors on reporting issues of nutrition, food safety, and health. She also developed a Kids and Chemistry program at her local grade school. Among her honors was her selection in 1992 as a *JAMA* Fishbein Fellow. She enjoys spending time with her family, which includes her four- and six-year old sons, her parents, and in-laws. In her free time, she enjoys running, biking, horseback riding, reading and writing, and traveling with her family.

Managing Medicine

Margaret A. Winker

Two out of three visits to a doctor result in a prescription for medicine, and the average person 65 years or older takes 6 medications each day. Medications have prolonged life and reduced disabling diseases for many people; for example, medicines to lower elevated blood pressure have markedly reduced the risk of stroke. However, medicines also can have adverse effects and can interact with other medicines. It has been estimated that one-third to one-half of people do not take their medicine as prescribed because of lack of information. Not taking medicine as prescribed can lead to treatment failure and adverse drug effects. Thus, it is very important to know what medicine you are taking and why, what side effects you should be aware of, and what you should avoid. It is also important to tell your doctor about all medicines that you taking, whether or not they were prescribed by a doctor and whether you take them all the time or just for certain symptoms.

Getting Started: Medication as You Age

This chapter provides some practical information and tips for taking medication. It also discusses some of the common reasons for taking medications and the types of medications most commonly taken by older people, as well as certain drugs older people should avoid taking. Not all available drugs can be discussed here, but for additional information, ask your doctor or pharmacist or consult the resources listed in the bibliography at the end of the book.

Defining Terms: The Basics

A medicine or drug is a substance used to produce a specific desired effect, usually the treatment of a disease such as hypertension or a symptom such as pain. Medicines may be taken by mouth, for example, hypertension medicines; injected under the skin, for example, insulin for diabetes; inhaled, for example, asthma medicines; applied in the eyes for glaucoma or in the nose for allergies; or applied to the skin in an ointment or patch. Regardless of the way medicines are taken, nearly all medicines can be absorbed into the body, cause side effects, and interact with other drugs.

In addition to prescription medicines, it is important to recognize that medicines also include over-the-counter pain medicine, herbal preparations bought at a health food store, or vitamin supplements. Although herbal preparations may be described as *natural,* many drugs exist in some form in plants (although not in a pure form) and many types of herbal preparations can have side effects, sometimes severe. Also the amount and potency of active ingredients in herbal preparations varies widely from sample and sample, unlike drugs produced by pharmaceutical companies that are regulated by the Food and Drug Administration. Impurities in herbal preparations are presumed to be responsible for some adverse effects, such as the association of a disease called eosinophilia-myalgia syndrome with tryptophan supplements.

A side effect or adverse effect is an unintended effect of the drug. Side effects may be mild and subside over time, such as a slight headache or stomach upset, or severe, such as kidney or liver failure. Most side effects are more common at higher doses of a drug but some can occur unpredictably at any dose.

A drug interaction is an effect one drug has on another drug, usually by slowing or speeding up how quickly a drug is cleared from the body or by affecting the way the body responds to the drug. Most drugs have the potential to cause a drug interaction; your physician or pharmacist or resource books can tell you whether the drugs you take may interact with each other.

Although more drugs are being made available without a prescription to treat specific illnesses, such as antifungal drugs to treat vaginal yeast infections and nicotine patches to help people stop smoking, most over-the counter medicines are used to treat symptoms, rather than specific diseases. Examples are medicines used to treat the symptoms of cold and flu or antacids and cimetidine to treat heartburn. On the other hand, many prescription medicine are prescribed for a specific disease or diagnosis, such as antibiotics for a bacterial infection, rather than for symptoms. Symptoms of one disease may mimic symptoms of another disease. Therefore, if an over-the-counter medicine does not improve symptoms, consult your physician.

Medicine Acts on Your Body and Your Body Acts on Medicine

People 65 years or older take more medicine than any other age group, and the effects of some medicines change as you age. Changes may occur in one of two ways: first, how and how quickly your body gets rid of the drug (what your body does to a drug, called pharmacokinetics). Usually, drugs are cleared more slowly as people age, so that the same dose of drug that is effective for a younger person may act longer and be too high a dose for an older person. Most drugs are cleared from the body by passing through the kidneys and being excreted in the urine. Some drugs must be metabolized by the liver first in order to be cleared in the urine. In general, the kidneys do not clear drugs as quickly as people age. For example, the drug hydrochlorothiazide, a diuretic used to treat hypertension that is cleared by the kidneys, can effectively treat hypertension in older people at half the dose needed for younger people. The liver also helps clear some drugs by changing, or metabolizing, their chemical structure into one that can be cleared by the kidneys. Some drugs are changed less efficiently by the liver as a person ages, but others are changed at the same rate.

Aging of the body can affect how long a drug stays in the body and whether the drug accumulates over time. As people age they generally lose muscle mass and increase the proportion of fat in their body, even if they do not gain or lose weight. Drugs that are fat-soluble, including many drugs that affect the brain (for example, benzodiazepines sometimes used for sleep or anxiety), tend to be retained longer in the body as a person ages, so such drugs generally are needed in smaller and less frequent doses. The total water in a person's body tends to decline, so water-soluble drugs generally also are given in lower doses as a person ages. These drugs are cleared by the kidneys, which tend to become less efficient as a person ages. For example, digoxin is a water soluble drug; older people tend to require smaller doses of digoxin than younger people.

What the drug does to the body, or how the body responds to the effects of the drug (called pharmacodynamics) can also change with age. While most drugs tend to be more potent in older people, some drugs (most notably some beta-blockers, used to treat high blood pressure and heart disease), may have less effect. The tendency of a person to have an adverse effect from a drug can also change with age. For example, some medicines with anticholinergic effects (choline is a type of messenger between cells within the body; anticholinergic effects occur because the drug interferes with the message), such as diphenhydramine (Benadryl and other brand names), tend to cause urinary retention (inability to empty the bladder). This tendency may never be experienced by a person with a normal bladder, but an older man with an enlarged prostate may develop urinary retention from the combination of the drug and the underlying disease.

Older people are not more likely to have adverse effects from drugs simply because of their age. Carefully controlled studies have shown that the frequency of adverse effects depends more on the total number of drugs that a person takes than on his or her age. Thus, being older is not a reason in itself to avoid necessary medications.

To summarize, what the body does to the drug and what the drug does to the body can change with age. While there are exceptions, the changes generally mean that older people are more sensitive to drugs and may require lower doses than younger people. Doctors prescribing medicines for older patients generally follow the adage *start low, go slow.*

Practical Points about Medication

Get a Medication Checkup

All medications you take should be reviewed with your doctor at least once a year (more often if necessary), just as you have regular checkups. The purpose of this medicine checkup is to determine if the drugs you are taking are effectively treating what they were intended to treat without producing unacceptable side effects and to determine if any medicines should be changed or can be stopped. When you review your medicine, bring all the containers of medicine you are currently taking with you to the doctor's office, including all over-the-counter medicines, vitamins, and herbal or natural preparations, and medicines you take even occasionally. Tell your doctor if you drink any alcohol and how much, or if you use other drugs, and whether you smoke cigarettes, since all these may interact with medications. In my experience it is essential to bring in the actual bottles of medicine, since otherwise you and your physician may not be discussing the same drug. If additional instructions need to be written on the bottles, or if some medicine needs to be discarded, that can be done at the same visit.

Even if your medication does not change as a result of this checkup, you can benefit by understanding your medicines better. You should understand why you are taking the medicines, what their potential side effects are, and instructions for taking them. Be sure you know whether there are any over-the-counter medicines you should avoid, if you should take your medicines with certain foods or not, or if you should not take alcohol or other drugs with your medicine. Finally, you should understand what to do if you miss a dose of medicine. Although missing a dose of medicine taken for arthritis pain may not be a problem, missing a dose of a drug such as a beta-blocker may be dangerous since stopping beta-blockers abruptly may worsen existing heart problems. Most medicines for chronic medical conditions need to be taken regularly at the same time every day, but if you miss a dose do not take a double dose unless you are instructed to do so.

Establish with your doctor a specific target or goal you wish to achieve by taking your medicine, such as blood pressure in the normal range if you have hypertension, better control of blood sugar if you have diabetes, or no chest pain and improved ability to function if you have heart disease. If you are taking a medicine for specific symptoms, identify the target symptoms and discuss with your doctor whether the medicine is helping your symptoms. When treating symptoms such as pain, urinary incontinence, or insomnia, it may help to record your symptoms for a few days before and after the medicine has been taken to help determine whether the medication has improved your symptoms.

Learn about Your Medicine

To promote better understanding of and compliance with medications, Congress passed a law in 1996 requiring that patients be provided with more useful information about the

prescription drugs they are taking.   Information provided
should include:

- the drug name, both the brand name and the nonproprietary (sometimes called *generic*) name;
- warnings relevant to the patient, including indications for
  use and the circumstances under which the drug should
  not be used;
- a list of precautions, such as things to avoid when taking
  the drug, risks to a pregnant or nursing mother or a fetus
  or infant, and risks to children;
- description of symptoms of adverse reactions;
- information about whether the drug is likely to produce
  tolerance to its effect or may be addictive;
- information about proper use of the drug, such as when
  and how to take it; and
- how to store the drug.

If you do not receive or do not understand any of this
information, ask your doctor or pharmacist to give or to
explain it to you.

In addition to information about a specific drug, for patients taking more than one medicine it is helpful to use a
medication list such as that shown in the box opposite. Such
a list should include the name of the drug, the reason for
taking the drug, the dose, the time of day the drug is to be
taken, possible side effects to look for, and the phone numbers
of your doctor and pharmacy. Keep the list with you to refer
to when you are out of the house or require emergency care
and cannot retrieve all your medicines, since your medical
records usually are not available to physicians caring for you
in emergency circumstances.

If you have a drug benefit as part of your health insurance or obtain your medications from a mail-order pharmacy
or use a generic form of a drug, remember that the appearance of pills may change even when the type of medicine
has not changed. For this reason it is essential that you or
a caregiver can read the label of the medication and understand the nonproprietary (the *generic* or non-brand) name of
the drug and the dose of the drug. Do not rely on the
appearance of the pills to determine when, why, and how to
take each medicine. Similarly, when you go to the doctor's
office, bring the bottles the pills came in, rather than individual pills or a description of what the pills look like. One
type of medicine may have many different appearances depending on the manufacturer and describing your medicines

Keeping Track of Your Medications

An example of a medication list with essential information provided. The list should include all over-the-counter medications as well as all prescription medicines. The list should be carried at all times in case of emergency.

Medication List

Date of last review: *11 / 21 /97*   Name: *Sheila Smith*

Medication	Indication	Dose	Time of Day	Other Information
Dyazide	High blood pressure	1 pill	7 AM	Call if dizzy or can't eat or drink because of illness
Aspirin	thin blood + prevent heart attack	1 table (325 mg)	with breakfast	call if blood in stool or black tarry stools
Glyburide	diabetes	2.5 mg.	7 AM	Eat 3 regular meals plus a bedtime snack
Acetaminophen	arthritis pain	1–2 tablets (500 mg)	can take up to 4 times per day	take as needed for pain – no more than 8 tablets per day – don't take if can't eat because of illness

Telephone Numbers

In case of emergency call: *Mrs. Amelia Harkins (sister) 555-3298*
Doctor's office/appointments: *Dr. Prendergast 555-7351*
Pharmacy: *555-6700*

in such a way may lead to confusion regarding which instructions pertain to which drugs. Such confusion could be dangerous.

Simplify Your Medicine Schedule

Although some medicines are to be taken only when needed, for example for pain, most medicines taken for chronic diseases need to be taken on a regular (at least daily) basis. For medicine to be effective, it is important for it to be taken as prescribed. However, remembering to take any medicine every day at the same time can be very difficult without some aids to help.

- **Take once-a-day medicines when possible.** The first step in helping to simplify the medicine schedule is to discuss with your doctor whether any medicines you are taking can be taken less often, or changed to other equally effective medicines that can be taken less often. Some medicines used to lower blood pressure, for example, can be taken once a day, while others have to be taken two or three times a day. Sometimes the medicines that can be taken less frequently also are more expensive, so discuss with your doctor what choice would be best for you.
- **Take medicines together whenever possible.** Most medicines can be taken at the same time without changing the effectiveness of the medicine or causing harmful effects. For example, most medicines that are to be taken once a day in the morning can be taken together in the morning with breakfast (unless the medicine must be taken on an empty stomach). The most common reason not to take medicines together is that it may cause stomach upset; if this occurs, take the medicines a few minutes apart. Some medicines should not be taken together with other medicines (take at least two hours apart), such as cholestyramine and psyllium (Metamucil, for example), which can prevent other medicine from being absorbed. Antacids also can prevent a drug from being absorbed. Other medicines, such as those used to treat diabetes, must be taken one hour or a half hour before breakfast so that the medicine is working in the bloodstream when breakfast is eaten. All medicines should be taken with plenty of water, usually a glass full.

  Medicine taken at other times of the day also may be taken together. However, medicine taken at bedtime should be taken with a full glass of water and swallowed before lying down. If you lie down before the medicine has passed into your stomach, the medicine may lodge in your throat or esophagus (swallowing tube) and cause irritation.
- **Use aids to help you remember to take pills.** Several types of aids are available to help you remember when to take medicine and remember which medicine you have already taken.
- **Medication schedule.** The simplest aid is a written schedule of your medicine. Write down which medicines are

Medication Schedule

7 AM	12 Noon	4 PM	10 PM
Digoxin 1 tablet		Enalapril 1 tablet	Coumadin 1 tablet
Furosemide 1½ tablets		Furosemide 1 tablet	
Enalapril 1 tablet			
Aspirin 1 tablet (with breakfast)			
Potassium 1 packet mixed in glass of orange juice			

to be taken at morning, afternoon, and night, and use it to refer to when you have questions or visit your doctor. An example is shown on the opposite page.

- **Pill box.** The pill box is available at drug stores and contains a separate compartment for each day of the week. Boxes are also available with separate compartments for different times of the day in addition to each day of the week. These boxes can also be used to carry a day's supply of pills when spending the day away from one's home. Pills should not be mixed in the same bottle for convenience, since many pills are similar in appearance and may be easily confused. The pill box is a safer alternative.

  The pill box can also aid in remembering which medicine has already been taken, and to use for people who have difficulty opening pill bottles. The pill box may be filled by a caregiver or visiting nurse at the beginning of each week. However, if the person taking the pills cannot remember whether he or she has taken medicine and might take extra doses, the person needs to be supervised for each dose of medicine.

■ **Medication calendar.** A medication calendar is used to check off which doses of medicine have been taken on which day. The doses for the week or month can be written down ahead of time and crossed off as they are taken. The medication calendar is especially helpful for medicine with a dose that may vary from day to day, such as the blood thinner warfarin. An example is shown on the next page.

While these techniques are especially useful for medicine taken on a long-term basis, they also can be useful for medicines taken for a short period of time, such as antibiotics. Antibiotics should be taken as prescribed to have the best chance of curing the infection and should be taken until all the pills are gone. Antibiotics should not be stopped as soon as symptoms resolve, because the infection may return.

Physical Problems with Taking Medicines

If you are unable to swallow pills, several alternatives are available. For example, potassium tablets are often large and can be taken as a liquid instead. Many drugs are available as suspensions. Unfortunately, suspensions are often more expensive than the pill form of the same drug and may need to be refrigerated. Your doctor or pharmacist can tell you if pills may be crushed and mixed with food. Sustained-release medicine cannot be crushed and other types of medicine may have special coatings to ensure that they are absorbed properly; ask first before you crush pills.

Child-safety caps can be difficult to open for a person with arthritis or a stroke. If you have difficulty opening pill bottles and live in a house with no small children, your pharmacist can provide you with bottles with snap-off or simple screw-on lids.

The High Cost of Medicines

Medicines are often expensive and represent one of the greatest health costs for people over 65 years of age. Drug companies have often invested years of research in developing new drugs and drugs can be expensive to produce and market. All these factors contribute to the high cost of medications. However, there are ways to reduce the costs of drugs. First of all, during your medication checkup determine if there are any drugs you no longer need to take or if any drugs can be substituted with less expensive brands, such as a generic form. Although certain drugs such as Coumadin generally

Medication Calendar

When medication doses differ from day to day, a calendar helps to keep track of what dose should be taken on which day. Here the daily doses of coumadin are written on the calendar, along with the days on which blood tests will be performed to determine whether the dosage should be adjusted. As each dose is taken, the day is marked to indicate the medicine has been taken. In this example, after the blood test on April 6th, the dose was reduced slightly (from from 5 mg for 2 days followed by 2.5 mg for 1 day to 5 mg alternating with 2.5 mg). The blood test result from April 13 will determine the dosing schedule for the next week.

APRIL   1998

			1	2	3	4
			Coumadin 5mg	Coumadin 5mg	Coumadin 2.5mg	Coumadin 5mg
5 Coumadin 5mg	6 Coumadin 2.5mg get blood test ✓	7 Coumadin 2.5mg	8 Coumadin 5mg	9 Coumadin 2.5mg	10 Coumadin 5mg	11 Coumadin 2.5mg
12 Coumadin 5mg	13 Coumadin 2.5mg get blood test ✓	14	15	16	17	18
19	20	21	22	23	24	25
26	27	28	29	30		

should not be substituted with generic drugs, most other drugs can be. Drugs that generally should not be routinely substituted with generic forms are those with a narrow *therapeutic window*—drugs for which the toxic dose is close to the therapeutic dose.

If you are unable to afford your medicine and must forgo necessities to purchase medicine, be sure to tell your doctor. Programs are available that may be able to help you pay for your medicines. Many forms of health insurance have a plan in which prescription medicines cost only a small copayment per prescription. Other plans are run by state or local governments and provide help in paying for essential medications for chronic diseases for individuals below a certain income level. Some drug companies have assistance programs available for patients who cannot afford their medications. Meeting with a social worker will help you learn more about assistance programs that are available. Always tell your doctor if you are not able to buy your medicine, since your doctor may be able to help find ways to make your medicine affordable.

Another way to reduce the amount you spend on drugs is to find a pharmacy that has lower prices for medications (national chains are often less expensive because they buy in bulk). However, keep in mind that you should purchase medications from one pharmacy whenever possible so that the pharmacist has your medications and medication allergies on record and can check for drug interactions. In addition, pills may be less expensive if purchased in the same containers as they come from the drug company, for example in bottles of 100 or 250 pills, since they do not have to be repackaged by the pharmacist. Your pharmacist can discuss options with you.

Do Not Share Medicines!

It is important never to share medicines, using a medicine prescribed for one person to treat another person, since a medicine that works to relieve the symptoms of one illness may not help another illness and may actually make another illness worse. One example is shortness of breath, which can be caused by emphysema (called chronic obstructive pulmonary disease by health professionals), pneumonia, angina, or heart failure, in addition to other diseases. Each of these illnesses has distinct treatments, and some medicines used to relieve symptoms of emphysema can worsen angina and vice versa. Sharing medicines can also lead to dangerous side effects from taking too much medication. Two people may need different drugs for the same medical condition because of other medical problems, or may take drugs that are the same chemically but are referred to by different brand names. If someone you know takes a medicine you think might help you, learn what you can about the drug and ask your physician whether the drug might be appropriate for you.

Commonly Used Medicines

Medicines Used to Treat Constipation

Many preparations are available for people who experience constipation. Medications often are not the best way to treat constipation, however, since constipation is a very common problem as people age and often results from lack of fiber and roughage in the diet, rather than from a specific medical condition. Many of the medicines used to treat constipation have side effects and are expensive, so it is best to increase intake of fruits, vegetables, and whole grains first when treating constipation. Drinking adequate amounts of water (several glasses per day) is also important. If increased fiber is not enough, drinking prune juice or eating prunes daily can help prevent constipation, as can psyllium taken with two 8 ounce glasses of water daily.

If these measures do not work, a number of preparations are available over the counter and by prescription. Over-the-counter laxatives should be avoided since, when taken on a long-term basis, they may produce dependence on the laxatives to achieve regular bowel movements. Colace or Senekot are stool softeners that can be helpful but expensive. They are useful for people with diabetes who should not drink large quantities of prune juice because of its sugar content. Medicines such as Milk of Magnesia or magnesium citrate can be effective but also may cause abdominal cramping and nausea and can lead to elevated levels of magnesium in the blood stream if taken in large quantities, especially if a person's kidneys do not function properly.

If constipation is severe and chronic or caused by medications (most commonly, narcotic pain medicine such as codeine or morphine), a regular bowel regimen is especially important. Such a regimen includes drinking plenty of water and other liquids, eating several servings that include fiber daily, and drinking prune juice. Lactulose is a liquid that acts by drawing water into the colon and softening stool; it is effective at relieving constipation and does not tend to create the dependence on laxatives that over-the-counter laxatives do. Lactulose can be taken in increasing doses as needed. It occasionally may be accompanied by cramping or bloating, although in my experience this is much less common with lactulose than with magnesium-containing preparations. Lactulose may take up to 24 to 48 hours to induce a bowel movement.

If constipation is severe and no bowel movement has occurred for several days, fecal impaction (large amounts of very hard stool in the colon that cannot be cleared by a bowel movement) may occur and necessitate disimpaction by gloved hand. Incontinence of stool and urine, as well as more severe medical problems, may be caused by fecal impaction. Thus, it is important that regular (at least every other day) bowel movements be maintained and a regular bowel program (fiber, prune juice, and/or psyllium taken daily with or without medication) be instituted for people who have chronic problems with constipation.

Medicines Used to Relieve Pain

Acetaminophen

The most commonly used drugs to relieve pain are those that can be purchased over the counter. Acetaminophen (Tylenol, and many less expensive generic forms) generally is safe and rarely interferes with other medicines. It can be as effective as drugs such as ibuprofen for arthritis pain if taken regularly. It should be taken in the smallest dose effective to relieve pain and no more than 4 grams per day, to avoid the rare but serious adverse effect of liver failure, usually seen with overdoses of the drug. Fasting for a few days or drinking alcohol while taking acetaminophen on a regular basis have been associated with liver failure in the cases that have occurred.

Aspirin and Other Nonsteroidal Anti-Inflammatory Drugs

Aspirin, or acetylsalicylic acid, is effective for a wide variety of aches and pains but can cause gastrointestinal upset and bleeding. Irritation of the stomach lining and gastrointestinal upset may be reduced by taking aspirin with meals and by using enteric-coated formulations of the drug. However, if aspirin is taken to relieve pain, using the enteric-coated form or taking aspirin with meals will delay the start of pain relief from the drug by delaying how quickly the drug is absorbed. Taking aspirin with antacids also will delay absorption of the drug into the body. When taken in small doses (80 mg to 325 mg per day), aspirin is effective in reducing the risk of heart attack and stroke in many groups of patients, likely because it reduces the tendency of the blood to clot. It should not be taken with blood thinners such as warfarin or in patients with bleeding disorders unless intentionally prescribed by a doctor to further reduce the tendency of the blood to clot.

Many other over-the-counter formulations such as cold formulas, etc., contain aspirin and people who have been advised to avoid aspirin should review the contents of all over the counter medicines before ingesting them. These same precautions and recommendations apply to most other drugs in the family called nonsteroidal anti-inflammatory drugs (NSAIDs), except that non-aspirin nonsteroidal drugs have not been shown to be effective in reducing risk of heart attack or stroke. Finally, all nonsteroidal anti-inflammatory drugs taken regularly can elevate blood pressure and may reduce the effectiveness of medicines used to lower blood pressure.

Indomethacin, most often used to treat an attack of gout or some rare types of arthritis, may be more likely to cause side effects such as gastrointestinal bleeding and confusion than other types of nonsteroidal anti-inflammatory drugs, although these adverse effects may occur with any of this class of drugs.

Salsalate is related to aspirin but is less likely to cause gastrointestinal upset. It can be effective in treating pain caused by arthritis. It can produce tinnitus when given in high doses, like aspirin. It does not prevent the blood from clotting and so is not useful in helping to prevent strokes and heart attacks.

Topical Preparations

Other pain medicines available over the counter include preparations to be applied to the skin. These medicines may be helpful for mild pain. Capsaicin is available for pain from shingles and some use it for arthritis pain with some success. Lidocaine ointment is available for skin surface pain, but may cause sensitization and a rash if applied more than once and should be avoided.

Control of Chronic Severe Pain

Many pain medicines are available by prescription. In general, chronic pain, such as that from moderate to severe arthritis or from cancer, should be treated with a regular dose of pain medicine (as opposed to "as needed") with additional doses as needed for breakthrough pain. A pain scale, used to rate pain severity, is useful to help determine whether pain control is effective and which medication schedule is best for treating and preventing pain.

Narcotic Pain Medicine

If acetaminophen or nonsteroidal anti-inflammatory drugs are not effective at controlling pain or cannot be tolerated because of side effects, narcotic medicines may be used alone or in combination with nonsteroidals or other analgesics. Tylenol (acetaminophen) with codeine is one common preparation. Codeine is often effective, but about 10% of the population are unable to convert codeine to morphine, the active drug, and may not benefit from codeine. Codeine is a narcotic and like all drugs in the narcotic family may be habit-forming when used long-term in some people. However, the possibility of becoming addicted to narcotics should not prevent patients and physicians from controlling severe pain. If you have been taking a narcotic drug for some time, including Tylenol with codeine, Darvocet, Vicodin (acetaminophen with hydrocodone), or others, you may experience mild withdrawal symptoms if you stop the drug suddenly. Withdrawal can be uncomfortable but can be minimized with a gradual reduction of drug dose. If you have been taking the medicine for several weeks or more, talk with your doctor before stopping the drug altogether.

The most common side effects of narcotics are drowsiness and constipation. Driving should be avoided when taking narcotic medicines. Although the side effects of these medicines tend to diminish over time, drowsiness and confusion should be monitored. A regular bowel program should be instituted before constipation occurs.

Some narcotic medicines are especially likely to cause side effects in older patients. Meperidine (Demerol is one brand name) is a narcotic that is metabolized into another drug that accumulates in fat and may cause confusion and seizures when taken over days. Because of the changes that occur as people age, older people are especially likely to experience side effects from meperidine and its use generally should be avoided. Propoxyphene (Darvon) also has a metabolite that may accumulate and cause confusion and heart problems in older adults. Pentazocine also should be avoided because of the possibility of seizures and cardiac toxicity.

Muscle Relaxants

Muscle relaxants or antispasmodics occasionally may be prescribed. These drugs are potent and have a high likelihood of causing side effects such as drowsiness and confusion. At least one panel of physician experts has recommended that older people not be given cyclobenzaprine, orphenidrate, methocarbamol, or carisoprodol because of these potential problems and the availability of other, safer, alternative medications.

Steroids

Steroids occasionally are used to treat pain. Because steroids taken by mouth cause many side effects, steroids are often given locally at the pain site. Injections of steroids into a joint such as the knee by a doctor experienced in the technique such may be very effective in reducing pain from acute injury or arthritis, although osteoporosis may be caused by repeated injections. Steroids taken by mouth are sometimes used to treat pain for diseases such as rheumatoid arthritis, usually with other drugs that help prevent the most serious problems with joints that occur with rheumatoid arthritis. Because of the many side effects that prednisone has on the endocrine system, the immune system, and bones, prednisone generally should not be used to treat pain from the most common form of arthritis, osteoarthritis.

Neuropathic Pain

Pain caused by inflammation or damage to the nerves, called neuropathic pain, can be treated with tricyclic antidepressant drugs or drugs used to treat seizures (such as phenytoin or carbamazepine), in addition to other types of pain medicine mentioned above. Tricyclic antidepressant drugs are discussed below under drugs used to treat depression and anxiety.

Drugs Used to Treat Problems with Sleep

The number of hours a person sleeps generally declines with age, so that a person who slept 8 hours at age 40 may sleep only 6 hours at age 80. While for some people this amount of sleep will be adequate, others do not feel adequately rested. Sleep complaints are most frequent among older people, who may have difficulty falling asleep or may wake up several times during the night. Some sleep problems may be caused by external factors, such as napping during the day or needing to urinate frequently at night, or medical problems such as heart failure or sleep apnea. Depression is a common cause of reduced sleep in older people. Whenever possible, external factors should be corrected first when trying to improve sleep. If sleep continues to be inadequate after correctable problems have been addressed, a sleep diary can be used to identify which difficulties with sleep cause the most concern. Factors that may contribute to problems with sleep should be explored before using a medication for sleep.

Several activities can help improve sleep. Regular exercise during the day, such as walking or using a stationary bicycle (no later than early afternoon, to avoid having exercise keep a person awake), has been shown to improve sleep in older people. Sleep hygiene is important and includes factors such as creating a relaxing bedtime ritual that is used each night, avoiding caffeine in the second half of the day and alcohol in general, and associating the bed with sleep and not reading or lying awake for long periods in bed after early morning awakening. Milk, warm or cold, may help sleep when taken at bedtime. Tryptophan has been used by some to help sleep, but some tryptophan supplements contained an impurity linked to the occurrence of eosinophilia-myalgia syndrome. Melatonin is a naturally occurring hormone that, when taken for sleep, is used in much higher doses than normally found in the body. While some studies have shown improved sleep for some people, others have found that taking melatonin at the wrong time of day can actually make sleep worse. Melatonin may be most useful as an aid for people traveling across time zones to avoid jet lag or for people doing shift work. Although current evidence is mixed, melatonin generally is not recommended for sleep in older people.

Medications used for sleep can help short term sleep problems, such as a person who has difficulty sleeping after a spouse has died or another major life event. However, the effectiveness of medications for sleep tends to diminish over time as tolerance develops. Sleeping pills can result in disordered sleep, in which the normal pattern of sleep is disrupted and very difficult to restore. Because of the lack of long term effectiveness and many side effects associated with sleeping pills, methods other than sleeping pills should be used whenever possible. A person chronically suffering from problems with sleep should be evaluated by a doctor to determine if a medical cause is responsible. Alcohol and sleeping pills should never be mixed; the combination reduces the drive to breath and can be deadly.

One commonly used class of sleeping pills is the benzodiazepines, which include medicines such as triazolam (Halcion), temazepam (Restoril), and flurazepam (Dalmane). These medicines can be useful for some people to restore sleep over the short-term. However, they reduce balance and increase the risk of falls in older people. Confusion, agitation, and inability of remember events (especially with short-acting drugs such as triazolam) may occur. Longer-acting drugs such as flurazepam can accumulate in the body, leading to a "hung-over" feeling the next day and reduced ability to drive and understand and react normally.

One drug that has recently become available is called zolpidem. Zolpidem is related to benzodiazepines but is less likely to be habit-forming. However, zolpidem can still cause confusion and memory difficulty in some patients. It is a relatively new drug, so its effects on balance and risk of falls are not yet known. It has been shown to be effective for improving sleep and may be useful for some patients who have not responded to the non-medication treatments listed above and who do not have a medical cause for their insomnia.

Diphenhydramine (Benadryl, Nytol, Sominex), a drug that is sometimes used to treat itching, is also used for sleep since one of its effects is drowsiness. However, diphenhydramine has many other side effects including dry mouth and constipation, and less commonly, confusion or inability to urinate, and so may be potentially harmful to older people. Diphenhydramine is included in many over-the-counter preparations for cold and flu, in varying doses; read labels carefully to determine if this drug is contained in an over-the-counter preparation.

Chloral hydrate is a less commonly used sleeping pill that has a rapid onset of action to reduce time in falling asleep, and stays in the bloodstream anywhere from 4 to 12 hours. As with other sleeping pills, it should never be mixed with alcohol. If taken in too high a dose over time, it has the potential for causing drug withdrawal and death.

Medicines that have been used in the past for sleeping pills but should be avoided if at all possible include meprobomate (Miltown), which can cause low blood pressure and severe withdrawal, in addition to confusion and incoordination; and the barbiturates secobarbital and pentobarbital, which can cause confusion, interact with alcohol to reduce respiration, and interact with many other drugs.

In people who are depressed or have a disturbance in mood with sleep problems, the tricyclic antidepressant drugs or a related drug, trazodone, are often prescribed. These drugs are discussed in more detail below. Tricyclic antidepressants have the advantage of causing fewer of the side effects listed above and are especially useful for patients in whom depression contributes to difficulty with sleep.

Drugs Used to Treat Depression and Anxiety

Depression is a medical medical condition that is often difficult to detect early in the course of illness without the use of screening tests. Two major classes of drugs are used to treat depression. One class, which comprises the tricyclic antidepressants (drugs such as nortryptiline, desipramine, and amitryptiline) and related drugs such as trazodone, has been available for many years. The other class, the selective serotonin reuptake inhibitors, or SSRIs, includes drugs such as fluoxetine, sertraline, and paroxetine, and has become available relatively recently. Both types of drugs are effective at relieving depression, although they generally take 4 weeks or so to affect mood, but each have side effects that should be taken into account when choosing one class over another. The drugs are occasionally used in combination, such as the use of trazodone in people taking SSRIs to help reduce problems with sleep.

Side effects of the tricyclic family of antidepressants include orthostatic hypotension (decreased blood pressure on standing that may produce dizziness), dry mouth, dry eyes, constipation, and occasionally, urinary retention or confusion. The tricyclics can affect the conduction of impulses through the heart and are usually avoided in people with heart disease. Newer drugs in the class, such as trazodone, tend to have fewer effects on the heart. The sedating effect of these drugs is often used to advantage by giving them at bedtime, since people who suffer with depression often have difficulty sleeping. The tricyclics often cause an increase in appetite, an advantage in older people with decreased appetite and weight loss as part of their depression. One tricyclic that is especially likely to cause sedation, dry mouth, dry eyes, and urinary retention is amitryptiline. While amitryptiline has been used more than other tricyclic drugs in treating some neuropathic pain syndromes, other drugs used to treat depression are usually preferable in older people because of these side effects.

The SSRIs have fewer effects on the heart and are less likely to cause a fall in blood pressure on standing and thus can be useful in treating depression in older people. However, they tend to cause agitation rather than sedation, and should be taken in the morning. (As mentioned above, trazodone is sometimes used at bedtime for a person taking SSRIs to help with sleep.) In addition, the SSRIs may reduce appetite in some people, an important problem for older patients who have lost weight with their depression and may be undernourished. Thus, weight and appetite should be monitored when using these drugs.

A less commonly used but effective class of drugs used to treat depression is the monoamine oxidase (MAO) inhibitors. These drugs are generally used to treat depression that does not respond to the other classes of antidepressant drugs. MAO inhibitors share many side effects with the tricyclic drugs, but the most difficult aspect of taking MAO inhibitors is the wide range of foods and medicines that must be avoided because they produce potentially life-threatening severe high blood pressure in the presence of MAO inhibitors. For example, people who take MAO inhibitors must be careful to avoid most cheeses, smoked fish, sausage, beer, and red wine, as well as several other foods. Many medicines available over the counter interact with MAO inhibitors, such as cold medicines, diet aids, and nasal decongestants. Many other prescription drugs should not be taken with MAO inhibitors as well, including the SSRIs. Thus, patients taking MAO inhibitors should understand which foods and medicines to avoid and carefully follow the instructions.

Methylphenidate, or Ritalin, is occasionally used to treat depression. It is a stimulant and may be used to treat people who are so severely depressed their health may be endangered by the four weeks or so the antidepressant drugs often need to take effect. Methylphenidate generally is used only for people whose depression is so severe that they require hospitalization.

Anxiety

Anxiety is a disorder that often occurs with depression. When anxiety occurs in a person who is depressed, treatment of the depression will often relieve the anxiety. Some people may not respond to antidepressant medication alone or may have only anxiety. In these people, anxiety medicine may be helpful. Buspirone is one antianxiety medicine with few side effects and does not tend to be habit-forming. However, the drug generally must be taken for 2 to 4 weeks before it begins to relieve anxiety.

The benzodiazepine class of drugs are also an effective treatment for anxiety. However, these drugs tend to be habit forming and can accumulate in the body of an older person. They can cause sedation and confusion and reduce balance,

Those Little Labels

Some medications may come with one or more little colored labels affixed to the container. They are intended for the specific medication and carry very brief instructions that are important for its use. If you think that they contradict what your physician has told you, call your physician.

While there are dozens of such labels available, explaining a few will help to understand their importance.

- **Shake well before using.** Some medications in liquid form have an active ingredient in suspension. If taken without shaking the active ingredient may have either risen to the top or settled to the bottom of the medicine bottle, resulting in either an insufficient dose or an overdose.

- **Take medication on an empty stomach.** As the first step in digestion, the body produces acid to break down food as it enters the stomach. Some drugs are also broken down (and inactivated) by stomach acid.

- **Take with food.** A wide number of medications, such as aspirin, are potentially irritating to the stomach, and food can act as a protective buffer against gastric distress.

- **Do not take dairy products, antacids, or iron preparations within 1 hour of this preparation.** These foods tend to impair the absorption of certain drugs, such as tetracyclines.

- **Avoid prolonged or excessive exposure to direct sunlight.** A few drug can cause photosensitivity in some people that can result in skin reactions, including rash and discoloration.

- **It may be advisable to drink a full glass of orange juice or eat a banana daily while taking this medication.** Some diuretics reduce the amount of potassium absorbed from the alimentary tract. These foods are a good way to make more potassium available.

increasing the risk of falls in some people. In general, shorter-acting benzodiazepines such as alprazolam and oxazepam are preferred over longer-acting benzodiazepines because they accumulate less in the body over time and cause less sedation. The very long acting benzodiazepines diazepam (Valium) and chlordiazepoxide (Librium) should be avoided in older people because of the increased likelihood of adverse effects.

Drugs Used to Treat Memory Loss

Treating Memory Loss

Dementia from Alzheimer's disease or small strokes (multi-infarct dementia) is a common and devastating problem, for which many possible treatments have been evaluated. However, no medicines have been found that prevent the disease or prevent progression of the memory loss. Only one class of drugs, the acetylcholinesterase inhibitors (which includes tacrine and donezepil), has been shown to improve memory in Alzheimer's disease consistently in controlled trials. This class of drugs does not prevent the progression of Alzheimer's disease but can improve memory in some people with mild Alzheimer's disease while the person is taking the drug. The improvement seen is equivalent to reversing 4 to 6 months of deterioration in memory. Both tacrine and donepezil can cause nausea and vomiting, although this effect is reportedly less common with donepezil. Tacrine can also cause reversible liver damage, so a blood test for liver function has to be performed every other week for at least three months while the dose of the drug is increased.

Some studies have suggested that estrogens, nonsteroidal anti-inflammatory drugs, and vitamin E and possible selegiline (an anti-Parkinson's drug), may improve memory or prevent Alzheimer's disease, but these studies have not been conclusive; some have only observed an association between people who used these drugs and a lower likelihood of having Alzheimer's disease. Drugs that have been shown to not be effective include cyclandelate and isoxsuprine. Lecithin has also been used, and while probably harmless, does not appear to be better than placebo (a dummy pill without medicine).

Dementia caused by multiple strokes, often so small they do not cause other symptoms, is another common cause of memory loss and is called multi-infarct dementia. While no treatment exists to reverse the damage caused by the strokes, stopping smoking, control of high blood pressure, and low-dose aspirin (325 mg per day or less) can help prevent subsequent strokes and hence help slow the decline in memory.

Other diseases may cause loss of memory and tests to detect them are performed as part of the medical evaluation for dementia. These diseases include depression, underactive thyroid (hypothyroidism), vitamin B_{12} deficiency, and syphilis that has gone untreated or undertreated for years. All of these conditions can be treated with medication and, if caught early in the disease, can help improve or at least slow the memory loss from the disease.

Treating Behavioral Problems

Drugs are sometimes used to treat the behavioral problems associated with memory loss. These drugs do not improve memory or slow the course of disease, but can help reduce specific behaviors that may put others at risk, such as hitting, biting, or kicking, and hallucinations (seeing or hearing things that are not there) or delusions (seeing or hearing something as something it is not).

Behaviors such as reversal of the sleep-wake cycle (people with dementia sometimes sleep during the day and are awake all night) are best treated by encouraging exercise and other stimulating activities during the daytime. If necessary, however, the sleep–wake cycle reversal can be treated with sedating antidepressants such as trazodone given at bedtime, while agitation may be treated with antianxiety medications such as buspirone. If these drugs are ineffective, low doses of a neuroleptic drug may be needed. Neuroleptic drugs are especially effective at reducing disturbing hallucinations or delusions, but can be very sedating and have several other side effects. The most commonly used drugs are risperidone, haloperidol, and thioridazine. The side effects of neuroleptics include sedation, dry mouth, urinary retention (inability to empty the bladder), and an increased risk of falls. Some people develop symptoms resembling those of Parkinson's disease (shuffling gait, a tremor in the hand at rest, overall stiffness, face appears like a mask). These should resolve once the drug is stopped.

An uncommon but potentially devastating side effect of neuroleptics is tardive dyskinesia, a movement disorder usually of the face (grimacing or lip smacking) that cannot be controlled by the individual. Tardive dyskinesia is most likely to occur with large doses of neuroleptics given over a long period of time, but occasionally can occur after small doses given for a short period. Tardive dyskinesia usually is not reversible even when the drug is stopped, but may get worse if the drug is continued. Thus, when using neuroleptics it is extremely important to identify specific target symptoms to be treated and review these target symptoms at each physician visit to determine if the drug is effective or necessary. Side effects should be assessed and signs of tardive dyskinesia should be specifically looked for in patients taking the drug.

Neuroleptic drugs are also used to treat psychiatric conditions that include psychosis (the most severe form of psychiatric disease), but the use of these medications for such psychiatric diagnoses will not be discussed here.

Drugs Used to Treat High Blood Pressure

High blood pressure in older people is usually defined as a systolic blood pressure greater than 160 mm Hg or a diastolic blood pressure greater than 90 mm Hg. If high blood pressure is found on two occasions with two separate measurements when a person has been sitting or lying down for 5 minutes, the individual has hypertension. Hypertension, if untreated, can lead to heart attack, heart failure, stroke, or death. Hypertension can be effectively treated through a combination of lifestyle changes and, if necessary, medications. Lifestyle changes that can help lower blood pressure include increasing the amount of regular exercise, losing weight if a person is overweight, reducing salt intake (some individuals are more *salt-sensitive* than others), increasing intake of food and vegetables, and stopping smoking and drinking alcohol. Meeting with a dietician to discuss your diet may be helpful to learn what foods to avoid and what foods to consume. If high blood pressure persists after these measures, medications to lower blood pressure generally are necessary.

Based on studies of the ability of antihypertensive drugs to reduce stroke and heart attack, experts recommend that for people with other medical conditions, the initial antihypertensive medications that should be prescribed to control high blood pressure are the thiazide diuretics, such as hydrochlorothiazide, or beta-blockers, such as metoprolol or atenolol. While these medications are recommended for people with hypertension in general, other medications a person is taking and other medical problems should be taken into account when choosing an antihypertensive medication. For example, diuretics can sometimes worsen or precipitate urinary incontinence and beta-blockers should not be used in people with asthma or emphysema. Beta blockers should not be stopped suddenly in people with heart disease because stopping the medicine may worsen angina. People with heart failure or diabetes may benefit from angiotensin converting enzyme inhibitors (ACE inhibitors) such as enalapril, lisinopril, or captopril. People who have angina may be treated with beta blockers or with calcium channel blockers, such as nifepidine, amlodipine, verapamil, or diltiazem. Men with prostate symptoms may be treated with prazosin or terazosin.

Because hypertension is a chronic problem that often requires taking medication for years, I prefer to treat patients with medicine that must be taken once or at most twice a day, to reduce the number of times a person must remember to take the medicine. Many drugs, for example, captopril and nifedipine, must be taken more than once a day, although nifedipine is available in a long-acting form that can be taken once a day.

Some physicians and researchers have been concerned about using nifedipine and other medicines in a subset of calcium channel blockers called the dihydropyridines to lower blood pressure. These drugs tend to increase the heart rate, which can increase the work of the heart. In addition, some researchers have observed an increased rate of heart problems among people who use dihydropyridine calcium channel blockers, while others have not. In general, I tend to prefer verapamil to the other calcium channel blockers, although verapamil can cause constipation, especially in older people. Although diuretics and beta blockers are recommended for initial treatment for hypertension, some doctors believe that ACE inhibitors and calcium channel blockers have fewer side effects than diuretics and beta blockers and so prescribe those drugs more often for their patients. In my experience, however, most people tolerate diuretics very well and many tolerate beta blockers. In addition, they are very inexpensive drugs, an important consideration for many patients.

All medicines used to treat high blood pressure can cause impotence in some individuals, but people who have impotence with one drug may benefit from another drug. If impotence is a problem for you and you are taking medicine for high blood pressure, you can discuss options for other blood pressure medicines or other treatments for impotence with your doctor.

Another side effect of high blood pressure medicine is orthostatic hypotension, or a fall in blood pressure when rising from sitting or lying down. Orthostatic hypotension may be accompanied by dizziness. Your doctor can check for orthostatic hypotension during your office visit, particularly if you have had dizziness or falls or near-falls. One way to combat dizziness when rising from bed is to sit on the side of the bed for a minute or so, dangling your legs. This pause before you stand up gives your blood vessels time to compensate for the change in position and can help prevent the fall in blood pressure and the dizziness you may feel when standing up.

Medicines that used to be commonly prescribed for high blood pressure include methyldopa and reserpine. These medicines lower blood pressure, but have many more side effects than other drugs now available. Thus, most physicians do not prescribe these drugs. Methyldopa accumulates in the body over time and can cause sedation or a low blood count (hemolytic anemia), and reserpine has been associated with an increased rate of depression. If you are taking either of these medicines and have questions about them, ask your doctor about alternatives before stopping any medicine. To avoid increasing risk of stroke or heart attack, antihypertensive medicine should not be stopped without blood pressure monitoring.

Drugs Used to Lower Cholesterol

Reducing high cholesterol levels has been shown to reduce the risk of heart disease in many populations of people. Reducing high cholesterol is especially important for people who already have heart disease or stroke, but most people without these conditions also should try to lower elevated cholesterol. A benefit from cholesterol lowering has not been shown for people who will survive less than 10 years, so these people generally should not be treated for high cholesterol. When considering treatment for high cholesterol, it should be remembered that stopping smoking, controlling high blood pressure, and getting regular exercise are also important ways to reduce the risk of heart attack and stroke.

Cholesterol consists of of several components that can be measured individually. Total cholesterol is used to screen for high cholesterol; the target cholesterol level is 200 mg/dL or less. Total cholesterol between 200 and 240 is considered borderline, and 240 and above is elevated; patients with cholesterol of 240 or above are considered at high risk for atherosclerotic disease (hardening of the arteries). Components of cholesterol that are measured include LDL (low-density lipoprotein — often referred to as *bad* cholesterol; a higher level means higher risk for atherosclerosis) and HDL (high-density lipoprotein — often referred to as *good* cholesterol; a higher level means lower risk for atherosclerosis). Elevated triglycerides also increase risk for heart disease and usually are identified because of a high VLDL level (very low density lipoprotein).

The first step in reducing elevated cholesterol is to reduce your intake of cholesterol and especially saturated fats. I have found it helpful for patients to meet with a dietician to discuss favorite foods and identify which foods should be avoided. Favorite foods often may be eaten in moderation; a dietician can help plan a diet that includes a variety of flavorful meals. Regular exercise, such as 20 minutes of walking at least 4 to 5 days per week, can help reduce weight and lower cholesterol. Reducing alcohol intake is necessary if triglycerides are elevated. If diet, weight loss, and exercise are ineffective in reducing cholesterol levels, and particularly if other risk factors for atherosclerosis are present such as smoking, hypertension, diabetes, or obesity, medications to lower cholesterol may be necessary.

Several types of cholesterol-lowering drugs are available. Cholestyramine is relatively inexpensive and has a sandy consistency; it should be taken with plenty of liquids to avoid constipation. Cholestyramine should be taken 1 hour before or 4 hours after other medicines to avoid interfering with their absorption. Colestipol is a drug similar to cholestyramine but more granular and with less taste. Since neither are absorbed into the bloodstream, both have few side effects other than bloating or nausea. They can be taken with fruit juice, applesauce, or flavored low-fat yogurt to make them more palatable, but again, plenty of water is needed to help prevent constipation.

Nicotinic acid is an inexpensive and effective drug, but must be gradually increased and taken with meals to minimize the common side effect of flushing of the face, neck, and trunk soon after taking the drug. Nicotinic acid can be toxic to the liver when taken in higher doses, and so a blood test to measure liver enzymes should be taken as the dose is increased. Liver toxicity may be more common with sustained-release niacin.

Several types of pills are available to lower cholesterol. These have the advantage of being easier to take, but are also more expensive and have more systemic effects than cholestyramine or colestipol. Gemfibrizol and clofibrate are effective (evaluated primarily in middle-aged men) but can cause gallstones. They have the advantage of lowering VLDL (very low density lipoprotein), so they are especially useful for patients who have high triglycerides.

The class of drugs called HMG-CoA reductase inhibitors are commonly used to lower cholesterol, and includes the drugs lovastatin, simvistatin, and pravastatin. These drugs are expensive and can cause gastrointestinal side effects, but are very effective at lowering LDL and are usually well tolerated.

Estrogen replacement therapy will often lower cholesterol in women and can be used as initial treatment for women interested in receiving estrogen replacement for other reasons.

Drugs Used to Treat Chest Pain or Angina

Pain in the chest may come from many sources: from the heart, the esophagus (swallowing tube) or stomach, the lungs, or the muscles and joints in the chest. Chest pain from lack of blood flow to the heart is classically described as a heavy pressure in the chest or ache in the left arm associated with shortness of breath or sweating and lasting minutes as opposed to seconds. However, heart pain, or angina, is described in many different ways, so any pain or pressure in the chest that lasts more a minute or recurs regularly should be evaluated by a physician. Angina may also be experienced as neck or shoulder pain with exertion, accompanied by shortness of breath. If the pain comes from the heart, medicine and/or surgery may be used to reduce the work of the heart or relieve the blockage in arteries that usually causes angina.

Several medicines are available to treat angina. Nitroglycerin is used to treat an episode of chest pain and acts by dilating (widening) the blood vessels, increasing the blood flow and lessening the work of the heart. When nitroglycerin tablets are placed under the tongue and allowed to dissolve, they are rapidly absorbed into the bloodstream and generally relieve angina pain quickly. Typically, when nitroglycerin is taken in this way it produces a tingling sensation under the tongue; nitroglycerin and other types of nitrates often produce a headache that resolves within 20 minutes or so, especially when nitrates are first started. If no tingling or headache is felt, the nitroglycerin may be outdated and, if so, should be discarded. Each bottle has an expiration date; a person with angina should make sure he or she has nitroglycerin on hand that has not expired. If possible, nitroglycerin tablets should be taken while sitting or lying down since they can cause dizziness by making the blood pressure fall.

If one nitroglycerin tablet does not relieve the pain after 5 minutes, another tablet may be taken. If a person with angina takes a total of 3 tablets without relief from chest pain, he or she should go to the emergency room as soon as possible because the chest pain may be caused by an impending heart attack, which usually will not resolve with nitroglycerin.

Other medicines are taken on a regular basis to prevent angina. Aspirin, usually 325 mg. or less each day, should be taken to help thin the blood unless a person is unable to or should not take aspirin. Aspirin should be taken with meals to reduce irritation of the stomach lining; aspirin can cause bleeding in the gastrointestinal tract. Isosorbide dinitrate is in the same class of medications as nitroglycerin but has a longer duration of action. Nitroglycerin can also be administered as a patch, from which the drug is absorbed through the skin and enters the bloodstream. Both isosorbide and nitroglycerine can cause headache when they are first started and may cause dizziness on standing. When a person takes nitrates over a period of time, tolerance may develop. For this reason, isosorbide may be more effective for some people because it is taken three times a day and the body is less likely to develop tolerance to the effects of the drug. When the nitroglycerin patch is used, it is usually placed on the chest, stomach, or upper arm first thing in the morning and taken off at bedtime, to prevent tolerance from developing. The patch is easier to use since it only needs to be applied once a day, but it generally is more expensive than isosorbide.

The other drugs commonly used to treat angina are beta-blockers and calcium channel blockers. Beta-blockers have been shown to reduce the likelihood of a second heart attack, but they should not be taken by people with asthma or emphysema. Some of the calcium channel blockers, for example nifedipine, nicardipine, and diltiazem, are used to dilate (widen) the blood vessels and thereby increase blood flow and reduce the work of the heart. Both groups of drugs may cause dizziness on standing, in addition to other less common side effects.

Drugs Used to Treat Heart Failure

Heart failure is usually experienced as a feeling of fatigue and shortness of breath, especially on exertion or lying flat. Fluid accumulates in the lungs and the dependent parts of the body, usually the feet and ankles for a person who is up and about. Most heart failure has one of two causes. The first, called systolic dysfunction (systole is the contraction phase of the heart cycle), occurs when the heart is unable to pump blood normally, usually because of poor blood flow through the vessels of the heart or because of past heart attacks. In the normal heart at least half the blood in the heart is pumped out with each contraction; in systolic dysfunction, the amount pumped out may be much less. The second cause, diastolic dysfunction (diastole is the relaxation phase of the heart), occurs when the wall of the heart thickens, preventing the heart muscle from relaxing and expanding normally. This reduces the blood flow into the heart. It is often difficult to tell which of these problems cause heart failure without performing an ultrasound test called an echocardiogram.

Heart failure often can be well controlled with medications. However, it is important to follow a low salt diet, since salt makes the body retain water and increases the amount of fluid the heart must pump. Nonsteroidal anti-inflammatory drugs can interfere with the action of diuretics and make the body retain salt and water, and should generally be avoided in people with heart failure.

Treatment for heart failure depends on the cause of the heart failure. The type of heart failure called diastolic dysfunction is usually caused by uncontrolled high blood pressure over many years that causes the walls of the heart to thicken, called left ventricular hypertrophy (thickening of the wall of the left ventricle, the main pumping chamber of the heart). Therefore, the main treatment for diastolic dysfunction is to control the blood pressure, which over time will reduce the thickening of the heart wall. Although few studies have been performed to help identify the best treatment for diastolic dysfunction, a diuretic may be used to help reduce the extra fluid that accumulates. Other antihypertensive medicines may be used to help relax the wall of the heart, such as beta-blockers or the calcium channel blockers verapamil and diltiazem.

Failure of the pump mechanism of the heart, or systolic dysfunction, is treated with a combination of two or more medications. The ACE inhibitors, most commonly enalapril, lisinopril, or captopril, has been shown to prolong life in people with heart failure and should be used in everyone with heart failure who does not have an allergy or other contraindication to the drug. ACE inhibitors may worsen kidney function in some people, so a blood test to check kidney function is usually performed before and after starting the drug. The ACE inhibitors can cause a dry cough and rarely, an allergic reaction called angioedema with swelling and sometimes difficulty breathing. People who experience these reactions or cannot tolerate ACE inhibitors for other reasons are usually treated with hydralazine, a medicine that acts in a way similar to the ACE inhibitors. However, hydralazine can cause a reversible abnormal immune response in the bloodstream in 5 to 15% of people and generally is used only for people who cannot take ACE inhibitors.

The other class of medicines most frequently used to treat systolic dysfunction are diuretics, often referred to as water pills. The diuretic most commonly used for heart failure is furosemide (Lasix), but metolozone (Bumax) also may be used. These diuretics usually cause frequent urination, especially in the first four hours or so after taking the medicine. They also reduce the potassium in the body, measured using a blood test, and so potassium supplements and/or foods high in potassium may be necessary. Foods high in potassium include bananas and many kinds of fruit juices. Maintaining potassium at a normal level is especially important when taking digoxin, since a low potassium level can cause irregular heart rhythms.

Digoxin is often used to treat heart failure and can improve symptoms such as shortness of breath, but, unlike ACE inhibitors, has not been shown to prolong life. Digoxin also is used to slow the heart rate in a heart arrhythmia called atrial fibrillation, which sometimes occurs with heart failure. Older people usually need a smaller dose of digoxin than younger people because of changes in body composition and kidney function. Digoxin needs to be carefully monitored since toxicity can occur at doses close to the doses used for treatment. Digoxin is usually monitored with a blood test for a person with heart failure or by measuring the pulse in a person with atrial fibrillation. A person with digoxin toxicity may have nausea and vomiting, may have a very slow pulse, and may see a halo around lights such as street lamps. (Van Gogh's painting *The Starry Night* may have been influenced by Van Gogh's use of foxglove, the plant from which digoxin was originally extracted.) Since digoxin toxicity can cause life-threatening heart arrhythmias, a person taking digoxin should be aware of these symptoms and contact a doctor if they occur.

Other medicines used to treat heart failure may include nitrates, such as isosorbide dinitrate. These medicines reduce the work of the heart and are most often used if narrowing of the arteries is thought to contribute to the heart failure.

Drugs Used to Treat Diabetes

Diabetes is an abnormal elevation of blood sugar in the body with inadequate production of insulin. A person with diabetes may experience increased thirst and appetite and may need to urinate frequently. These symptoms are not always severe and so doctors often screen for diabetes using a blood sugar test. Identifying and treating diabetes is important because (1) uncontrolled diabetes can cause severe imbalances in the bloodstream requiring admission to the hospital and intensive treatment, (2) diabetes increases the risk of heart disease, stroke, peripheral vascular disease, kidney failure, blindness, and nerve damage. These problems can be reduced and even prevented with good medical care and attention to diet and proper treatment.

Of the two types of diabetes, Type I (insulin-dependent) and Type II (non-insulin dependent), Type II diabetes is the more common type of diabetes people acquire as they age. People with Type I diabetes have low levels of insulin because their pancreas cannot produce enough, whereas people with Type II diabetes often have elevated levels of insulin but still not enough to control blood sugar, usually because they are overweight. People who can produce insulin may still require treatments with insulin if drugs are unable to stimulate the body's production of insulin.

The first step in controlling the blood sugar is reducing calories, fat, and sugar in the diet, weight loss, and exercise. Exercise, such as walking 20 minutes each day, should be done at least four or five times a week. Exercise and following a diet should help reduce weight and improve blood sugar. The diabetic diet consists of eliminating as much as possible refined sugars (candies, cakes, syrup, etc.) and saturated fats (butter, cheese, red meats) and increasing complex carbohydrates such as starches and whole grains and monounsaturated fats (canola oil or olive oil). This diet reduces the load of sugar on the body that requires control with insulin and reduces the fats in the diet that increase risk of heart disease and stroke. The diabetic diet should be explained by a dietician, who can review with you what you eat every day and make suggestions about how you can improve your diet and still eat many of the foods you enjoy.

If diet, exercise, and weight loss do not control blood sugar, the next step, in addition to continuing these measures, is to use medicine to control the blood sugar. The most commonly used pills to control blood sugar are glipizide and glyburide, which increase the release of insulin in the body. Both are effective at lowering blood sugar, but glyburide stays in the body longer than glipizide, particularly in older people. Pills should be taken one-half hour before breakfast in the morning, and one-half hour before dinner if taken twice a day. Other medications available recently to treat diabetes are metformin and acarbose. Metformin has the advantage of lowering blood sugar directly without increasing insulin levels, but can only be used in people with normal kidney function. It also has the rare adverse effect of lactic acidosis, which can be life threatening and may be more common in older people. Another newer drug is acarbose. Acarbose is a drug that is taken with the first bite of each meal and delays the absorption of sugars during meals, lessening the increase in blood sugar. It can cause diarrhea and gas, and experience with it in older patients is currently limited.

Two medications used to control diabetes before glipizide and glyburide became available were chlorpropamide and tolbutamide. However, chlorpropamide tends to accumulate in older people and is more likely to cause dangerously low blood sugar. Tolbutamide is shorter acting but is less widely used now that newer drugs are available. Glipizide and glyburide are preferred in older people.

Many drugs can affect the way diabetes medicine is cleared from the body. The most common of the non-prescription drugs to affect diabetes medicines are alcohol and salicylates, which can lower the blood sugar level. Tell your doctor if you use either of these drugs.

If diet and oral medicines do not control the blood sugar, insulin injections may be necessary. Insulin is most commonly used in two forms, NPH, a long-acting insulin, and regular, or short acting insulin. People with mild diabetes may be able to take a single injection of NPH or NPH and regular each morning before breakfast, while those with more severe forms of diabetes have to have injections twice or even three times a day.

Monitoring blood sugar is important for people who take either insulin or oral medication, and can be done by the patient or caregiver by performing a fingerprick to test blood sugar in a glucometer. It is done most often when a new medicine is started or the dose of medicine is changed.

Insulin injections require good eyesight to ensure that the correct amount of insulin is drawn up into the syringe, manual dexterity to inject insulin in the appropriate place, and good memory to ensure that the insulin is taken at the appropriate time. If one or more of these factors is a problem, either an oral medication should be tried if possible or a responsible caregiver or visiting nurse involved to help ensure that the medicine is given appropriately. If eyesight is a problem, a caregiver or nurse can draw up several day's worth of insulin and store it in the refrigerator for the diabetic patient to use.

Low blood sugar may occur with any drug treatment for diabetes. Low blood sugar is dangerous and should be prevented or, if it occurs, treated as soon as possible. A blood sugar monitor is useful to test for low blood sugar;

the level considered too low should be discussed with your doctor, but a sugar level less than 60 mg./dl. nearly always is too low. Symptoms of low blood sugar include weakness, palpitations, sweating, and anxiety. Symptoms can be relieved by consuming refined sugar, for example by drinking orange juice or sucking hard candies. Low blood sugar may not always cause symptoms, especially in people who have had diabetes for many years. One common cause of low blood sugar is skipping meals or eating meals irregularly. Therefore, regular meals should be eaten consisting of three reasonably small meals a day with a snack at bedtime to prevent the blood sugar from dropping too low during the night. Another common cause is illness. If a diabetic person becomes ill with reduced appetite, nausea, or vomiting, the diabetic medicine dose should be reduced and the doctor contacted.

Drugs Used to Treat Heartburn and Ulcers

Heartburn or stomach upset are common symptoms that can often be treated simply by avoiding the offending food or taking an antacid. Sometimes, however, these symptoms can signal an ulcer. If an ulcer is present, bleeding may occur and can be life-threatening if severe. Therefore, ulcer disease generally requires treatment with medication.

For many years the only medicine available to treat ulcers was antacids. While these medicines can often help to heal an ulcer, they have to be taken frequently, up to every two hours, and can cause diarrhea and other gastrointestinal problems. They also should be taken at least an hour apart from other medicine so that they do not interfere with absorption of the other drugs. More recently, the histamine-2 receptor blockers (H_2-blockers) cimetidine, ranitidine, and famotidine (among others) were developed to heal ulcers using a twice a day or once a day medicine. These medicines are effective but often must be taken for months or even years to prevent recurrence of the ulcer. They also have side effects; cimetidine can interact with many other drugs because it inhibits liver enzymes that help clear drugs from the body, and all the H_2 blockers can cause confusion.

Researchers established in the last decade that bacteria called *Helicobacter pylori* are responsible for most ulcer disease, and treating people with these ulcers with a combination of medications, including an antibiotic to kill the bacteria, usually heals the ulcer and prevents recurrence. Treatment for Helicobacter pylori consists of several possible combinations of drugs, usually including one or two antibiotics, an H_2 blocker, and/or omeprazole, a medicine that reduces secretion of acid into the stomach. Some medicines are very expensive but only have to be taken twice a day, while others are less expensive and have to be taken several times a day. Regardless of which drug regimen a person takes, it is extremely important to take the medicine for the entire time prescribed so that no *Helicobacter pylori* remains and the ulcer is healed.

Other medicines sometimes used to treat ulcer disease or other stomach and intestinal problems are sucralfate, misoprostol, and omeprazole. Sucralfate is used sometimes to treat ulcer disease, but sucralfate pills are very large and may be difficult to swallow. Doctors sometimes recommend taking sucrafate as a slurry. Misoprostol may be used to protect the stomach lining from the effects of nonsteroidal anti-inflammatory drugs, usually for people who have had problems from nonsteroidal anti-inflammatory drugs but must continue to take them. Omeprazole can be used to reduce the secretion of acid that causes inflammation of the esophagus. Its use has not been extensively studied in older people.

While medicines are an important part of treating ulcer disease, other factors influence ulcer disease. The most common and severe of these is cigarette smoking. Smoking is a major risk factor for ulcer disease. Other factors, such as spicy food or coffee, probably do not cause ulcer disease, although alcohol can contribute to irritation of the stomach lining. Milk and other foods are not effective treatment for ulcer disease.

Drugs Used to Thin the Blood

When blood clots form in the body, they can cause life-threatening problems such as stroke or pulmonary embolus (a blood clot that lodges in the lung). Therefore, if a blood clot is found or is very likely to form, blood thinners may be used. In addition, people who have a high likelihood of forming clots because of an artificial heart valve or a heart rhythm irregularity called atrial fibrillation are often given blood thinners. Warfarin (coumadin) is the most commonly-used blood thinner. Since coumadin prevents the blood from clotting normally, people taking coumadin must report to their doctor if they develop a severe or constant headache (since a severe headache may signal bleeding inside the brain), bleeding that will not stop, or blood in their stools or black, tarry stools (often a sign of bleeding in the stomach in people not taking iron).

Coumadin must be carefully monitored to ensure that the blood is thinned enough but not too much. Blood tests generally are performed at least weekly at first until the correct amount of coumadin is established. The coumadin dose is adjusted by using the international normalized ratio (INR).

Many drugs interfere with how coumadin is cleared from the body. Aspirin and nonsteroidal drugs also reduce the ability of the blood to clot and should not be taken with coumadin unless a physician specifically recommends the combination (for example, in people who have had clotting in spite of being treated with adequate doses of coumadin). Vitamin K counteracts the effects of coumadin, so if you take vitamins you should read the label to determine if it contains vitamin K. Eating large amounts of leafy green vegetables can also increase vitamin K and reduce blood thinning, so intake of green leafy vegetables should be kept constant or avoided while on coumadin.

Dipyridamole used to be given frequently to stroke patients, usually in addition to aspirin, to help prevent stroke. However, the medicine was found to not be effective and to have side effects, in addition to being much more expensive than aspirin. Therefore, dipyridamole is rarely used now except for people with artificial heart valves or other less common problems.

Drugs Used to Treat Glaucoma

Eye drops are commonly used to treat glaucoma. Many different medications can be administered as eye drops to try to prevent damage to the eye by lowering the high pressure caused by glaucoma. Eye drops should be administered by tilting the head back, gazing upwards, squeezing out a drop from the bottle, and then holding the inside corner of the eye shut for a minute or so to let the fluid absorb. Many older people have problems administering drops in their eyes because of limitations from arthritis or other problems. Ask your doctor if you are unsure how to use eye drops or if you have pain in the neck or head as you place them in your eye.

The medicine most commonly administered in the eye is timolol. Timolol is a beta-blocker. Although timolol used for glaucoma is given in the eye, it can be absorbed into the bloodstream. Thus, a person with asthma or emphysema may experience difficulty breathing or other breathing problems with timolol eye drops. Betaxolol is another type of eye drop similar to timolol, but is less likely to cause difficulty breathing.

Pilocarpine is another medication for glaucoma given as an eye drop. Pilocarpine can cause reduced vision initially when it is given, because it limits the ability of the pupil of the eye to change size to focus or let in more light. It can also cause eye or brow pain. Other eye drops used less commonly are carbachol, echothiopate, and epinephrine. Echothiopate can prolong the action of medicine used for general anesthesia, so it is essential to bring your bottles of eye drops with you or tell the doctor exactly what you are taking any time surgery requiring general anesthesia might be considered. Epinephrine can be absorbed into the bloodstream and affect the heart; any chest pain or shortness of breath while using epinephrine drops should be brought to the attention of the doctor immediately.

Acetazolamide and neptazane are medicines taken by mouth that may be used to treat glaucoma. These medicines are usually used if glaucoma cannot be controlled by eye drops alone. A blood test is often performed to monitor the acid level in the bloodstream. Side effects that occur uncommonly include confusion, increased problems with controlling urine, and, rarely, stones in the urinary tract.

Drugs Used to Treat Asthma or Emphysema

Asthma, or constriction of the tubes in the airways reducing ability to breath, and emphysema, or chronic obstructive pulmonary disease, are common causes of shortness of breath in older patients. Asthma usually is worsened by smoke, pollens, or infection and often starts when a person is young. Emphysema is caused by smoking, which destroys the normal air cells of the lungs and leads to air trapping in the lungs. Despite the different causes of these breathing problems, many of the medicines used for treatment are similar.

The initial medicines used to treat asthma and emphysema are given through inhalers. Inhaled medicine has the advantage of being delivered directly to the lungs and minimizes the side effects seen with oral medicines. However, all inhalers must be used properly to be effective. The best way to learn how to use an inhaler is for someone to demonstrate for you at the doctor's office and then watch you while you practice to ensure that you feel comfortable with the technique. The timing of pushing down the inhaler while inhaling must be precise and can be tricky for many people. If you have difficulty using an inhaler correctly, a spacer can be attached to the mouthpiece of the inhaler. The spacer enables you to breathe normally to inhale the medicine, rather than timing a breath while pushing down the top of the inhaler.

Storing Medications

Like everything else we ingest, medications are perishable and should be stored properly. The medicine cabinet in the average bathroom is often not the best place—it is too warm and humid an environment. Find a cool, dry, well-lighted spot somewhere else at home. The kitchen is a convenient spot (but not a cabinet over the stove). Some other hints that might be useful are:

- Keep medications in their original containers and keep the tops securely fastened.
- Remove the little ball of cotton that comes in some containers. It can absorb moisture from the air.
- Do not leave medications in a car for long.
- Some medications need to be stored in the refrigerator, but should never be put in the freezer.
- Get rid of medicines that may be too old or contaminated with other substances. Among things to look for are

  - Creams and ointments that have hardened or changed color, or whose containers are cracked or leaking.
  - Liquids that have thickened or changed color.
  - Aspirin and acetaminophen that have an odor. A sharp, acidic odor, like that of vinegar, indicates that the medication is old and should be thrown out.

- Dispose of out-of-date medications by pouring them down the toilet, not by putting them in the garbage.

The most commonly used inhaled medicines are beta-agonists and inhaled steroids. Beta-agonists, most commonly metoproterenol or albuterol, are best used for acute worsening of symptoms rather than as a regular medicine. If taken in high doses, all beta-agonists can cause tremor and irregular heart rate. Salmeterol is a newer long acting beta-agonist useful for preventing attacks, but is not effective for an acute attack. Inhaled steroids are extremely important to use in preventing attacks, but will not relieve an acute attack. Inhaled steroids should be used on a regular basis, rinsing out the mouth after using the inhaler to prevent oral thrush (yeast infection of the mouth).

Oral steroids may be necessary when symptoms become severe, such as sever attacks precipitated by bronchitis or other lung infection. Steroids are generally prescribed in a high dose initially followed by a rapid taper to maximize the immediate response but minimize side effects. The tapering schedule should be followed closely to reduce side effects, unless symptoms rebound. Because of the many effects steroids can have on the body when ingested over the long term, including diabetes, osteoporosis, cataract, and reducing the function of the immune system, oral steroids should be avoided unless absolutely necessary to control the disease.

Ipratropium (Atrovent) is another commonly used inhaled drug and is often used for people with emphysema. Like other inhalers, it must be inhaled properly to be effective. It is useful in preventing but not in treating symptoms. Side effects include a dry mouth, and people with glaucoma must be very careful when using the spray to ensure that none of the medicine is sprayed in the eye, since the medicine may make glaucoma worse.

Cromolyn sodium is used most commonly for asthma, often for children. It is inhaled and is used to prevent symptoms rather than treat them. It is often used for asthma precipitated by specific situations like seasonal allergies or exercise. It may produce irritation and dryness of the mouth, and cough.

Theophylline is an oral medicine used to treat both asthma and emphysema. It was one of the first medicines used to treat these disorders, but as more inhaled medicines with many fewer side effects have become available, its use has declined. Many drugs can raise or lower the level of theophylline in the blood stream, and blood tests must be performed to monitor theophylline levels since too high a dose can cause severe side effects such as heart arrhythmias and seizures. Difficulty sleeping, restlessness, tremor, and nausea may also occur with the drug.

Estrogen and Progesterone

Estrogen is often used to treat women who are going through the menopause or *change of life*. Menopause is often associated with a decline in estrogen in the body, which can result in hot flashes or vaginal dryness and itching. Over years, low estrogen can result in a loss of bone causing osteoporosis and increasing the risk of bone fracture. Estrogen can be effective in relieving these symptoms and can reduce the risk of osteoporosis and reduce elevated cholesterol. However, estrogen can cause endometrial cancer (in women who still have their uterus) if not cycled with progesterone and can increase the risk of blood clots. Some researchers believe it increases the risk of breast cancer.

Endometrial cancer can be prevented either by obtaining regular screening vaginal exams from a physician to determine if changes that precede development of cancer are occurring, or by using progesterone in combination with estrogen. The combination can be given one of two ways. The first is to cycle the two, for example by using estrogen for 20 days followed by progesterone for 10 days, which mimics the hormonal cycles the body goes through during the years when a woman is menstruating. The second way is to take the estrogen and progesterone together. Both methods usually produce vaginal bleeding, similar to a period, but when the two hormones are given in combination the bleeding may eventually stop altogether.

A woman deciding whether to take estrogen should discuss the benefits and risks of treatment with her doctor and make the choice that is right for her. Sometimes trying estrogen therapy for a few months is useful in helping to decide whether hormone replacement will improve the target symptoms.

A mammogram is recommended before starting estrogen since in a woman with an undetected breast cancer, the cancer might grow more quickly if the woman takes estrogen. As for all women over the age of 50 years, annual mammograms are recommended. Pap smears and vaginal exams also should be performed each year for women who have not had a hysterectomy.

For women who do not want to take estrogens orally, estrogen may be applied topically to the vagina to treat vaginal symptoms or to the urethra for urinary stress incontinence associated with thinning of the tissue around the urethra. However, when used regularly as a vaginal application, estrogen is absorbed into the bloodstream and so cycling with an oral progesterone is still recommended in women who have their uterus.

Drugs Used to Treat Urinary Symptoms from an Enlarged Prostate

Most men experience at least some enlargement of the prostate as they age. While surgery may become necessary for some, many of the symptoms associated with an enlarged prostate wax and wane over time and may not require treatment or may be improved with medicines. The most common symptoms are urinary frequency, including needing to urinate frequently in the middle of the night, hesitancy when urinating, dribbling after urinating, and feeling that the bladder has not emptied completely.

Nighttime urination is often distressing because it disrupts sleep. It can be alleviated by minimizing fluids at dinnertime and after, but sometimes medications are necessary to reduce the need to urinate at night.

The medications most frequently used for symptoms from an enlarged prostate are terazosin or prazosin. These drugs are effective for many men and take effect almost immediately. The drugs generally are taken at bedtime because a common side effect with these drugs is orthostatic hypotension, or a fall in blood pressure when standing up, which can cause dizziness. This is most likely to occur with the first dose, but may persist. For this reason, the lowest effective dose should be used. Terazosin may cause this side effect less frequently than prazosin. These drugs also lower blood pressure throughout the day and can be used as a treatment for hypertension in addition to treating urinary symptoms.

Another drug that has been used is finasteride. However, finasteride is expensive, requires 4 to 6 weeks before its effect, and is no more effective (likely less effective) than terasozin or prazosin. Because finasteride may affect the prostate specific antigen (PSA) level, the PSA should be checked and a prostate exam performed before the drug is started.

Vitamin Supplements

The importance of adequate nutrition to maintain health and prevent disease has been increasingly recognized in the last several years. In general, a high fiber, low fat (less than 30% of total calories) diet with at least 5 servings per day of fruits and vegetables produces a variety of health benefits, from lowering the risk of certain types of cancer, such as colon cancer, to lowering the risk of heart disease, to lowering high blood pressure. Increased intake of soluble fiber, such as that found in cereals, is associated with a reduced risk of diabetes. However, the role of vitamin supplements has been less clear. The health benefits of a high-fiber, low fat diet cannot be achieved by taking a pill containing vitamin and mineral supplements. On the other hand, older people are less likely to get some important nutrients, because of difficulty keeping fresh fruits and vegetables when access to a store with such foods is limited, dentition is not adequate to chew or dentures are poorly fitting, or the food consumed is prepared in an institutional setting. In these circumstances and possibly in others, vitamin supplements may be appropriate.

There is some evidence that older people have different nutritional requirements for vitamins and minerals than younger people, although a separate Recommended Daily Allowance (RDA) for nutrient intake for older people has not been established. Current RDA recommendations are the same as for younger people. Older people do appear to have different requirements for at least some vitamins and minerals, however. For example, calcium is an important component of bones and adequate calcium intake is essential for older women and men to help prevent osteoporosis. Recommendations from experts are to get at least 800 mg of calcium each day; some experts recommend up to 1200 mg per day.

Vitamin D is also important to maintain bone and prevent osteoporosis. Vitamin D is found in many foods, but in order for the body to convert the pre-vitamin D found in foods to active vitamin D, the person must have sun exposure on a regular basis. A person who lives in the community who leaves the home for shopping and the like will have adequate sun exposure, but someone who is homebound or who lives in a nursing home may have insufficient exposure to the sun. In order to get the beneficial effects from the sun, the person must be exposed to ultraviolet rays; sitting in the sunlight shining through a window will not provide the necessary exposure. In addition, sunblock at a level of 8 or higher will prevent the beneficial effects of the sun. Weekly sun exposure for several minutes is generally adequate for the body to produce active vitamin D.

Folate is an important nutrient that has been associated with a reduced risk of atherosclerosis (hardening of the arteries). Folate is found in fresh fruits and vegetables, as well as in vitamin supplements. Vitamin B_{12} is important for proper functioning of the nervous system, including the memory. Although B_{12} is found in many foods and dietary intake is usually adequate, B_{12} may be less well absorbed in older people. Low vitamin B_{12} can be detected by a blood test.

Vitamin E is thought by researchers to be needed in larger amounts in older people than in younger people. Vitamin E is found in nuts and vegetable oils. Some research has suggested that vitamin E can improve the function of the immune system.

When considering whether to take a vitamin supplement, it is important to understand how vitamins are absorbed and stored in the body. Certain vitamins, vitamins A, D, E, and K, are fat soluble and cannot be cleared by the body as quickly as the water-soluble vitamins (the B vitamins and vitamin C). Thus, it is important that any supplement be in the range of the recommended daily allowance. Some supplements contain *megadoses* of vitamins (the amount of vitamin is several times as high as the RDA); these can cause adverse effects such as liver problems if they are fat soluble, or kidney stones if they are water soluble. In general, a multivitamin providing vitamins, calcium, and trace elements such as selenium in doses comparable to those recommended as part of the RDA should be sufficient to benefit from such elements in the diet and to avoid the potentially harmful side effects of megadoses of vitamins.

Topical Medicines to Apply to the Skin

Many preparations are available over-the-counter and by prescription to treat a variety of skin problems. While such preparations cannot be discussed in detail here, it is important to understand a few basic concepts about topical preparations. First, there are three basic kinds of preparations. First are skin softeners or lotion, which usually have a cream or ointment base. Skin lotion can be helpful to soften the drying of the skin that occurs with aging and help make the skin more resilient to injury. Many types of skin lotion have additives to give them a pleasant fragrance. However, the fragrance in lotion can cause an allergic reaction, so if an area that has had lotion applied to it becomes red or itchy, the lotion should be stopped and a lotion without fragrance (such as Lubriderm or Cetaphil) applied. Similarly, many lotions have vitamin E and/or an extract from the aloe vera plant added to them as an aid to healing. Whether these additives help aid healing is unclear, but they can cause allergic reactions on the skin and cause red, itchy, inflamed skin.

Another type of topical ointment is antibiotic ointment, used to help heal cuts or scrapes and help prevent them from becoming infected. Two of the most common antibacterial ointments are Polysporin and Neosporin. However, Neosporin contains neomycin, which can often produce an allergic reaction, so in general Polysporin is better to use. If redness spreads in the area of a cut or if the cut swells or oozes, an infection is likely setting in and needs a doctor's attention.

Finally, lotion may be used to reduce itching from eczema, insect bites, or poison ivy. Hydrocortisone cream or ointment (such as Cortaid) is available over-the-counter to control such itching. However, hydrocortisone is a steroid and if the itching is caused by an infection, it can potentially make the infection worse. If itching persists or if redness increases while using the ointment, see your doctor to find out whether an infection might be causing the problem. Stronger steroid creams or ointments are available only by prescription and should be used only as directed. If these stronger steroids are used for a prolonged time, they can cause thinning of the skin that may not be reversible and should always be used with a doctor's supervision.

Conclusion

The medicines used to treat illness and prevent disease are some of the major advances physicians and researchers have made in the last 40 years. However, medicines are potent and potentially dangerous if taken incorrectly. Your doctor should prescribe medicines that are effective and as affordable as possible for you, stop medicines that are ineffective or unnecessary, and give you the information you need to take your medicines appropriately and know what warning signs to look for. Your responsibility is to understand what your medicines are for, to take them as prescribed, and to tell your doctor if you have any questions or problems with your medications. Always tell your doctor about other medications you take, any over-the-counter preparations you use, and any alcohol intake or other drug use. Bring your medications with you to your doctor's appointment and discuss their use and any questions you have. By being informed about your medications, sharing your questions and concerns with your doctor, and taking your medication as prescribed, you will be able to get the most out of your medication to treat medical illness and prevent disease.

Marshall B. Kapp, J.D., M.P.H., holds professorships in both the departments of Community Health and Psychiatry at the Wright State University School of Medicine in Dayton, Ohio. He also serves as the Director of the school's Office of Geriatric Medicine and Gerontology and teaches at the University of Dayton School of Law. A graduate of the George Washington University Law School, he was drawn to the needs of dependent populations for personal reasons—a brother who is mentally retarded. After completing a master's degree in public health at Harvard, he joined the Health Care Financing Administration's Division of Long-Term Care, where he worked on the regulation of intermediate-care facilities and nursing homes. During that period his interest in long-term care and aging developed. He has written extensively on the subjects of patient autonomy, confidentiality, informed consent, and protective services. He has made a particular effort, with considerable success, to explain elder law to health care providers through his many journal articles and books, which include *Older Adults' Decision-Making and the Law, Patient Self-Determination in Long-Term Care,* and *Our Hands Are Tied: Legal Tensions and Medical Ethics.*

The Law and the Elderly

Marshall B. Kapp

Almost every aspect of modern life in the United States involves legal issues and implications. A person's interaction with the law is likely, if anything, to increase as he or she ages. Thinking about the law and lawyers tends to make most people nervous. This chapter aims to reduce some of that anxiety and to assist older individuals and their advocates to make the best, most effective use of available legal rights and opportunities to enhance their quality of life and maintain as much control concerning personal decisions as possible.

Succinctly put, "law" is the body of enforceable rules and prohibitions that is established by a jurisdiction's constitution, legislature, executive agencies, and courts. By both embodying and exhibiting important social attitudes and by ordering and implementing actions by society, the law exerts a major impact on the daily lives of older persons in a variety of ways. Some of these are identified and explained in this chapter. The reader is cautioned that the laws concerning many of the topics discussed here may vary considerably among the different states. While this chapter provides general information, one should always consult his or her own state's laws and expert legal counsel before making decisions or taking actions that have potentially significant legal consequences.

Issues in the Workplace

Age Discrimination

The Age Discrimination in Employment Act (ADEA) was passed by Congress and signed into law in 1967, as a sequel to the federal 1964 Civil Rights Act. Coverage of the ADEA has been expanded by amendments several times since the original enactment, and many states have enacted their own counterparts to the federal legislation.

Building on the Civil Rights Act's focus on racial equality, Congress in passing the ADEA intended to protect people against discrimination in the workplace based exclusively on their age. The ADEA, as amended, imposes on most private and public employers, employment agencies, and unions nondiscrimination obligations (namely, the responsibility to treat everyone equally regardless of age) concerning hiring, termination, promotion, training, and other terms and conditions of employment or retirement. The earlier widespread practice of mandatory retirement at a specified age has now been prohibited. Unequal treatment of particular workers or applicants is justified under the ADEA only on the basis of reasonable factors other than age (RFsOA), such as the inability of an individual to perform the essential functions of the position satisfactorily, or where age is a Bona Fide Occupational Qualification (BFOQ), as in piloting an airplane or working in public safety. The U.S. Supreme Court in 1984 explained when chronological age may be used in this fashion in *Western Air Lines, Inc.* v. *Criswell*. Older persons who have been unfairly discriminated against may have their rights enforced through complaint to the Equal Employment Opportunity Commission (EEOC) and ultimately through a civil lawsuit for monetary damages and equitable relief (such as job reinstatement) in federal district court. Many states have enacted statutes and enforcement mechanisms that parallel what is available at the federal level.

Health Insurance

The ADEA also requires that any private health insurance coverage that an employer offers to its other workers must be offered equally to workers who choose to stay in the workforce after age 65. The employer's plan is the primary payer with respect to the Medicare coverage that the older individual also receives. This means that the employer's plan pays first, and Medicare then pays eligible expenses that are not covered by the employer's plan. The reverse order of priority is true for any private insurance coverage provided to retirees of a company. The main federal law governing employee benefits, including health insurance, is the Employee Retirement and Income Security Act (ERISA).

When an employee or the employee's eligible dependents (spouse and dependent children) would otherwise lose coverage under an employer's plan because of certain events, they are eligible to continue their group health coverage—at their own expense—for a limited period of time (18 to 36 months, depending on circumstances). This provision is called COBRA continuation coverage, named after the 1985 Consolidated Omnibus Budget Reconciliation Act. In the case of an employee, qualifying events include termination of employment and a reduction in hours. For a dependent, qualifying events include those two as well as the employee's death, divorce or legal separation of the employee and spouse, or the employee's becoming entitled to Medicare.

Disability Claims

If a person becomes unable to continue working because of a work-related injury, that person may be entitled to monthly income checks and health and rehabilitation benefits under the state's Workers Compensation program in which employers are required to participate. Other sources of income for disabled former workers are private disability insurance policies and the Social Security Disability Insurance (SSDI) program. At age 65, SSDI discontinues and an eligible individual converts to Social Security retirement benefits.

Early Retirement

Early retirement plans have become popular in this era of corporate "right-sizing." Early retirement plans are permitted under the ADEA, but certain restrictions on these plans are established by the 1990 federal Older Workers Benefit Protection Act. In addition, 1991 amendments to the ADEA provide that an employee's decision to accept an early retirement offer will not be considered voluntary, and therefore not a valid waiver of rights the employee might otherwise have had, unless the following conditions of the waiver are met:

- It is written in understandable language;
- It explicitly refers to rights or claims under the ADEA;
- It does not apply to rights or claims arising after the date the waiver is signed;
- It provides the employee additional consideration (in other words, something additional of value) for signing;
- It advises the employee to consult an attorney before signing;

- It gives the employee at least 21 days to consider the agreement or at least 45 days if the waiver is part of an exit incentive or employment termination program;
- It is revocable by the employee for at least 7 days after being signed; and
- If the waiver is part of an employment termination program, the employee must be provided details as to whom the program applies.

Medical Decision Making

Informed Consent and Confidentiality

In contemporary American society, older persons have a legal right (consistent with the ethical principle of autonomy discussed in Chapter 10) to control a broad range of facets concerning their own medical treatment, now and in the future. This section outlines legal principles and processes relevant to the exercise of that control.

The starting point is the doctrine of informed consent. There are three essential elements that must be present for a patient's choice about treatment to be considered legally valid. First, the patient's participation in the decision making process and in the ultimate decision must be voluntary—that is, free of force, fraud, duress, overreaching, or other ulterior form of constraint or coercion on the part of the health care provider.

Second, the patient's agreement must be informed. A patient has the right to be presented, in understandable lay language and under conditions likely to encourage comprehension, with the following types of information so that he or she may make a legally valid medical choice:

1. Diagnosis;
2. The nature and purpose of the proposed intervention;
3. The risks, consequences, or perils of the intervention;
4. The probability of success;
5. Reasonable alternatives;
6. The result anticipated if nothing is done;
7. Limitations of the professional or health care facility; and
8. The health professional's recommendation.

The third fundamental element of legally effective consent is that the patient must be mentally able to think rationally regarding personal care. When the patient lacks sufficient mental capacity, a substitute or proxy decision maker must be involved (discussed below).

In the course of receiving medical care, the older patient or his surrogate usually shares a substantial amount of personal information with members of the health care team. The patient has a reasonable expectation that this information will be held in confidence by those team members, and the latter have a legal responsibility to fulfill the patient's expectations in this regard. If this trust is violated, a patient may have recourse in a civil damage suit based on both statutory (legislative) and common (judge-made) law and the state's professional practice acts and implementing regulations. State practice acts provide that violation of a duty of confidentiality is a potential ground for revoking, denying, or suspending a health professional's license to practice.

However, the patient's right to confidentiality is not absolute or immutable. There are several exceptions to the general rule. The first exception is that a patient may waive, or give up in a voluntary, competent, and informed manner, his right to confidentiality. This occurs daily in the health care area to make information available to third-party payers (such as Medicare and Medicaid), quality-of-care evaluators and inspectors, and other public and private entities, including nursing home ombudsmen and patients' legal representatives. Second, when the rights of innocent third parties (such as highway drivers and passengers) are jeopardized, the general requirement of confidentiality may yield.

Third, the patient's expectation of confidentiality must give way when a health professional is mandated by state law to report to specified public health authorities the existence of certain enumerated conditions (such as infectious diseases or elder abuse or neglect) that are observed or suspected in a patient. Finally, health professionals may be compelled to reveal otherwise confidential patient information by the force of legal process, that is, by a judge's issuance of a court order requiring such release in the context of litigation. This is a possibility in any type of lawsuit where the patient's physical or mental condition is in dispute.

Health care professionals often presume that it is all right to share information about an older patient's treatment with that patient's available relatives. If this practice is inconsistent with the patient's wishes, the patient should make very explicit as early as possible in the treatment relationship his desires concerning the release or nonrelease of medical information to specific other persons.

Advance Planning

To maximize the likelihood of continued control over one's own medical treatment, older individuals should plan ahead for possible future times when crucial medical decisions may need to be made, but the individual will not be personally capable at that moment of making and expressing treatment preferences reached through a rational decision making process. The two most important current legal devices for advance health care planning are the living will and the durable power of attorney. Authorizing legislation for both of these devices has been enacted in virtually every state.

The living will is a form of instruction directive, in which a presently capable person documents his future medical treatment wishes. The written forms for accomplishing this vary. Model forms for each state may be obtained from Choice in Dying and from one's particular state medical and legal associations; an example of this legal instrument is provided in this chapter. Since it is impossible to specify prospectively in a document every potential medical contingency, an alternative form in which the person enumerates chosen values (for instance, the desire to live as long as possible or the desire to avoid pain at all costs) rather than specific medical interventions may turn out to be more helpful when the time comes to implement the directive.

The durable power of attorney for health care is a written document (see example in this chapter) executed by a competent individual that names another person as proxy or agent, usually called the attorney-in-fact, with authority to make specified decisions on behalf of the patient in the event of the patient's future mental incapacity. This advance planning device is very useful for people who have another person whom they trust, and whom they expect to continue to be available for this purpose, to whom decision making power may be delegated. The execution of a durable power of attorney should be supplemented by honest conversations with the designated agent, to assure that decisions made in the future are consistent with the patient's actual values and preferences; one cannot otherwise assume that his chosen agent will always or even usually guess correctly about the patient's wishes in specific future treatment scenarios.

The Patient Self-Determination Act (PSDA) passed by Congress in 1990, in the aftermath of the United States

Supreme Court's holding in *Cruzan* v. *Director, Missouri Department of Health* imposes a number of requirements on hospitals, nursing homes, health maintenance organizations, preferred provider organizations, hospices, and home care agencies that participate in Medicare and Medicaid. Among these are mandates:

1. That the provider create and distribute to new patients or their proxies a written policy on advance directives, which may reflect particular organizational values but must be consistent with state law;
2. That the provider inquire at the point of admission or enrollment whether the patient has previously executed an advance directive; and
3. If no advance directive has been executed previously and the patient currently retains sufficient decisional capacity, that the provider inquire whether the patient wishes to execute such a directive now.

Another form of advance directive for medical decisions is the "Do Not" order. Written "Do Not" orders from an attending physician to other members of the health care team are predicated on prospectively made decisions to withdraw or withhold certain types of medical interventions from a specific patient. Most attention so far has been devoted to Do Not Resuscitate (DNR) orders (also known as No Codes), or instructions by the physician to refrain from attempts at cardiopulmonary resuscitation (CPR) in the event of a cardiac arrest. However, Do Not Hospitalize and Do Not Treat orders also are potentially significant, especially in the long-term care setting.

Legally, deciding about Do Not orders should take place according to the same substantive principles and procedural guidelines that apply to other treatment choices. Older individuals should take the initiative to discuss the issues raised by Do Not Orders and other possible treatment questions with their physicians, as well as their families, in a timely, open, and honest fashion. The individual should expect sufficient, updated information about likely benefits and burdens, and must be allowed to reevaluate any decision in light of changes in physical or mental condition that might alter the possible benefit/burden ratio of different treatment alternatives. A Do Not decision may be revoked or modified at any time.

Living Will

A sample living will. Copies of such a document should be given to and discussed with one's physician and family.

INSTRUCTIONS	**FLORIDA LIVING WILL**
PRINT THE DATE	Declaration made this _____ day of _____, 19____.
PRINT YOUR NAME	I, _____, willfully and voluntarily make known my desire that my dying not be artificially prolonged under the circumstances set forth below, and I do hereby declare:
	If at any time I have a terminal condition and if my attending or treating physician and another consulting physician have determined that there is no medical probability of my recovery from such condition, I direct that life-prolonging procedures be withheld or withdrawn when the application of such procedures would serve only to prolong artificially the process of dying, and that I be permitted to die naturally with only the administration of medication or the performance of any medical procedure deemed necessary to provide me with comfort care or to alleviate pain.
	It is my intention that this declaration be honored by my family and physician as the final expression of my legal right to refuse medical or surgical treatment and to accept the consequences for such refusal.
	In the event that I have been determined to be unable to provide express and informed consent regarding the withholding, withdrawal, or continuation of life-prolonging procedures, I wish to designate, as my surrogate to carry out the provisions of this declaration:
PRINT THE NAME, HOME ADDRESS AND TELEPHONE NUMBER OF YOUR SURROGATE	Name: _____ Address: _____ _____ Zip Code: _____ Phone: _____
© 1996 CHOICE IN DYING, INC.	

(Continued)

Living Will *(continued)*

I wish to designate the following person as my alternate surrogate, to carry out the provisions of this declaration should my surrogate be unwilling or unable to act on my behalf:

PRINT NAME, HOME ADDRESS AND TELEPHONE NUMBER OF YOUR ALTERNATE SURROGATE

Name: _____

Address: _____

_____ Zip Code: _____

Phone: _____

ADD PERSONAL INSTRUCTIONS (IF ANY)

Additional instructions (optional):

I understand the full import of this declaration, and I am emotionally and mentally competent to make this declaration.

SIGN THE DOCUMENT

Signed: _____

WITNESSING PROCEDURE

Witness 1:

Signed: _____

Address: _____

TWO WITNESSES MUST SIGN AND PRINT THEIR ADDRESSES

Witness 2:

Signed: _____

Address: _____

© 1995
CHOICE IN DYING, INC.

Courtesy of Choice In Dying, Inc.   6/96
200 Varick Street, New York, NY 10014 212-366-5540

The Health Care Surrogate

A durable power of attorney of attorney designates an individual as an agent or surrogate for health care. It is an important task and one that all parties should discuss thoroughly. The surrogate and any alternate surrogates should be prepared to faithfully follow the signer's legal wishes, even when those wishes may not entirely accord with the surrogate's own.

INSTRUCTIONS	

FLORIDA DESIGNATION OF HEALTH CARE SURROGATE

PRINT YOUR NAME

Name: _____

(Last)   (First)   (Middle Initial)

In the event that I have been determined to be incapacitated to provide informed consent for medical treatment and surgical and diagnostic procedures, I wish to designate as my surrogate for health care decisions:

PRINT THE NAME, HOME ADDRESS AND TELEPHONE NUMBER OF YOUR SURROGATE

Name: _____

Address: _____

_____ Zip Code: _____

Phone: _____

If my surrogate is unwilling or unable to perform his duties, I wish to designate as my alternate surrogate:

PRINT THE NAME, HOME ADDRESS AND TELEPHONE NUMBER OF YOUR ALTERNATE SURROGATE

Name: _____

Address: _____

_____ Zip Code: _____

Phone: _____

I fully understand that this designation will permit my designee to make health care decisions and to provide, withhold, or withdraw consent on my behalf; to apply for public benefits to defray the cost of health care; and to authorize my admission to or transfer from a health care facility.

ADD PERSONAL INSTRUCTIONS (IF ANY)

Additional instructions (optional):

I further affirm that this designation is not being made as a condition of treatment or admission to a health care facility. I will notify and send a copy of

© 1996
CHOICE IN DYING, INC.

(Continued)

The Health Care Surrogate *(continued)*

FLORIDA DESIGNATION OF HEALTH CARE SURROGATE — PAGE 2 OF 2

this document to the following persons other than my surrogate, so they may know who my surrogate is:

PRINT THE NAMES AND ADDRESSES OF THOSE WHO YOU WANT TO KEEP COPIES OF THIS DOCUMENT

Name: _____

Address: _____

Name: _____

Address: _____

SIGN AND DATE THE DOCUMENT

Signed: _____

Date: _____

WITNESSING PROCEDURE

TWO WITNESSES MUST SIGN AND PRINT THEIR ADDRESSES

Witness 1:

Signed: _____

Address: _____

Witness 2:

Signed: _____

Address: _____

Courtesy of Choice In Dying, Inc.
200 Varick Street, New York, NY 10014 212-366-5540

6/96

Surrogate Decision Makers

In situations where the patient is neither currently capable of making a decision nor has executed a valid advance medical directive, decision making authority may devolve or pass from the patient to someone else by operation of a statute, regulation, or judicial precedent. Family consent statutes in over half the states set forth legal authority empowering specifically designated relatives to make particular kinds of medical decisions on behalf of incapacitated persons who have not executed a living will or durable power of attorney. Older individuals who do not execute advance directives ought to familiarize themselves with the normal legal progression of decision making authority in their own state to make sure that it comports with their wishes (and to take action if it does not).

In addition to family consent statutes, courts in an increasing number of states are formally recognizing the authority of the family to exercise an incompetent person's decision making rights for him. Just as notably, most of these judicial decisions explicitly establish legal precedent for families to act in future cases without the need for obtaining prior court authorization. As a general matter, even when there is neither an advance directive nor any specific statute, regulation, or court order delegating authority to a substitute decision maker for an incapacitated patient, it has long been a widely known and implicitly accepted medical custom for families to be relied on as the decision makers.

In some cases, though, informal substitute decision making by the physician and family members may not work. Family members may disagree among themselves. They may make decisions that seem to be at odds with the earlier expressed or understood preferences of the patient or that clearly appear not to be in the patient's best interests. The family may request a course of conduct that seriously contradicts the physician's or facility's own sense of ethical integrity. When such situations happen, the various interested parties may resort to petitioning a court to appoint a guardian or conservator with the power to make decisions on behalf of the incompetent patient (see guardianship discussion below).

Timely, thoughtful family discussions and advance care planning and documentation can assist the older person to reduce the possibility that this sort of acrimonious scenario will unfold in his own life. Such planning, designed to maximize personal autonomy, is especially advisable for older individuals who are among the increasing number of aging persons growing older today without meaningful relationships with any family members or friends, and who might otherwise fall into a state of legal and medical limbo that can put them in jeopardy when questions of legal authority are called into play.

In Anticipation of Death

Many older individuals wish to maintain as high a degree of personal autonomy as feasible not just regarding medical treatment decisions, but concerning related post-death choices as well. Two spheres in which the law in each state encourages and facilitates this attitude of planning for one's own death are autopsies and organ donation.

In every state, an individual while still mentally capable may document future wishes concerning an autopsy of his own body after death, granting or refusing permission. Practically speaking, even when the deceased has earlier given consent, most hospitals are quite reluctant to conduct an autopsy without also obtaining the family's approval. Thus, it definitely behooves an older person who feels strongly about this matter to discuss it thoroughly in advance with members of the family who might pose a problem later. In the absence of an earlier written expression of wishes by the deceased, the autopsy decision ordinarily rests exclusively with family members, in a priority order specified by state statute. There are exceptions, however, where no one's consent is required, for situations in which the unusual or suspicious circumstances surrounding a person's death compel the party signing the death certificate to report the death to the applicable local coroner or medical examiner (depending on the jurisdiction), who is then the official who makes the autopsy decision.

A similar situation exists for organ donation. An individual may indicate — often on the back of an automobile driver's license — a desire to donate particular organs (or the entire body) at the time of death for transplantation or educational purposes, although discussion with family members to curtail subsequent subversion of the individual's wishes is advisable.

Consumer Rights and Long-Term Care

Although most older persons are relatively healthy and independent, there is a significant likelihood that the majority of individuals who achieve old age will, at some point or points in their lives, need one or more forms of long term care (LTC) temporarily or for a longer period of time. For both institutional and community-based LTC, there are a constellation of legal rights available to consumers designed to protect them against abuse and exploitation and to help them maintain as much autonomy over large and small treatment and residential decisions as possible.

Involuntary Psychiatric Commitment

Involuntary commitment (variously labeled involuntary institutionalization, involuntary hospitalization, or civil commitment) is one route by which a person may gain entry into a public mental health facility or a private facility that is licensed by the state to accept and be paid for treating involuntarily committed patients. It is a route that disproportionately and frequently inappropriately affects the elderly. The elderly account for more than one fifth of state mental hospital patients and 5% of new admissions. Moreover, most patients with Alzheimer's disease or a related dementia who enter a public mental health institution do so through the involuntary commitment process.

Before commitment (other than for a short-term emergency) may occur, the state must satisfy a number of both substantive and procedural hurdles that are in place to safeguard the rights of the proposed patient. Substantive criteria for involuntary commitment require the state to prove, by at least a standard of clear and convincing evidence, that the individual is mentally ill and dangerous either to himself or to others. An array of procedural safeguards, mandated by federal or state constitutional due process or equal protection clauses or created by state statute or judicial decision, characterize the civil commitment process. These include, in most states, a right to representation by legal counsel, to have appointed psychiatric and/or psychological experts of one's own choosing, to a jury trial, and to periodic judicial review of the factual justification for continued commitment.

Even after a person has been committed to a mental institution, he or she still retains a variety of constitutional and statutory rights. Among other things, the individual is entitled to communicate with the outside world and, in the absence of a separate judicial finding of substantial decisional incapacity, to consent to or refuse medical treatment including psychotropic drugs and other forms of mental health intervention.

Because intrusions by the government into individual freedom must be based on the least restrictive or least intrusive alternative principle under constitutional due process, there has been a significant trend in recent years toward outpatient civil commitment. Under this approach, an individual who is found to satisfy the criteria for commitment may be ordered by the court to comply with an outpatient treatment regimen as a condition of not being placed involuntarily inside a public mental institution.

Nursing Facilities

Nursing facilities or homes are the place of residence for about 5% of all persons over age 65 in the United States at any moment in time, and half of all persons who will live to the age of 65 are projected eventually to spend part of their lives in a nursing home. The federal Nursing Home Quality Reform Act, passed as a portion of the Omnibus Budget Reconciliation Act (OBRA) of 1987, establishes a host of nursing facility requirements, tied to Medicare and Medicaid reimbursement, intended to promote important resident rights. Among the more significant requirements imposed by the law are those relating to the following:

- Ensuring resident privacy and decisional rights regarding accommodations, medical treatment, personal care, visits, written and telephone communications, and meetings with others;
- Maintaining the confidentiality of personal and clinical records;
- Guaranteeing facility access and visitation rights to persons of the resident's choosing;
- Requiring issuance of notice of rights at the time of admission;
- Implementing admissions policy requirements;
- Ensuring proper, substantially limited use of physical restraints and psychoactive drugs;
- Protecting resident funds that are being managed by the facility;
- Ensuring transfer and discharge rights and issuing related notices;
- Requiring a minimum amount of nursing and social work coverage;
- Requiring comprehensive resident assessments and individualized care plans in accordance with those assessments; and

- Requiring state prescreening of all prospective nursing home admittees and prohibiting admission of individuals with mental illness or mental retardation unless they specifically need nursing facility services.

In addition to these federal requirements, regulation of nursing facilities by individual states under their licensure authority is extensive, with specific provisions relating to quality of care and resident rights often exceeding those imposed on the federal level. Nursing homes are also heavily regulated under state and local fire and building codes and similar business-related safety provisions.

Home Health Care

Many older people receive formal (that is, paid professional) LTC services in the home, often in conjunction with informal home care provided by family and/or friends. When formal home care services are delivered by a home health agency, the law provides specific rights to protect the well-being and autonomy of the home care consumer.

Home care providers are subject to state licensure requirements, and a serious deviation from those requirements may jeopardize a provider's continued legal permission to stay in business. Additionally, home health agencies that participate in the Medicare and/or Medicaid programs must comply with federal certification requirements to receive payment for their services. Among the enumerated items included in the federal certification provisions and most state licensure statutes are the right of the home care consumer to:

- Be fully informed in advance about the care and treatment to be provided by the agency, to be fully informed in advance of any changes in the care or treatment to be provided by the agency that may affect the individual's well-being, and (except with respect to an individual adjudged mentally incompetent) to participate in planning care and treatment or changes in care or treatment;
- Voice grievances with respect to treatment or care that is (or fails to be) furnished, without discrimination or reprisals for voicing those grievances;
- Have the confidentiality of his or her clinical records maintained; and
- Have one's property treated with respect.

In addition to these regulatory protections, a home care consumer who fails to receive services promised by an agency may have redress in a civil lawsuit based on a breach or violation of contract theory. A civil lawsuit predicated on a negligence theory (negligence being an unintentional but blameworthy form of tort law) may be available to a home care consumer who suffers a serious injury as a direct result of the service provider's deviation from acceptable professional standards. Individuals who feel they have been wronged in either of these ways should consult a personal injury attorney.

Financial Decision Making

Thus far, this chapter has concentrated on the topics of decision making and advance planning in terms of the older individual's involvement in medical and residential choices. We now turn in this section to financial or estate planning, which is an area with important implications for the older person's quality of life, the medical and residential choices available to that person, and the person's ability to give a financial legacy to others of his selection while alive and after he has died. For example, failure to initiate financial planning at an opportune time may jeopardize a person's future eligibility for certain public benefits, especially Medicaid coverage for nursing home care. Further, virtually all financial planning decisions (either made consciously or by default) carry substantial tax implications that can affect the future financial viability of the individual or his heirs.

Estate Planning

Comprehensive estate planning has many components, depending on the assets, family situation, and desires of the individual. Ideally, an estate planning team should be composed of a knowledgeable attorney, accountant, financial advisor, and insurance agent who are working together for the client.

Probably the best known element of estate planning is the testamentary will. This is a legal document, executed by a competent adult, that controls the distribution of the person's material property after his death. It also names an executor (called an administrator or a personal representative in some jurisdictions) to carry out the testator's (the person who made out the will) wishes regarding that distribution. Practically every person with any assets who cares at all about who will eventually receive those assets should consider executing a testamentary will. When a person dies, his will is carried out under judicial supervision through a process called probate.

Depending upon one's unique financial resources and needs, various forms of trust arrangements may be available to help accomplish specific financial objectives held by the individual. Trusts come in two basic categories: revocable and irrevocable. Revocable trusts can be changed at any time, and typically the person who sets up the trust (the "trustor" or "settlor") can be both a trustee and a beneficiary. Irrevocable trusts cannot be changed once established.

Within these two basic categories, there are a multitude of variations. Trusts are classified according to when they are created, who benefits, how assets are distributed, and myriad other factors. Among the particular types of trusts that a person should discuss with members of his financial planning team are the following:

- **Credit-shelter trust.** A common estate planning device, it is designed to allow married couples to reduce or avoid estate taxes when they die.
- **Disclaimer Trust.** Designed for the couple who do not yet have enough assets to need a credit-shelter trust, but may need one in the future.
- **Marital-deduction Trust.** Used to leave any money to a spouse that does not go into a credit-shelter trust, free of estate tax when the trustor dies. The most popular form of marital trust is the Qualified Terminable Interest Property Trust, or Q-TIP. With that instrument, the surviving spouse gets the trust income but, when the spouse dies, the assets themselves go to whomever (for instance, the trustor's children) was specified in the trust documents.
- **Living or Inter Vivos Trust.** A revocable trust formed while the trustor is alive, usually becoming irrevocable and testamentary at the trustor's death.
- **Life Insurance Trust.** An irrevocable vehicle into which the trustor either places money for life insurance premium payments or an existing policy itself.
- **Qualified Personal Residence Trust.** A QPRT allows a person to get a home or vacation property out of the taxable estate.
- **Charitable Remainder Trust.** This trust permits one to leave assets to a favored charity and get a tax benefit, yet retain income while alive.

- **Charitable Lead Trust.** The opposite of the previous vehicle, here a trust pays a charity income from a donated asset for a specified period of time. When the term is up, the principal goes to the donor's beneficiaries with reduced estate or gift taxes.
- **Generation-Skipping Trust.** This is used to leave a large amount of money to grandchildren with reduced estate taxes.

Additional financial planning tools are available for consideration in particular situations. One is the concept of joint property ownership. An older person may add the name of a spouse, adult child, or anyone else to a checking or savings account or other financial asset account. This may make it easier to carry out banking transactions. Both joint tenancy with right of survivorship and tenancy in common are joint ownership arrangements involving two or more names on a single account. But only the form incorporating survivorship allows one joint tenant to automatically receive, on the death of the elderly individual, what is left in the account without having to go through the probate process, and pay the otherwise associated estate taxes, for the account proceeds.

Some joint accounts allow either owner to transact business and sign financial instruments, others require the signature of all joint owners for any transactions, and still others restrict the ability of one or another owner to unilaterally withdraw funds. Local law and banking practices determine which planning avenues are possible. Obviously, before entering into a joint account a person must have a high level of trust in the judgment and integrity of the party to whom he is granting joint ownership status over his real and personal property.

Another type of financial planning available to many older persons is to give assets away, while one is still alive and competent, to family members, friends, or nonprofit charitable entities. The seemingly straightforward act of making a gift is fraught with tax and Medicaid eligibility implications about which one should consult a knowledgeable financial planning team in a timely manner.

Funeral Arrangements

The law gives individuals the right to preplan their own funerals. Paying in advance for one's funeral offers one the chance to control important details of that event, relieves family members of the burden of making these arrangements during a stressful time for them, or substitutes for the absence of family and friends in assuring that one's last wishes are followed. Before entering into a funeral preplanning agreement, one should check on the right to cancel the agreement in case one moves or changes one's mind. Money paid in advance should be paid only into a trust or escrow account maintained by the funeral director.

Federal Trade Commission (FTC) regulations require funeral directors to disclose specific information about the funeral and to refrain from engaging in unfair business practices. These federal regulations help protect individuals who preplan their own funerals, as well as relatives or friends of deceased persons who have not preplanned.

When Planning Has Not Occurred

This chapter has explained some of the merits of planning ahead, both medically and financially. If adequate planning has not taken place and the concerned individual becomes seriously cognitively impaired and unable to competently make autonomous major life decisions, those decisions probably will still need to be made and carried out from time to time. Instead of the concerned individual maintaining control and direction over those choices, however, third parties will end up exerting authority and taking actions that may or may not be consistent with the fundamental values and preferences of the person whose life is being affected.

We have already discussed delegation of decision making authority from a person incapacitated in decision making to someone else through a durable power of attorney executed in advance by the individual while still capable. As noted, in most cases naming one's own agent in advance is the most likely way to maintain a high degree of autonomy later. We have also outlined how decision making authority may be transferred legally through the operation of family consent statutes and practically through the custom of service providers turning to next of kin.

Guardianship

In the absence of these legal and pragmatic forms of power transfer, in situations where the formal locus of decision making authority must be clear (such as major transactions involving financial institutions), the legal mechanism most likely to be invoked to achieve such formal clarification of authority is the mechanism of guardianship. Guardianship is a legal relationship, authorized by a state court (in most states in the probate division), between a ward (the person whom a court has declared to be incapacitated to make particular decisions) and a guardian (whom the court appoints as the surrogate decision maker for the ward).

Terminology regarding this relationship varies somewhat among the states, with the surrogate decision maker referred to in some states as a conservator or committee. In most states, a court-appointed surrogate with total authority over the ward's personal and financial matters is called a plenary guardian, one with authority over financial issues only is a guardian of the estate or conservator, and a surrogate decision maker concerning personal (such as medical and residential) questions is a guardian of the person. To avoid confusion, the reader should familiarize himself with the language used in his specific jurisdiction.

The ethical justification for judicial imposition of a surrogate decision maker for an incapacitated individual in the realm of both personal and financial decisions is found in two fundamental and related principles. The principle of nonmaleficence instructs us to "do no harm" to others (primum non nocere). The related principle of beneficence instructs us to help others who need assistance, to affirmatively "do good." These ethical principles have been transformed into the legal doctrine of parens patriae, the inherent authority and responsibility of a benevolent society to intervene, even over objection, to protect people who cannot protect themselves. Thus, instead of abandoning cognitively incapacitated individuals to a superficial, meaningless autonomy to make harmful decisions or to neglect their own basic needs, the state may exercise its authority to protect even unwilling disabled individuals from their own folly or deficits.

Judicial appointment of a guardian to make decisions on behalf of a person who has been adjudicated incompetent means that the ward no longer retains the power to exercise those decision making rights that have been assigned to the guardian. The legal system historically has treated guardianship as an all-or-nothing proposition, global findings of incompetence being accompanied by virtually complete disenfranchisement of the ward. The trend lately, however, has been toward statutory and judicial recognition of the concept of limited or partial guardianship, which accounts for the decision-specific nature of mental capacity and the ability of some people to make certain kinds of choices rationally but not others. Under this arrangement, a guardian is given power to make only those kinds of decisions that the court finds the ward unable to make personally.

Alternatives to Guardianship

A number of alternatives to plenary, private guardianship exist for assisting older individuals with cognitive impairments to navigate through the vicissitudes of daily life. Some of these alternatives are planned by the individual in anticipation of future need, and some are put together in the absence of advance planning.

Planned Alternatives

This chapter has already discussed joint bank accounts, various forms of living trusts, durable powers of attorney, and living wills as examples of the legal and financial strategies that have evolved to enable individuals, while still mentally and physically capable of making and expressing their own rational choices, to plan ahead for the contingency of future incapacity. Other planning mechanisms include direct deposit of checks and personal money management services.

We encourage advance financial and health care planning by currently capable persons to foster continuing autonomy and to help ensure that, when the current exercise of autonomy is no longer feasible, decisions are made and implemented for the individual in the least intrusive or restrictive manner reasonably available. The least restrictive alternative (LRA) principle is a matter both of ethics (the principle of autonomy) and constitutional law under the Fourteenth Amendment Due Process clause. A central objective of advance planning is to keep private decisions within the private, nonjudicial sphere.

Unplanned Alternatives

Unfortunately, the majority of people who become incapacitated in decision making have failed to take good advantage of the available advance planning opportunities. For this bulk of the cognitively impaired population, alternatives to standard plenary, private guardianship fall into two categories: alternative forms *of* guardianship and alternatives *to* guardianship.

Recognition of the LRA principle has fueled a modern trend, noted above, toward limited or partial—as opposed to global or plenary—guardianship orders when the proposed ward is able to rationally make certain decisions but not others. Judges are encouraged today to distinguish as precisely as possible those areas where even a minimal level of decisional capacity is lacking from those areas where, with adequate assistance and support, the individual could autonomously, albeit perhaps imperfectly, manage.

For a growing number of older persons whose cognitive impairments could technically qualify them for guardianship, plenary or limited, the most pressing practical problem is the unavailability of family members or close friends who are willing and able to assume guardianship responsibilities. Some state legislatures have created public guardianship systems, by which a government agency itself acts as guardian of last resort or contracts out these services to a private entity. In a few localities, religious or other private community agencies have organized volunteer guardian programs, at least to help meet temporary needs. When the proposed ward has sufficient financial assets, the services of a new cottage industry of private, for-profit professional guardians are on the market for purchase by the courts.

In the absence of these alternatives, the cognitively incapacitated individual with no family or friends often literally "falls between the cracks." Important decisions, such as those involving medical treatment, by default go without being made until an emergency has developed and consent to treatment can be presumed as a matter of law. In these situations, health care providers usually end up functioning as unappointed patient surrogates, frequently with no real inkling of the patient's own pertinent values and preferences.

Even when advance planning for incapacity has not happened, some form of official guardianship for the cognitively incapacitated older person is by far the exception rather than the rule. One unplanned alternative to guardianship is the representative payee ("rep payee") system established by federal law for handling government benefit checks on behalf of incapacitated beneficiaries. Authorization of a surrogate to receive and manage the checks is accomplished through a simple administrative process involving almost nothing more than the filing of an application. Some states have created a counterpart system for state benefit checks.

Another significant means of surrogate decision making for cognitively impaired older individuals is Adult Protective

Services (APS). Every state has created an APS system to provide a constellation of social, legal, medical, and basic maintenance services to older community-dwelling persons in need. These services ordinarily are accepted by the beneficiary voluntarily, and the most pressing issue is how to obtain enough resources to satisfy the individual's needs. State APS statutes usually contain provisions, however, authorizing involuntary imposition of services, over the older person's objections, in emergency circumstances based on a very abbreviated application and hearing. APS really is only a quasi-alternative to guardianship, because once an emergency has abated the APS agency must go through the entire formal guardianship process before proceeding with further intervention over the individual's objection.

Using Lawyers Effectively

Although most older people are independent, intelligent, and able to speak up for themselves and make plans for the future, sometimes professional assistance is advisable. At many points in this chapter, the reader has been admonished to seek personal legal counsel to be advised about, and to protect and promote, his rights under the law in specific circumstances. This final section discusses briefly methods to help older persons use attorneys most effectively to fulfill their goals.

One Attorney or Several?

Once a decision has been made to seek out the services of an attorney, the first issue to be confronted is whether one attorney will be sufficient or a potential conflict of interest makes the hiring of multiple attorneys a better way to proceed. For instance, when we contemplate the drafting of a testamentary will, durable power of attorney, or other legal instrument that affects the interests both of the older person for whom the instrument is being prepared and of that person's family members, a conflict among the interests of the various respective parties is not difficult to imagine. Put baldly, what is best for the relative (who may be the one initiating the legal service and even paying the bill) who expects to be named in the legal instrument an heir, executor, agent, and/or trustee, may not be the most advantageous course of action for the older individual in his own right. If one attorney conducts the transaction on behalf of all the parties, an ethical concern about who exactly is the "client" might arise. If raised later by someone who feels he was disadvantaged by the legal action taken, such a concern potentially could be the basis for litigation in which a judge invalidates the whole transaction. These concerns are exacerbated when the older person (the ostensible "client") had some degree of cognitive impairment at the time the legal instrument was created or other legal activity occurred.

In such situations, the older person and supporting family or friends should seriously consider hiring separate lawyers whose exclusive allegiances to their individual clients would be clearly defined. Although the associated trouble and expense certainly is not necessary for every routine legal transaction affecting both the older person and his family, retaining multiple counsel probably is a wise investment when more complicated planning and transactions, involving substantial amounts of money or property, are involved and/or there is apprehension that some disgruntled person may later claim that family members or friends who profit personally from a transaction were using undue influence or duress and not acting in the older person's best interests.

Finding the Attorney or Attorneys

Once a decision to retain a lawyer (or lawyers) has been made, where does one find the right professional for the task at hand? Forming a good client–attorney relationship is in many respects not unlike a marriage. Elder law is an established specialty today. Among places to seek out appropriate attorney recommendations are one's personal physician (especially if the physician has a large geriatric practice), the hospital or nursing facility social worker, the local Area Agency on Aging, local organizations such as the Alzheimer's or Parkinson's Disease Associations, and, of course, other older persons and their families who are or who have been in similar situations to one's own. Most local bar associations operate lawyer referral services; if this resource is used, one should ask specifically for the names of attorneys who specialize in elder law. An even better strategy is asking for a recommendation from the National Academy of Elder Law Attorneys (NAELA) (headquartered in Tucson, Arizona), which maintains a roster of certified legal specialists in this field.

The potential client ought to interview an attorney before formally hiring him; usually the attorney will charge a fee for this initial consultation, but it is worth paying this fee to make certain that the attorney has the necessary expertise and experience to handle the particular matters of concern to the client. Among the questions that should be posed at the interview are the percentage of time that the attorney devotes to elder law practice, whether the attorney is a member of the NAELA and its state counterpart, whether the attorney has been involved in his or her state or local bar's elder law committee, and whether the attorney has published articles and/or given public presentations on elder law topics.

Legal Fees

Legal fees are a source of great apprehension for many potential clients. The issue of fees should be brought up explicitly at the initial interview, and the client has a right to insist on specific information, in writing, about the amount and calculation of those fees before a binding agreement about representation is formed. There is nothing improper or untoward about comparing among, and negotiating professional fees with, law firms with whom one is engaged in a sort of courtship ritual.

Law firms are businesses, which must sell their services within an increasingly competitive economic marketplace. Most firms will quote new prospective clients a standard fee structure, usually based on an hourly rate. Other firms charge an agreed-upon amount in return for a designated package of legal services (for example, drafting a will, a living will, and a durable power of attorney), regardless of the actual time it takes the firm to provide those services.

Besides those provided by privately practicing attorneys retained directly by older persons or their surrogates, legal services for the elderly are available from a variety of other sources. These sources include: pro bono (donated) services by the private bar; legal aid offices funded through the federal Legal Services Corporation, the Older Americans Act, or local charitable contributions; and law school clinical programs. Information on reduced or nonfee legal services for the elderly generally may be obtained from one's local bar association, long term care ombudsman's office, legal aid office, United Way, or Area Agency on Aging.

Conclusion

For older persons dealing with legal issues that affect their lives in ways both large and small, knowledge and understanding are powerful allies. This chapter has tried to strip away some of the mystery and confusion that too often engulf senior citizens' impressions of the legal system and inspire unease and apprehension. I hope that, armed with the information provided here, the reader in partnership with his or her attorney can better use the law to responsibly take advantage of the rights and opportunities that society has provided to its older members.

Laurel E. Beedon, D.Ed., is a Senior Policy Advisor on the Economics Team of the Public Policy Institute at AARP, where she specializes in Social Security, Supplemental Security Income, and disability policy research. She previously worked at the Social Security Administration's Office of Research and Statistics, served on faculties of George Washington University and Virginia Polytechnic Institute and State University, and was on the staff of the Joint House–Senate American Indian Policy Committee. She has written and published numerous articles in her areas of expertise. A transplanted Minnesotan, now living outside Washington, DC, she is a volunteer mediator for the Superior Court of the District of Columbia, and she relaxes by playing classical piano and quilting.

Achieving Financial Security

Laurel E. Beedon

Planning for the future, whether you are 25 or 55, can seem a daunting task. The younger a person is, the easier it is to put it off until next month or next year—there seems to be plenty of time. The older a person is, the harder it is to find the time—and the energy. No matter what your age, it is always worth the effort. In preparing for a financially secure and independent future, you should focus first on the "three legs of your retirement income stool," Social Security benefits, pensions, and savings and investments. Then, evaluate additional sources of financial security, such as health care coverage, the value of real estate, life insurance, work, gifts, wills and trusts, and the income safety net for those over age 65—Supplemental Security Income (SSI).

Financial Planning

Although no simple formula exists to calculate your exact financial requirements during retirement, most financial planners point out that you will need close to 80 percent of preretirement earnings to continue the same lifestyle. By completing the form that follows you can determine if Social Security and pension benefits, along with interest from investment and savings, will provide that level of minimum income. The completed form will give you an idea of approximately how close—or far—you are from that goal.

With some idea of your projected retirement income, you can begin planning for a secure financial future. Remember that every good long-term plan has a short-term component.

Before considering long-term investments, place the equivalent of three to six months salary in a "back-up" savings. Keep this money in an interest-bearing checking or savings account, so that it can be withdrawn without any penalty to cover inevitable, but unpredictable, expenses, such as a major illness or injury that may result in time out of the workforce, unplanned car or home repairs, or even the loss of one's job.

After "back-up savings" are established, additional savings can be used to begin making a commitment to retirement. Planners recommend that you put 90 percent of current earnings toward current expenses—such as, the mortgage, food, gas, and insurance premiums—and 10 percent toward the future—savings and investments.

However, even a quick look at the dramatic increases over the past few years in the numbers of people living into their 80s and 90s (the oldest old, those people 85 and older, is the fastest growing segment of the population) is a persuasive argument for trying to achieve an 80:20 ratio. The government may project a life expectancy of slightly more than seventeen years for sixty-five year olds, but that is only a statistical average. If you accept this number as your personal projection for planning your retirement and are lucky enough to live to 90, you will go broke at 82.

Social Security: The First Leg

Social Security is first of the three legs on the retirement income stool. If a job is covered by Social Security, both the employee and employer contribute toward Social Security and Medicare by paying FICA taxes. For Social Security, the employee and employer each contribute a total of 6.2 percent of an employee's wages up to a maximum of $68,400 in 1998. For Medicare, each contributes 1.45 percent of all earnings. Self-employed individuals who qualify for these benefits pay both as employer and employee.

If wages are stopped or reduced because of retirement, disability, or death, the retiree and/or family members will receive benefits. Although Social Security was never intended to replace a person's entire income, it does provide a broad, stable base on which to plan for one's future.

Qualifications for Benefits

To receive benefits, you must earn Social Security credits. In 1998, for each $700 you earned on a job covered by Social

Figuring Retirement Worth

Use a work sheet like this to calculate both annual income and savings at retirement.

Estimated annual Social Security benefit at full retirement age	$ _____
Estimated annual pension amount	
Employer sponsored plan(s)	$ _____
Individual plan(s)	
IRA	$ _____
Keogh	$ _____
Annuity	$ _____
Other	$ _____
Estimated total annual income	$ _____
Savings and investments	
Certificates of Deposit	$ _____
Stocks	$ _____
Bonds	$ _____
Mutual Funds	$ _____
Savings accounts	$ _____
Other	$ _____
Life insurance cash value	$ _____
Estimated total savings	$ _____

Security, you received one credit — up to a maximum of four credits. When you have earned forty credits, you qualify to receive benefits at retirement age.

Social Security credits do not need to be earned consecutively and are carried from job to job. Thus, if you change jobs or leave the workforce for a period of time before reaching eligibility, the earned credits remain on your record. You can add to them by returning to the workforce or moving to another job.

Retirement Age

Currently, you can receive full retirement benefits at the age of 65. However, beginning in the year 2000, the age will increase until it reaches 66 in 2009 and 67 in 2027.

You can retire at age 62 and still collect Social Security, but the payments will be permanently reduced because of the extra years you will be receiving benefits. At present, the reduction is 20 percent, but when the full-retirement age reaches age 67 in 2027, the reduction for early retirement will have increased to 30 percent.

Similarly, if you choose to wait until after the age of 65 to collect Social Security, your benefit will increase by a percentage called the delayed retirement credit (DRC). The percentage will increase annually until it reaches 8 percent in 2008.

If you decide to defer retirement benefits, you should still apply for Medicare approximately three months before you turn 65 years of age. Medicare does not begin automatically.

Applying for Benefits

You must apply for Social Security and Medicare benefits. Therefore, between three and six months before you intend to retire (or immediately if you are applying for disability benefits), make an appointment to visit your local Social Security office or call the Social Security Administration at its toll-free number.

When you apply for Social Security benefits, bring the following documents:

- Your Social Security card or a record of your Social Security number;
- Birth certificates for you and your children, if they are also applying. If you do not have a birth certificate, check with the Social Security Administration for information about other acceptable documents;
- Your marriage certificate (or other acceptable proof of marriage) if you are applying for spousal or widow/widowers' benefits;
- Evidence of recent earnings, such as your most recent W-2 or self-employment tax return;
- Proof of the worker's death, if you are applying for survivor's benefits;
- A list of hospitals or other health care facilities where you have been treated and a list of attending physicians if you are applying for disability benefits;
- Your checkbook, savings book, or other papers from your financial institution with your name and account number if you want to have benefit checks deposited directly into your account.

If you do not have a specific document, check with the Social Security Administration about acceptable substitutes.

The lack of a document should not keep you from applying for benefits.

Amount of Benefits

Employment Covered by Social Security

The amount of your Social Security payment depends on the number of years you have worked in jobs covered by Social Security and your average earnings over a 35-year work life. If you worked fewer than 35 years but have at least 40 Social Security credits (approximately ten years of covered work), you still qualify for a benefit, but it will be proportionately lower. For an average earner who retired at age 65 in 1998, the Social Security benefit was $938 per month; for someone earning the maximum wages subject to Social Security taxes, it was $1,342.

What makes Social Security an exceptionally secure base for retirement is that, unlike most private pension plans, it does not lose its value because of inflation. Monthly benefits increase automatically every January to accommodate any rise in the cost of living.

If you return to work after you have started receiving benefits, your wages (on which you will pay FICA tax) may also increase your benefits. The Social Security Administration automatically recalculates your benefit to include the additional earnings.

Family and Disability Benefits

Social Security is often viewed as just a retirement system. However, Social Security provides other benefits, including financial protection should you become severely disabled during your working life, as well as benefits for your family. These family benefits extend to:

- Your spouse, if 62 years of age or older;
- Your spouse if under 62 years of age, but caring for your child who is under 16 years of age or, if disabled, is under the age of 22;
- Your former spouse, if 62 years of age or older and if married to you for at least ten years, divorced from you for at least two years, and not remarried;
- Your child, if 17 years of age or younger;
- Your adult child, if severely disabled before 22 years of age;
- Your widow/widower, if 60 years of age or older or 50 years of age and severely disabled;

- Your aging parents, if dependent on you for more than one half of their support.

The amount of these benefits vary as follows:

- Your spouse receives 50 percent of your retired worker's benefit amount at 65 years of age. Your spouse's benefit is reduced for early retirement in the same way your benefit would be.
- Your divorced spouse can also receive 50 percent of your retired worker's benefit amount. These benefits do not affect the amount of your benefits or those of your current spouse.
- Your child receives 50 percent of your retirement benefit amount.
- Your widow/widower receives 100 percent of your benefit amount at 65 years of age. This amount will be reduced if you take early retirement.
- Your two parents receive up to 75 percent and one parent up to 82.5 percent of your benefit amount.

The limit to the amount of benefits that a family can receive based on one worker's record is called the Family Maximum. It is based on the principle that a family should not receive more in benefits than the worker earned on the job.

If you are so severely disabled that you are unable to work at any job for at least a year or you are expected to die, you and your family members can qualify to receive disability benefits. This assumes that you have earned the required number of Social Security credits.

Whenever you qualify for more than one benefit, you will receive the amount that is higher. The benefits are not added together.

The Windfall Reduction

If you are planning to receive a pension from a government job or a job not covered by Social Security and if you also have enough credits to receive Social Security benefits, a formula may be used to lower the amount of your Social Security benefit. How much depends on the number of years you contributed to Social Security.

The Public, or Government, Pension Off-Set

If you are planning to receive a pension from work not covered by Social Security and you are eligible to receive Social Security benefits based on your spouse's record, the public pension off-set can reduce your Social Security benefits by as much as two thirds of your government pension payments.

Continued Earnings

If you decide to work and receive Social Security benefits, but are between the ages of 62 and 69, the Social Security Administration does not consider you fully retired. As a result, your benefit will be reduced accordingly.

If you are under 65 years of age, every $2 of earnings over the limit, which was $9,120 in 1998, reduces your Social Security benefit by $1. If you are 65 through 69 years of age, your Social Security benefit will be reduced by $1 for every $3 you earn over the limit, which was $14,500 in 1997.

The earnings limit also applies if you are receiving benefits as a spouse, child, or parent who cares for a young child. In addition, certain rules apply specifically to the first calendar year that you receive benefits.

Check if the earnings limit rules apply to you; the penalties for noncompliance are fairly heavy. Note, however, that earnings from savings, investments, pensions, and other "unearned income" do not count as income under the limit.

Social Security Benefits and Taxes

Depending on your income, Social Security benefits may be subject to taxation. For this purpose, income is calculated by adding one half of your Social Security benefit to other adjusted gross taxable income plus tax-exempt interest income (including interest earned on savings bonds used to finance higher education for yourself or a dependent) and amounts earned in a foreign country that are excluded from gross income.

Based on this calculation, if you are married with an annual income between $32,000 and $44,000 or if you are single with an annual income between $25,000 and $34,000, up to 50 percent of your benefit may qualify as taxable income. If you and your spouse have an income of more than $44,000 or if you are single with an income of more than $34,000, up to 85 percent of your benefit can be taxed.

Your Social Security Record

Employers report employee earnings quarterly and annually to the Internal Revenue Service. Self-employed individuals report their annual net earnings on their income tax returns.

Because the benefit you ultimately receive is based on these reported earnings, check with the Social Security Administration every three years to be sure that your earnings have been properly recorded.

You can request Form SSA 7004, called the Request for Earnings and Benefit Estimate, from the Social Security Administration by calling their telephone information line, visiting your local Social Security office, or downloading the form from the Internet. After filling out and returning the form, you will receive a Personal Earnings Benefit Estimate Statement (PEBES). The PEBES gives you the opportunity to check your earnings record and also provides you with an estimate of your future Social Security benefits based on those earnings — a great retirement planning tool.

Private Pensions: The Second Leg

Pensions are the second leg of your retirement income stool. There are several types of employer-sponsored plans, as well as plans you can provide for yourself. Because pension plans vary enormously from benefit levels to early retirement provisions, you must review your plan, ask questions now, and determine how much retirement income security your pension will provide.

This section focuses on private pensions. However, if you participate in some form of public pension plan, the same admonitions hold — find out about your pension so you can plan your future.

Employer-Sponsored Plans

The two basic types of employer-sponsored pension plans are defined benefit (DB) and defined contribution (DC) plans. The first places the primary responsibility for your pension with your employer; the second places the primary responsibility with you.

Defined Benefit Plans

After you meet the plan requirements, DB plans provide you with a guaranteed, defined benefit based on a specific formula. Generally, your employer is entirely responsible for administering and funding the plan. The Pension Benefit Guarantee Corporation, a government agency, insures at least partial payment of your pension should your employer go out of business.

DB plans are designed to equal approximately 40 to 60 percent of your preretirement earnings. The benefit calculation formula for most DB plans is based on years of service and total earnings. Sometimes, the amount of your Social Security benefit is included in the calculation. This is called pension integration. Check with your plan administrator or read the plan description to determine whether integration applies to your pension. Integration could lower the amount of your pension benefit to 20 or 30 percent of your preretirement earnings.

Defined Contribution Plans

Unlike defined benefit plans, a DC plan is generally funded by a combination of employer and employee contributions and the benefit amount is not guaranteed. Depending on the plan, the amount of the contribution can be fixed or can fluctuate. It could, for example, be a percentage of either your salary or the company's profits. The amount of your benefit depends on how successfully these contributions are invested. If the investments are profitable, you could receive a substantial sum at retirement. If not, this leg of your retirement stool could be very short.

On the positive side, no matter how much is invested, the money grows, in your name, tax free, until you withdraw it at retirement. Unlike DB plans, in which each employer holds the funds until you retire, the money in your DC account can be rolled into another tax-deferred retirement account that you control. Four types of DC plans are discussed below.

401(k): A 401(k) is a plan with advantages for both you and your employer. For your employer, it may be easier to administer and more affordable than most DB plans. For you, it means tax-free savings, and if you leave your job, control of your money.

You can participate in a 401(k) offered by your employer by directing him or her to deduct a percentage of your taxable earnings, up to $10,000 in 1998, and deposit that sum into an account in your name. Some employers also match your contributions. This could mean, for example, for every $2 you contribute to your future well-being, your employer contributes another $1. Thus, you earn a bonus for doing something for yourself! If this type of matching is offered where you work, be sure to take advantage of it by saving as much as you can.

In addition to building your retirement savings, taxes on both the annual deposit amount and on the overall interest accrued are deferred until you withdraw your 401(k) savings at retirement. Note that as with many other investments, 401(k) plans are not federally insured.

When you withdraw your 401(k) savings at retirement, you will have to pay taxes on it. Be sure to check on the option of five-year forward averaging when you withdraw your 401(k). It allows you to withdraw your money all at once, but pay taxes as if you had withdrawn it over a five-year period. (Five-year averaging will not be available after 1999.)

If you withdraw cash from your 401(k) before your retirement, you are taking money away from yourself. If you must, however, the majority of company plans allow you to take a loan from your 401(k). Such loans are limited to 50 percent of your vested balance or $50,000 in any 12-month period, whichever is lower. You have up to five years to pay the money back into your account. The interest, if your plan has an interest clause, is paid back to your account. Your plan may also allow you to make a hardship withdrawal (usually from the money you have contributed) if, for example, you have very high medical expenses.

403(b): A 403(b) provides salary reduction savings options for people who work in such nonprofit organizations as schools or hospitals. With a 403(b), a contribution is subtracted from your taxable income and is tax deferred until you withdraw it. Annual contribution levels are based on a formula that includes years of service, earlier contributions, and current salary. As with a 401(k), the level of contributions are limited. As with 401(k)s, you should take advantage of this plan.

Profit-Sharing Plans: This type of DC plan is based on your employer's profits. If the business does well, so can you. (Just remember, businesses do not always do well.)

Employees do not contribute to this plan. Rather, each participant receives a portion of the total contribution made by the employer. Although an employer who provides this type of plan is not required to contribute it annually, the law requires that contributions be "recurring and substantial."

An Employee Stock Ownership Plan (ESOP): An ESOP is a DC plan that contributes to your retirement in the form of company stock. If you work in an up-and-coming enterprise, this is an opportunity to purchase stock without paying a broker. In addition, you do not have to pay taxes on the value or the interest earned until you retire, unless you leave your job and cash out your stock. As with other tax-deferred plans, if you change jobs, you can "roll" (transfer your funds, tax free, from one retirement plan to another) your stock into an individual retirement account (IRA).

If you leave your current job, be sure to roll over your tax-deferred retirement money within the sixty-day time limit. Otherwise, even if you intended to reinvest the money, you will have to pay a significant penalty. If you take your tax-deferred pension money in a lump sum, 20 percent will be taken off the top. If you have not reinvested that money within 60 days, the full amount of your payout is subject to federal and state taxes. This amount could well exceed 20 percent. If you are under age 59½, you will also have to pay the 10 percent penalty for withdrawing your retirement savings before retirement age. (The payment does not apply if you left your job after reaching age 55.)

The simplest solution for this potential problem is to have the full amount of your tax-deferred plan transferred directly to an IRA or other qualified plan you may already have. If the money does come to you, take that money plus an additional 20 percent of your own (remember 20 percent was taken off the top) and put it in an IRA or qualified plan. You will not lose the 20 percent, and when you file your income tax, you will receive a credit.

Information on Private Pension Plans

To plan for retirement, you should learn about your company's pension plan by asking the following questions about qualifications, benefits, payments, and survivor benefits.

1. Is a pension plan provided by this company? Employers are not required to provide a pension plan.
2. Is my job category covered by the plan? Even if your company has a pension plan, your job category may not be covered. For example, if you work fewer than 20 hours per week or 1,000 hours per year, you may not qualify.
3. What are the eligibility requirements? Most plans have age and service requirements for participation in the pension plan. In general, you can begin to earn benefits if you have reached the age of 21 and have completed one year of qualified employment.
4. How long do I have to work before I am vested (that is, before you have the right to a pension at retirement)?

    Most employers have plans with either five-year 100% vesting or three- to seven-year gradual vesting. As you move from job to job, keep accurate records of your vested pensions so you know what you are owed and can be sure to collect it. If you are considering changing jobs, check to see how far you are from being fully vested with your current employer. You may want to hang on six months or a year longer until you have earned a pension. That small benefit seems unimportant now, but it may mean a great deal when you reach age 70.

- What happens if I am laid off or fired?
- What if I take time off to return to school or care for a sick spouse?

5.   How will my pension be calculated?

- Does the benefit formula include my Social Security benefit?
- Is there a different formula for early retirement?
- Does the formula include my work after age 65? Employers are not required to contribute to your pension after age 65.
- What is the formula with a joint and survivor annuity? The joint and survivor annuity will lower your benefit while you are alive, so that your spouse can receive a benefit after you die. The joint and survivor provision is automatic for most pensions. If you decide to forego it, both you and your spouse must waive the benefit in a notarized spousal consent form provided by the pension plan administrator.

6.   When can I begin to receive benefits?

- Can I receive a benefit before the full-retirement age?
- What if I continue to work after reaching the full-retirement age?

7.   Will my benefits increase after I retire? Although Social Security and federal pensions are adjusted annually to keep beneficiaries even with inflation, most private pensions are not. If your plan is one of the few that does, great. If not, your financial retirement plan needs to provide for increases in the cost of living.

To answer all of these questions, you should consult the plan documents, your benefit statement, and the plan administrator.

The Plan Documents: Two important documents describe your pension plan—the Summary Plan Description (SPD) and the official plan document. The SPD, which outlines the plans rules and requirements, is written in everyday English. You are entitled to a free file copy from your plan administrator. For an in-depth description, the official plan document is also available. Your employer may charge you for a copy, but is required by law to provide the document, if you request it in writing.

In addition to the plan documents, the plan administrator must automatically provide you with a copy of the Summary Annual Report, which summarizes the financial report each plan must file with the U.S. Department of Labor.

Your Benefit Statement: Many employers automatically inform employees about pension benefits. If your employer does not, you are entitled to request in writing a free individual benefits statement annually. This statement will include the value of your total pension benefit. Be sure to differentiate between the amount projected as your retirement income and the amount you have earned to date.

The Administrator: If you feel more comfortable speaking directly to a person or have specific questions after going over the documents, make an appointment to speak with your pension plan administrator.

Individual Retirement Plans

Individual Retirement Account (IRA)

If your employer does not provide pension opportunities, a good way to create that second leg of your retirement stool is open an individual retirement account. IRAs were designed to encourage individuals, through tax incentives, to save for their own retirement. Although some of the rules have changed, an IRA is a smart investment in your future. You can open or contribute to your IRA as late as the date for filing your federal income taxes (April 15th) and still get the tax advantage for the preceding year.

Tax-Deferred IRA: You can contribute up to $2,000 to an IRA annually, if you are under the age of $70\frac{1}{2}$ and are employed. During the years that you work and contribute to an IRA, the interest, dividends, and capital gains earned will grow and compound tax free until you withdraw the money at retirement.

Tax-Deductible IRA: In addition to taking advantage of an IRA's tax-deferred growth, you can deduct your annual $2,000 IRA contribution or part of it from your income tax depending on your adjusted gross income (AGI). Even if only part of the

$2,000 is deductible, you can still contribute the full amount and take advantage of the tax deferred savings.

If neither you nor your spouse participate in a retirement plan at work, you may each deduct all $2,000 of your annual IRA contribution. Even if you and/or your spouse participate in a retirement plan at work, you may still qualify for a tax-deductible IRA based on income. If you are married, file taxes jointly with your spouse, and your AGI is $50,000 or less, each of you can make a fully deductible contribution. If you file jointly and your AGI is between $50,000 and $60,000, for each $1,000 above $50,000 your IRA deduction is reduced by $200.

If you are single and your AGI is $30,000 or less, you may deduct the full $2,000 annual contribution to your IRA. If you are single and your AGI is between $30,000 and $40,000, for every $1,000 you earn above $30,000, your IRA deduction is reduced by $200. Thus, if your income is $35,000 you can still deduct $1,000 from your income tax — a deduction that is still worth the effort. Under the 1997 Tax Act, these income levels will increase gradually to $80,000 for married taxpayers filing jointly by the year 2007 and $50,000 for single taxpayers by the year 2005. The Act also removes the restriction that prevents an individual who is not an active participant in an employer-sponsored retirement plan from making a deductible IRA contribution if his or her spouse is an active participant in such a plan, provided that their joint income is less than $150,000. There are additional new provisions that apply to the taxable year beginning January 1, 1998.

Roth IRA: A new "backloaded" IRA that accumulates earnings tax free until retirement has been added by the 1997 Tax Act. Remember that money is taxed as income *before* you deposit it in your Roth IRA. Contributions to a Roth IRA cannot be deducted on your tax return, but when you begin to withdraw funds from your IRA at retirement, you will not have to pay taxes on the interest earned. (This is opposite to the way a regular IRA works.) This IRA is available to anyone within certain income levels. Contributions are limited to $2,000 less the amount of contributions to deductible IRAs. To qualify for the full contribution, the income limit is an AGI of $95,000 for singles and $150,000 for married taxpayers filing jointly. You can still make a partial contribution if your AGI is below $110,000 for singles and $160,000 for couples. No Roth IRA contributions are allowed beyond this income level.

Spousal IRA: Annual contributions of $2,000 are allowed for spouses who are not earning wages. Whether or not the working spouse participates in a retirement plan, you can take a full deduction of $2,000 as long as your AGI as a couple does not exceed $150,000.

Another advantage of an IRA is that it allows annual contributions for spouses who are not earning wages.

Education IRA: As of 1998, individuals who qualify can put up to $500 in an education IRA for a designated child under age 18. The contributions are nondeductible but the earnings are tax-free and penalty-free as long as they are used for higher education. Single taxpayers with an AGI of up to $95,000 and married taxpayers with an AGI of up to $150,000 get a full contribution. If you earn more than these limits, your allowable contribution shrinks; for singles the maximum phases out at $110,000 and for couples at $160,000. A child may have one or more education IRAs, and parents, grandparents, friends, and even the child may contribute, but the total of contributions from all sources must not exceed $500 or the surplus will be subject to a 6% excise tax for every year it remains in the accounts. This is obviously not the sort of account that one can quietly set up to surprise a child years later when she goes to college.

Withdrawals: IRAs were created to promote retirement savings. Thus, significant penalties are incurred if you decide to use the money before you retire. Withdrawing money from an IRA account before you reach age $59\frac{1}{2}$ is considered a "premature withdrawal." With few exceptions, there is a 10% penalty in addition to payment of accrued taxes. The exceptions are if the owner of the IRA dies, becomes permanently disabled, or sets up a plan to make withdrawals from your IRA in equal amounts each year for your remaining life-expectancy, and if there is a distribution to an alternate payee, for example in a qualified domestic relations order (QDRO) from a court. In recent years, three new exceptions have been added: higher education expenses, catastrophic illness, and first-time home purchases.

Between the ages of $59\frac{1}{2}$ and $70\frac{1}{2}$, you may withdraw your IRA contributions at any time for any amount. If that withdrawal is based on contributions that were tax deductible, the amount you withdraw, including the earned interest, is taxed as income in the year of withdrawal. If, however, the withdrawal is based on a nondeductible contribution, you have already paid tax on the contributions and only the earnings will be subject to tax on withdrawal. Keep track of which is which. Otherwise, untangling the tax-deferred form the nondeferred parts of your various IRAs can be difficult.

By April 1 of the year in which you reach the age of 70½, you must begin to withdraw money from your IRA by December 31 of each year. If you delay your first payment until March 31 of the following year, you are still required to take your distribution for the current year as well. The distribution amount is based on your life expectancy or the joint life expectancy of you and your beneficiary.

Simplified Employee Pensions (SEP)

If your employer does not provide a pension plan investigate a SEP, which is low cost, low effort, and low maintenance for your employer. It offers employees tax advantages and control over their own investments. Generally, SEP-IRAs are subject to the same withdrawal rules as regular IRAs. The money is yours, but if you withdraw it before the age of 59½, you will incur a penalty and be required to pay income tax on interest earned. And, as with regular IRAs, you must begin to withdraw the money by age 70½. Contributions are limited to 15% of earned income or $30,000, whichever is lower.

SEP-IRA: A SEP-IRA is established and maintained by an employee, but the employer makes all the contributions. For the employee, this means control over the money contributed and deferred taxes on interest earned. For the employer, it means minimum paper work and a tax deduction for all contributions. If you are self-employed, even part-time self-employed, you can benefit from tax advantages as both employer and employee.

To establish a SEP-IRA, your employer fills out the unusually short IRS Form 5305 SEP, which allows contributions of up to 15% of your earnings or $30,000, whichever is lower, to be contributed each year on your behalf. All you and the other employees have to do is set up IRAs into which your employer can make deposits.

Savings Incentive Match Plan for Employees (SIMPLE): Small firms with fewer than 100 employees might offer a SIMPLE, a salary reduction plan that works much like a 401(k). In 1998 eligible employees may contribute up to $6,000 a year. The employer contributes and may match up to 3 percent of an employee's pay or contribute 2 percent of the pay of all eligible workers, whether or not they all contribute. You are immediately vested in the money your employer contributes, but if you withdraw that money in the first two years, you will owe taxes and a large penalty.

Keogh

A Keogh is a pension/savings option that allows a self-employed person to be treated as a employee. Contributions to your Keogh are fully tax-deductible and earnings from the investment are tax deferred until the money is withdrawn—presumably at retirement.

Even if you are working full-time and have pension coverage from your employer, any additional income you earn as a self-employed person allows you to set up a Keogh—not just if you are a physician or the owner of a small specialty store, but if you teach violin in the evenings or sell cheese cakes to your friends for their dinner parties. If, however, you employ others in your business, you must contribute the same percentage of income to their accounts as you do to your own.

A profit-sharing Keogh allows you to change the amount of your contributions from year to year. If you are unsure of what your annual profits will be, this is probably the plan for you. You can invest as much as 15 percent of your net self-employment income, up to $30,000.

A money-purchase Keogh allows you to shelter more of your self-employment earnings—up to 25 percent, with a $30,000 cap. This shelter is particularly useful for earnings from a second job. However, you must contribute the same percentage to the Keogh each year or face tax consequences. If your self-employment income is steady, this may be the plan for you.

A paired plan combines the advantages of the money purchase and the profit sharing plans. The paired plan allows you to contribute a fixed amount to a money-purchase plan and vary contributions to a profit-sharing plan up to a total of 20 percent of your earnings, with a $30,000 cap.

Annuities

A basic annuity is a contract issued by an insurance company, bank, or brokerage firm that, in return for your investment over time, guarantees to pay you a set amount of money either in a lump sum or over a period of time—usually your life. Earnings on annuity investments are tax deferred until you withdraw the money at retirement. However, the annual contribution amount is not deductible.

An annuity should not be confused with a life insurance policy, simply because you can purchase both from an insurance company. Life insurance builds up principal to be paid to your beneficiaries upon your death. In contrast, an annuity spends down principal by making structured payouts after you retire.

Although a guaranteed benefit from an annuity sounds very secure, remember that the better the guarantee, the lower the benefit and the higher the cost. Also, if you decide on a fixed monthly amount that is satisfactory now, in five years that amount may be significantly eroded by inflation.

Although variable rate annuities allow you to move your investment among the funds offered by an annuity tax free, if you want your money before age $59\frac{1}{2}$, there is a 10% penalty in addition to income taxes and a surrender fee. Just having an annuity involves costs — usually a contract maintenance fee, an assets management fee, and an administration fee. The moral of the story is the same as that of any investment tale — do your homework. Define what you want this investment to accomplish and decide whether it achieves that goal. Rating information about annuities is available from Best's Insurance Reports.

A life annuity provides monthly payments as long as you are alive. When you die, payments stop — even if you have only received one payment. If you are not concerned about benefits for your spouse or other dependents after you die, this may be an option. Another version of annuity guarantees a minimum number of payments, so if you die before the guaranteed number has been made, your estate will receive the guaranteed amount.

A fixed rate annuity guarantees you a fixed rate of return for a set period of time. By guaranteeing the interest rate, the insurer is assuming the investment risk.

With a variable rate annuity, your premiums are invested in mutual funds. Although the annuity shelters your earnings from taxes, your payment depends on the success of the investment portfolio. In other words, you assume the risk. What you must consider here is whether a variable annuity is a better investment for you than just investing yourself in a range of mutual funds.

Savings and Investments: The Third Leg

Social Security and pensions provide two important legs on your retirement income stool, but to maintain your financial balance, you must provide the third leg by saving and investing on your own. Many options are available, including savings and checking accounts, certificates of deposit, bonds, stocks, and mutual funds. Some involve taking risks.

The Right Mix

The conventional wisdom from financial advisers is that the younger you are, the more your money should go into potentially high-return, but riskier, investments, such as stocks. The older you get, the more those dollars should be moved to more secure options, such as bonds, that will preserve your assets and give you a steady stream of income. However, as a result of increasing life-expectancy, rising costs of health care, and decreasing support from pension plans, some advisers recommend that you stay with higher risk, high-return investments longer—even into retirement.

Before investing, calculate how risk will affect your potential retirement income. Look at the worksheet on which you estimated your income from Social Security benefits, pension payments, and interest from current savings and investments. Determine how much additional income you need to reach approximately 80 percent of your preretirement income. If your answer is not much, you can probably afford low-risk investments with low rates of interest. However, if you have a very low pension or a small Social Security benefit and no savings, you may decide to take greater risks to achieve a higher rate of return. (There are other ways to reduce the gap, such as living more frugally or working.)

It is easy to calculate the impact of various interest rates by using the "Rule of 72." Just divide 72 by the interest rate you will receive (or expect to receive) from your investment. The result is the number of years it will take to double your money. Thus, if you are able to save $1,000 at 7% interest, it will equal $2,000 in just over ten years (72/7=10.28). That same $1,000 at 10% interest will double in slightly more than seven years.

Savings and Investment Options

The terms "savings" and "investments" are often used interchangeably. In fact, they are not the same, and the difference is important to you as you make decisions about your money. When you put your money in savings, it earns interest but the principal amount never changes. (It may lose value because of inflation, but that is a different matter.) In contrast, with an investment, you expect the principal to change — hopefully to grow. What follows are some of the available options.

Low-Risk Savings

Checking and saving accounts are good places to keep your month-to-month expense money and some of your back-up funds. You can also purchase a CD at a bank, credit union, or similar institution, which means you are, in essence, lending your money for a specified period of time at a fixed rate of interest. At the end of the period, usually one to five years, you receive your money and the interest earned. Unless the CD is part of an IRA, the interest is taxable. If you decide to withdraw your money before the designated period, you will have to pay a penalty.

A money market deposit account is an interest bearing account, available from financial institutions, that is invested in short-term securities. If you deposit in a money market account from a FDIC-insured institution, your principal is guaranteed up to $100,000. The risk is obviously lower, but so is the return.

Bonds

A bond is an interest bearing security that represents the debt of a company or a governmental entity. As a bond holder, you are paid interest over a specified period of time. In addition, when the bond matures, you are paid its face value. Unlike a stockholder, who owns a share of the company, as a bondholder, you are a lender who is paid for the use of your money.

Bond price changes have the opposite effect from changes in interest rates. When interest rates drop, bond values increase, and when interest rates go up, the market value of bonds fall.

Bonds are not without risk. If you sell your fixed-rate bond before maturity, for example, and the market interest rates have gone up, the value of your bond is reduced. It is also possible that the principal of your bond will not be repaid. The probability can be reduced (not eliminated) by researching the bond and its rating before making your purchase. As with stocks, the higher the risk, the higher the potential gain. Bonds are evaluated by independent analysts, such as Standard and Poor's or Moody's, which determine the ability of the issuer to pay interest and principal to the bondholders.

The bonds that financial advisers consider the safest are rated A or above by Standard and Poor's or Moody's. Bonds in the C range and below are considered speculative and in danger of default.

U.S. Treasury Securities: These are attractive investments that are free from state and local taxes. *U.S. Savings Bonds* (Series EE and HH) are a secure and easy-to-make investment. You can purchase them without any sales charge through your bank or savings institution or directly from a Federal Reserve Bank. Series EE, sold at discount, are priced from $25 to $10,000, and can be converted to Series HH bonds at maturity. HH bonds are fixed-income and pay interest twice yearly. You do not have to pay state or local income tax on Series EE bonds and federal income tax can be deferred until the bonds mature or are cashed in.

You can use the proceeds of EE bonds, tax free, to pay education costs, if you are over age 24. This could be the boost your child's college fund needs. However, Series EE Bonds issued after May 1, 1995 have no guaranteed rate of interest. Instead, they earn interest at the market bond rate. EE bonds held six months to five years will earn a rate equal to 85 percent of the average yield on six-month Treasury bills. Bonds held longer will earn a rate equal to 85 percent of the average yield on five-year Treasury bonds and notes during the preceding six months. Interest is added to each bond's redemption value on December 1 and June 1. Keep those dates in mind when you are cashing in your bonds so you earn the maximum interest.

U.S. Treasury Bills (T-Bills) are government bonds sold with 3-month, 6-month, and 1-year maturities for a minimum of $10,000. You purchase the bill at a price lower than the face value and receive the difference between what you paid and face amount when the bills mature.

U.S. Treasury Bonds are long-term investments, with initial maturities of ten years and minimum denominations of $1,000. The principal is paid at maturity and interest is paid twice a year.

U.S. Treasury Notes fall between a bond and a bill in length of term. Treasury notes are issued for one to ten years in denominations of $1,000 or more. Interest is paid twice a year, and the principal is paid on maturity.

Municipal Bonds: Two types of municipals are issued by state, county, or other small, government subdivisions. Public purpose bonds are exempt from federal tax and, if issued in your own state, exempt from state income tax. Private purpose bonds are taxable unless specifically exempted.

If you have money that is already tax sheltered, such as an IRA, Keogh, or SEP, you may want to put other nonsheltered money into municipals.

With insured municipal bonds, the issuer purchases insurance to protect the investors if a default should occur. Because insurance costs money, these bonds have a lower yield.

Corporate Bonds: Corporate bonds represent the obligation of the issuing corporation which promises to repay your loan with interest. Such bonds are guarantee rated by the corporation's ability to pay. The safest bonds receive the highest ratings.

Junk Bonds: Junk bonds fall at the bottom of the bond ratings, because they are high-risk, although potentially high-yield bonds. If you have a nervous streak, these are probably not for you.

Stocks: The Long-Term Winners

Historically, stocks offer the highest potential short-term risk and the highest potential long-term return on your investment. Their values rise and fall as business cycles and economic conditions change. Regardless of the daily ups and downs of the market, however, stocks have consistently performed better than bonds and other cash investments over the long term.

Sound great? Maybe, but if you decide to invest in individual stocks, make the commitment to do your homework. Think about how much risk you want to take; then do your research. Read and ask questions and look into at least 10 to 20 specific stocks in a wide range of industries. Consider joining an organization that can provide you with specialized information, such as the American Association of Individual Investors. (A less-threatening plunge may be investing in mutual funds, which are discussed later).

Stock is a share in the ownership of a company. If you purchase stock, neither your principal nor your rate of return is guaranteed. If the company makes a profit, you will receive a dividend in the form of cash or additional stock from the corporation's earnings.   If the company is not successful, neither are you.

Preferred Stock: If you own preferred stock, your dividends are paid, at a specified rate, before they are paid to holders of common stock. If dividends are not paid in any one year, they accumulate and must be paid to you before dividends are paid to holders of common stock. For these privileges, preferred stock does not have the same appreciation potential as common stock.

Common Stock: Common stocks are basic units of ownership in a public corporation. As the stockholder, you are an owner of the risks as well as the profits of the entity in which you invest.

Blue Chip Stock: Blue chip is an unofficial designation for stock issued by a company that is known for quality and its ability to make money. (For example, IBM and GM were considered blue chip stocks in the early 1980s.)

Income Stock: Many financial advisers recommend that you purchase this type of stock for your retirement, as it provides a steady income rather than growth.

Growth Stock: Financial advisers recommend this stock for people with a long-term focus. A growth stock is expected to grow faster than the economy, beating both inflation and the stock market in general but because its value can fluctuate, it has potential for both large profits and significant losses.

Mutual Funds

If you are not confident in your ability to pick and choose the right stock or bond intelligently and prefer not to deal with a financial planner, then mutual funds may be the right investment for you.

An investment company creates a mutual fund by selling shares in the fund to individual investors and then pooling the resources. A professional manager invests the funds in a range of securities that make up the fund's portfolio. The value of the shares rises or falls depending on the performance of the securities in the portfolio. A fund may be comprised of all stocks, all bonds, or a mixture of both.

For some people, mutual funds mean losing control of their money. If you are one of these, you may want to stick with individual stocks and/or bonds. Other investors, however, find mutual funds an attractive investment option for the following reasons:

- A mutual fund is a convenient alternative to researching, buying, and selling individual stocks.
- A mutual fund does not require investment of large sums of money. Many mutual funds have plans in which you

can invest $50 a month. If you are just starting to invest, this could be an easy way to begin.

- A mutual fund, by buying and selling large amounts of securities at one time, costs you less than buying and selling individual securities on your own.
- A mutual fund, by owning shares in a number of different securities rather than individual stocks and/or bonds, spreads out your risk.
- A mutual fund is managed by an investment professional.

Mutual funds earn money in several ways. A fund may receive dividends and interest on the securities it owns; you as a shareholder are paid in dividends. A fund may also sell the securities it owns at a price higher than the purchase price. This capital gain (minus any capital loss) is generally distributed to investors at the end of the year. Finally, a fund may hold securities that have increased in price. Because this increases the value of your shares, you make a profit called a capital gain when you sell them. Usually, you can decide either to receive a payment for distribution and dividends or you can have it reinvested in the fund to buy more shares.

Taxes: You will owe taxes on distributions and dividends in the year that you receive them. You will also owe taxes on any capital gains you receive when you sell your shares. If, however, your mutual fund is part of your tax-deferred retirement savings, such as an IRA, your taxes will be deferred according to IRA regulations.

If you invest in a tax-exempt fund, such as municipal bonds, some or all of the dividends will be exempt from federal, and sometimes state and local, income tax. Taxes must be paid on capital gains of funds kept longer than six months and sold at a profit.

Guidelines for Investing: Just as when you invest in individual stocks and bonds, you are taking a risk when you invest in a mutual fund. You may lose some or all of the money you invest if the securities held by the fund decrease in value. Over the long run, however, this type of investment can be more profitable than "safer" investments, such as money market accounts or fixed-rate annuities.

Some banks and credit unions also sell mutual funds. Although it is legal for them to do so, the fact that these funds are sold in a financial institution does not mean they are insured by the federal government or guaranteed by the institution that sold them.

Before investing in a mutual fund, consider these guidelines.

- Reexamine your long-term goals and your comfort zone. Are you relying on this investment for stability, growth, and/or a steady stream of income? How much risk do you need to take to reach your income goal? How much risk makes you uncomfortable?
- Research the annual rankings. Many financial publications include annual fund rankings. Do not become too excited about a one-time winner. Look for funds that both meet your goals and have above-average, long-term returns—check a five-to ten-year record. Has a fund earned above average returns in both good and bad economic times? Choose several of the most consistent performers and send for their prospectuses. The most complete reference for mutual funds is Morningstar Mutual Funds, which is updated every two weeks.
- Read the prospectus carefully to determine the types of investments a fund holds, the fund's goals, the fees charged, information on who manages and advises the fund and how well the fund has performed in the past.
- Review the information about fees before you invest; this information is included in the prospectus. A front-end load, charged when you purchase shares in the fund, usually serves as a commission for the broker or salesperson who assists you. It cannot exceed 8.5 percent. A deferred load can be charged when you sell all or part of your investment. No-load does not necessarily mean no cost. All funds charge an annual management fee. Depending on the fund, this fee could be as much as the front-end sales fee. Some funds charge to reinvest your dividends or switch your shares to another fund within the same family. Compare how the fees charged by various funds will affect your investment.

Types: There are more than 7,000 mutual funds for sale on the market—those with high-risk aggressive growth, those with safe, low returns, and those in between. Listed below are some basic types of funds. These descriptions can help you decide what funds might meet your needs. After you make your investment, review your funds regularly.

Of the several types of mutual funds, *money market* involves the lowest risk. Although money markets are limited by law to certain high-quality, short-term investments, they are not guaranteed by the federal government and should not be confused with a money market account. Money market

Keeping What You Save

The elderly are a special target of scams and frauds, since they are often available at home alone and usually have a desire to increase their fixed incomes. The con artist may make his (or her) alluring offer in magazine or newspaper ads, by door-to-door selling, or through an unsolicited telephone call. While most merchandising done in this fashion is legitimate, one should always be on guard for the swindlers—they are a persistent, hard working group. The golden rule here is "If it sounds too good to be true, it probably is." Here are a few things of which to be wary:

- Miracle health products that are pitched with phrases like "scientific breakthrough" or "secret formula"; have long lists of unrelated conditions they can "cure"; and carry doctors' testimonials.
- A "no risk" investment opportunity. Except for U.S. Government bonds and treasury notes, *all* investments carry risk. Were it really risk free, would the salesman need to seek you out?
- A free gift that requires a processing fee.
- A 900 or 809 area code telephone number that you must call to find out if you won a prize or to receive detailed instructions. Calls to the 900 area code are charged the caller at high rates with the called party getting part of the charge. The 809 area code is in the Caribbean and, unlike in the U.S., caller-paid numbers are not in a special area code. Calls to some of these numbers could be billed to you at rates of up to $25 a minute while the con man rambles on about prizes and deals that do not exist.

If you find yourself confronted with a suspicious offer:

- Do not let yourself be hurried into making a decision. "This offer is only available right now" is a favorite conman's tool.
- Ask for references from the firm—a bank and satisfied customers in your neighborhood.
- Request all claims, total costs, and guarantees to be in writing.
- Do not hand over cash under any circumstances.
- Get a second opinion from your accountant, banker, or attorney.

Finally, if you are a victim of such a crime, do not be ashamed to admit it. Report the crime to the police. You might get your money back or at least help put a swindler out of business.

mutual funds try to keep their value stable and to provide regular distribution of income, which is determined by short-term interest rates.

An *aggressive growth* fund involves the highest risk, but also can produce the largest gains over the long-term. It seeks maximum capital gains by investing in stocks of small companies and/or developing industries in which rapid growth is projected.

A *growth* fund is less risky than an aggressive growth fund because it invests primarily in the stocks of established companies whose growth is expected to exceed inflation.

A *growth and income* fund emphasizes appreciation and current income by investing in stocks of established companies that offer consistent dividend payments and steady price appreciation. As a result, this type of fund is less volatile than the growth or aggressive growth funds.

Index funds purchase a portfolio that matches a particular index, such as the Standard and Poor's 500, an index of European stocks, or an index of bonds. The fund's portfolio will track, exactly, the ups and downs of the particular index. (This means your level of risk is exactly average.)

Balanced funds are similar to the growth and income funds in objective, in that the goals are income and long-term growth. The difference is that a balanced fund usually invests approximately 40 percent of its portfolio in bonds, which provide steady dividends, little appreciation, and lower risk than stock-only funds.

A *fixed income or bond* fund invests in corporate, government, or municipal securities that pay interest on a regular basis. The risk varies depending on the type of bond mix in which the fund specializes.

Work: The Poor Man's Pension

Although for most people financial security is part of successful aging, not everyone can afford to retire. The three-legged stool represents the ideal—a combination of three sources of income on which a person can "sit" during one's later years, but the real and the ideal are not always the same. For some people the stool may be wobbly. Because work can help to stabilize the stool, consider the following practical factors concerning leaving work before full-retirement age, accepting part-time work, and assessing the attitudes of management toward older workers.

Early Retirement

Before you decide to retire early, consider the impact of this decision on your retirement income. Generally, early retirement reduces the amount of your pension and Social Security benefits because it reduces the number of years that contributions are made to your accounts and increases the number of years you are expected to receive benefits.

Thus, if you participate in your employer's defined benefit pension plan and remaining on the job is an option, your final pension benefit amount could be increased significantly just by working at your job another two to five years. Talk with your plan administrator and obtain an estimate of the increase in your benefit for each additional year you remain employed at the company. Even if your pension plan is not a defined benefit plan, the longer you work, the longer you can contribute to your 401(k) or IRA or other tax-deferred plan.

The same is true for Social Security benefits. Because benefits are computed based on the 35 highest earning years, your nonearning years before age 62 can reduce your benefit amount. On the other hand, for each year that you work beyond full retirement age (up to age 70), you receive a percentage increase in your benefit. This is called delayed retirement credit.

Another advantage of waiting to retire is that you will not tap into your savings and investments to live. You may, in fact, be able to save and invest additional funds on your own.

Part-Time Work

If you need to supplement the income you receive from Social Security, pension, and interest on savings and investments, part-time work may be a solution. It enables you to earn a salary, but leaves you with more discretionary time than if you worked full time. Some employers offer "phased retirement" that allows you to gradually reduce your work hours without decreasing your pension benefits. Check with your plan administrator to find out what options are available.

When you consider employment, calculate the impact of the extra income on your Social Security benefit. Remember, if you work part time and are under the age of 65, your benefit can be reduced by $1 for every $2 you earn over the limit of $9,120 (in 1998); if you are between the ages of 65 and 69, your benefit can be reduced by $1 for every $3 of earnings over the $14,500 limit (in 1998).

In addition, employers may consider part-time workers as independent contractors rather than as employees. This means that you must pay both the employee's and the employer's portion of your Social Security and Medicare taxes, which comes to 15.3 percent of your earnings up to the taxable maximum (and 1.45 percent for Medicare alone on all earnings greater than that). On the other hand, independent contractors can benefit from various small-business tax advantages. If you are thinking of starting a business or buying into a franchise with your retirement funds, consider all the possibilities—what happens if you are not successful? Can you afford to lose all of your investment? A session with an accountant or attorney who specializes in small business may be helpful in you identifying various options.

If you need benefits such as health or disability insurance in addition to salary, keep in mind that part-time jobs are considerably less likely to provide these benefits.

Attitudes of Management

An AARP commissioned study examined which factors most influenced employers' decisions concerning older workers. According to the findings, the traits that managers identified as most desirable included flexibility, adaptability to change, and the capacity and willingness to exercise independent judgment. Therefore, older workers should pay attention to the job market; identify skills that are in demand; receive training in those skills, and demonstrate flexibility and adaptability to technology.

Life Insurance

Life insurance, very simply defined, provides protection for your family should you suddenly die. This protection is important for families with young children. However, for older people who are no longer supporting a family, for single individuals, and for married couples with two incomes and no children, this coverage may not be as essential.

Before you purchase life insurance, think carefully about whether life insurance is the best way to meet your needs. For example, how much will the policy cost over the long term and does that cost make sense when compared with the return. Is there a cheaper way to accomplish your goals? Are the benefits provided by this policy useful over the short-term—the long-term? Can the terms of the policy be adjusted to a changing lifestyle without losing everything already invested?

If you decide to purchase life insurance, learn whether your employer or an organization to which you belong offers a group policy. Group rates are usually much more attractive than those offered by insurance agents or company representatives.

Finally, if you have contributed the maximum allowable amount to other tax-deferred savings and still have money to shelter, insurance/savings plans may be a good option. But only if you have reached the maximum on other options. Remember that investment in a tax-deferred IRA or Keogh, for example, will give you the same tax advantages without having to pay interest to borrow money or premiums that include the costs of administering the policy.

Before purchasing a policy, learn about your options and ask the right questions.

Term Insurance

Term insurance is the simplest, lowest cost life insurance you can purchase. In the event of your death, a benefit is paid to your beneficiary(ies). Most term policies are guaranteed to be renewable annually as long as you pay the premiums on time. In most cases, a physical is required only when the policy is purchased. (Sometimes, when joining a group policy, no physical is required.)

You can also purchase a term policy for a specified period of time. This is useful, for example, to help see your children through college. You can then redirect your insurance dollars to retirement-oriented investments.

For young and middle-aged people, term premiums are generally lower than those for whole life or the other hybrids of life insurance. In most cases, the premiums increase on a yearly basis, though some insurers offer policies that have no increases for the first five or ten years. As you grow older, the risk that you will die and that your beneficiary(ies) will collect on the policy becomes greater. Thus, the premiums increase rapidly. For most people, this is not a problem— by age 65, the reasons for your life insurance policy have graduated from college.

If you think you will need life insurance after reaching the age of 60 or 65, several options are available. Some advocates recommend locking in your premium amount by purchasing whole life insurance. Some insurers allow you to convert from term to whole life insurance and give you credit for the premiums you have already paid. Others enable you to keep the annual premiums the same, but decrease the coverage. Explore carefully all of the options.

Whole Life Insurance

This type of policy includes a death benefit and a kind of "savings plan" that becomes tax-deferred over time. Usually, the amount of the death benefit stays the same, although some policies have increasing death benefit options. Whole life insurance is a long-term proposition. Therefore, if you need insurance coverage for only a few years, whole life is probably not the best alternative.

Thus, always read the policy carefully. A guaranteed issue policy may sound like a great buy because, "everyone is accepted and no health questions are asked," but for the first few years of this type of policy, death benefits are limited to the premiums paid—full death benefits are paid only if the death is accidental.

The amount of your premiums that becomes savings is the cash value of the policy. As long as these savings accrue, they are tax-deferred. You can borrow against this cash value or you can cancel the policy and receive a lump-sum payment. An insurance policy, however, is not like your savings account. Because commissions and administrative costs are subtracted when you purchase your policy, you will not have much in the way of cash value for the first ten or so years of the policy. Also, if you die before repaying any amount borrowed from the cash value, the unpaid amount of the loan will be deducted from the death benefit your family will receive.

In general, whole life premiums are higher than those for term life insurance, but they remain the same from year to year. The premium amount is based on your age, health, and sex, so the younger you are when you purchase this kind of policy, the lower your premiums will be.

Other Variations

Universal life insurance is basically a term-life policy with an investment feature. This allows the premium rates and death benefits to be adjusted to adjust to your changing needs. The money that accumulates receives interest.

Variable life insurance is a hybrid of a whole life policy that offers you a number of investment options for the cash value portion of the policy. As long as these investments grow, they are tax-deferred. If the money stays in the policy until the insured dies, the proceeds are tax-free. The value of these policies also fluctuates with the market; thus, the purchaser of the policy is assuming greater risk.

Health Care Coverage

As most people grow older, a major concern is providing for health care during retirement. Because most people qualify for Medicare, familiarize yourself with its benefits, as well as those of Medicaid. In addition, you should consider the possibility of both Medigap insurance and long-term care insurance.

Medicare

Just as Social Security provides a base of income for retirement, Medicare provides a base of health care for retirement. Part A, Hospital Insurance, helps pay for in-patient care and some home health care. Part B, Supplemental Medical Insurance, helps pay for doctor bills, out-patient treatment, and related services.

Part A is financed through the FICA taxes paid by all workers and their employers. Part B is financed one-quarter through monthly premiums paid by beneficiaries and three-quarters from general revenues of the federal government.

You can apply to receive Medicare, both Part A and Part B, when you turn 65, whether or not you continue to work. Medicare is also available if you have been receiving Social Security Disability Insurance benefits for two years.

Eligibility

If you are eligible for Social Security benefits, you automatically apply for Medicare Part A when you apply for Social Security benefits at age 65. At that time, you will be asked if you also wish to apply for Medicare Part B. If you choose to enroll, the Part B premium will be deducted from your Social Security check. If you do not apply for Social Security retirement benefits at 65, you must apply for Medicare when you turn 65 or you will not be enrolled. Until you retire, you will be billed in advance every quarter for your Part B coverage.

A spouse, who is 65 years of age, may also receive Medicare Part A benefits based on your work record, if you are eligible for Social Security benefits. This applies even if you are not yet 65 years of age.

If you are not eligible for Social Security benefits, you can receive coverage by paying a monthly premium: in 1998 the premium for Part A was $339.90 per month if you had fewer than 30 quarters and $187 if you had at least 30 quarters but fewer than 40. For Part B the premium was $43.80 per month. You must buy into both parts.

Benefits

Medicare covers only services that are determined to be medically necessary and charges that are defined as reasonable.

Part A: Hospital Insurance: When you enter the hospital, you will be required to pay a deductible, which was $764 in 1998. This deductible can be no more than the actual charges. After the first 60 days in the hospital you will be required to pay a daily charge, which was $191 in 1998. After 90 days, you may choose between paying the full per day amount yourself or paying a daily charge, which was $382 in 1998, for up to 60 nonrenewable "lifetime reserve" days. Medicare has a 60 day "benefit period." This means that if you require another hospitalization more than 60 days after the last hospital admission, you will have to pay another deductible in addition to the fees already described.

Medicare provides limited benefits at, and has very strict qualifying rules for, skilled nursing facilities. These services are available only if your hospital stay was at least three days and must begin within 30 days of your discharge from the hospital. You pay nothing for Medicare allowable expenses for the first 20 days. After that, you pay a daily fee ($95.50 in 1998) for the next 80 days. Medicare does not pay any benefits after 100 days of care in the "benefit period." Medicare does not pay for custodial nursing home care.

Part A also covers other services, including specific home health services, such as physical therapy and some rehabilitation equipment, if you are confined to your residence. These services must be prescribed by your physician, be part-time or intermittent, and be provided by a home health agency that is certified by and participates in Medicare.

Hospice Care benefits for the terminally ill are limited to 210 days, unless at that time you are recertified as being terminally ill. The total amount you will have to pay for a "period of hospice care" is limited. Medicare also covers some drug and respite provisions (to relieve the load on family caregivers) related to hospice care.

Psychiatric Hospital Care is covered by Medicare for up to 190 days of in-patient care during a person's lifetime. Care in a nonparticipating hospital may be covered if it is the closest facility in an emergency.

Part B: Supplemental Medical Insurance: Even if you do not qualify for Medicare Part A, you can enroll to receive Part B when you reach 65 years of age as long as you agree to pay the premium, which is adjusted every January. If you do not elect to receive Part B when you first became eligible at the age of 65, there is an open enrollment period from January through March every year. However, for each 12-month period you were eligible and did not apply, your premium will be increased by ten percent.

With some exceptions, Part B pays 80 percent of the approved charges for medical expenses after the annual deductible of $100 has been paid. Some of the expenses covered by Part B are:

- physician's and surgeon's fees for house calls, office visits, or services provided in a hospital;
- diagnostic tests, including x-rays and laboratory and other tests (some clinical diagnostic laboratory tests are not subject to the $100 deductible or the 20 percent copayment);
- physical therapy provided in a doctor's office or by an institutional provider or an independent physical or occupational therapist;
- mammograms;
- radiation therapy;
- drugs that you cannot administer yourself;
- pneumococcal and flu vaccine (there is no cost sharing for this service and the $100 deductible does not apply);
- ambulance services, if your condition allows no other kind of transportation;
- rental of durable medical equipment, such as oxygen tanks or a wheelchair.

Noncovered Expenses

You might imagine that with Medicare Parts A and B and the Addition to Part A, you are all set. Unfortunately, as comprehensive as the list may seem, Medicare will by no means cover all your health care expenses. For example, routine physicals, prescription drugs taken at home, private nurses, eye exams, and glasses are not covered.

Medigap or Medicare Supplemental Insurance

Because there are "gaps" in Medicare coverage, many people purchase Medigap insurance, which provides coverage for those health care costs not paid by Medicare, such as the deductible Medicare requires of you on admission to the hospital, a private duty nurse, and prescription drugs.

Legislation to impose minimum standards and simplify choices in selecting Medigap insurance became effective in 1992. If you had a Medigap policy before the 1992 law took effect, you are not required to switch, but you may want to check the options. All insurers who provide Medigap policies must offer, in addition to their other plans, a plan with only a core package of benefits. The core benefits are:

- Coverage for Part A hospitalization expenses not covered by Medicare from day 61 through day 90 in any Medicare benefit period and for Part A hospital charges while using the lifetime in-patient reserve days;
- Coverage for up to 365 additional days of hospital in-patient coverage after Part A coverage has been exhausted;
- Coverage for the first three pints of blood;
- Coverage for the 29 percent coinsurance on Part B expenses (subject to the $100 deductible).

There are nine standard Medigap plans, in addition to the basic plan that insurance companies are required to offer. These plans provide additional features in various combinations, such as skilled nursing facility care, medically necessary emergency care while in a foreign country, basic prescription drug coverage, and at-home recovery benefits. Not every insurer offers all nine standard plans and all nine are not yet available in all states.

To select the plan that is appropriate for you, read and compare the plans as they apply to your life style and physical condition. For example, if you never travel out of the country, you do not need coverage for emergency medical care on foreign soil. On the other hand, if you use expensive heart medication daily, you may find an insurance premium for drug coverage is lower than the actual cost of the prescriptions. Then, look carefully at the premium amounts and the conditions under which they can increase.

Remember that one comprehensive policy is all you need; be careful not to purchase insurance for the same thing twice. Take your time reaching a decision, read the policy yourself and, if you choose, have an informed friend or attorney help. Read the policy again before you sign it and be careful not to sign a blank form.

The law requires insurance companies to provide you with an outline that describes each plan's benefits. If you sign up for a policy and then change your mind, you have 30 days to cancel the policy and get a full refund of all the premiums you have paid.

Medicaid

Medicaid is a means-tested program that provides health care assistance to individuals with very limited income and assets. If you are over the age of 65 and meet the strict financial criteria, Medicaid provides payment for medical costs not covered by Medicare.

The eligibility requirements vary from state to state. However, in all but 11 states, if you qualify to receive Supplemental Security Income (SSI) benefits or your state's welfare benefits, you qualify for Medicaid. In 1998, the SSI income limit for an individual not receiving wages was $494 per month and for couples $741. The asset limits were $2,000 and $3,000 respectively.

Coverage

For Medicaid recipients and Qualified Medicare Beneficiaries (QMBs), individuals whose income falls below 100 percent of the federal poverty level (in 1997, $7,525 annually for an individual and $9,484 for a couple) and whose assets do not exceed twice the SSI allowable amount, Medicaid pays Medicare premiums, coinsurance payments, and deductibles.

For those who fall between 100 and 120 percent of the federal poverty level and meet the QMB asset levels, Medicaid pays the Medicare Part B premium.

Long-Term Nursing Home Care: Medicaid can help pay for long-term care, but myriad federal and state rules apply.

In states where the SSI eligibility rule applies, an individual is allowed what SSI allows: personal assets worth no more than $2,000 and income that is no more than $494 per month for individuals and $3,000 and $741 for couples.

Many older people, who do not meet the low-income and asset requirements to receive Medicaid, assume that they will qualify for Medicaid-covered, long-term care either if they put them in a Medicaid Qualifying Trust or give their assets to their children. However, 1993 changes in the law have made both of these options much more difficult to accomplish.

If you are thinking about a Medicaid Qualifying Trust, be aware that this type of trust is irrevocable and leaves no access to the principal by you, the grantor, your spouse, or your trustee. Additionally, the new rules require that the trust be created at least 60 months before your application for Medicaid.

If, on the other hand, you decide to make a "gift" of your assets, they must be transferred at least 36 months (the old rule was 30) before you apply for Medicaid benefits.

To avoid impoverishing the remaining spouse when one goes into a nursing home, there are higher Medicaid asset and income caps. These caps vary from state to state. For example, the amount of monthly income excluded ranges from 150 percent of poverty to $1,870.50. The asset cap ranges from the greater of $14,964 or one half of the couples assets, up to a maximum of $74,820.

Because of the complex relationship between income and assets and the ability to qualify for Medicaid, you should consider consulting an attorney or financial adviser who specializes in Medicaid issues in your state before you take any action. A knowledgeable professional can help you save both money and aggravation.

Long-Term Care Insurance

Medicare and Medigap both exclude long-term nursing home care from their coverage. Although Medicaid is an option for people who meet the income and asset tests, others may consider purchasing insurance to protect themselves if long-term care becomes necessary.

Because long-term care insurance is a relatively new type of insurance, premiums and benefits vary widely. If you are interested in this type of insurance, be sure to investigate at least three or four providers to find the combination of cost and benefits that best suits your needs.

Planning for Difficult Times, an AARP publication, lists seven questions to ask about long-term care insurance policies before you put your money down: (1) Does the policy cover care in any licensed care facility? (2) What are the policy's time or dollar limits? (3) How does the policy exclude coverage for "preexisting conditions?" (4) Does the policy provide coverage for Alzheimer's disease or other psychiatric conditions? Is clinical diagnosis required? (5) Is the policy renewable? (6) What is the annual premium for the policy? How does that compare with the cost of other long-term care policies? (7) Is the insurance company from which you are considering buying the policy, financially secure? Look at the reports from the various rating services such as Standard and Poor's or Duff and Phelps.

Your Home: More Than a Roof over Your Head

The asset most often neglected in discussions of retirement income is your home—probably the biggest single investment you have ever made. Not only is it a place in which to live, it also can be a source of income through home equity conversions, home equity loans, and the exclusion from taxes of gain on the sale of your home.

Home Equity Conversion

If you own your home (or have paid off most of your mortgage) and you want to stay in it, a home equity conversion may be the way for you to turn that investment into cash to supplement your income. Often called a Reverse Mortgage, it works just as its name suggests. Your mortgage is reversed—as the owner, you borrow an amount each month (or periodic lump-sums) against the value of your house. As you receive income, the loan balance increases (including the interest that compounds over time.) When you die, move, or sell the property, the entire amount of the loan must be repaid to the creditor—usually with the sale of the house.

The amount you receive from a reverse mortgage depends on the amount of your current mortgage, if any; your age; and your life expectancy. If you die soon after the agreement is signed, your estate owes the lender all the monthly checks you received, with interest, as well as all or part of the appreciation in the value of the house since the mortgage was signed. On the other hand, if you live long enough, the payments received could exceed the value of your home. Keep in mind that the monthly amount you receive will not increase.

The cost of a home equity conversion varies depending on closing costs, interest charges, and application fees. The costs may be minimal to you, but hard on your beneficiaries. Remember that when you die, your estate must pay off the loan. If you want your youngest child to have the family homestead after you die, a reverse mortgage is probably not what you want.

Reverse mortgages can provide you with a place in which to live and a monthly income, but they are also financial agreements that involve your home. If you are considering using your home in this way, protect yourself. Do your research and discuss the options with your children, financial adviser, and/or your attorney. Your best protection against a mistake is always knowledge.

Home Equity Loan

A home equity loan or home equity line of credit is not the same as a home equity conversion. A home equity loan means that you are borrowing against your home. As with any other loan, you must make monthly payments. If you default, the lender can foreclose, and you could lose your house.

Exclusion of Gain on the Sale of a Principal Residence

If you sell your principal residence and make a profit, you may exclude up to $250,000 ($500,000 in the case of a married couple filing a joint return) of gain from your taxes. You may use this exclusion as often as every two years, but only if you have lived in the house for at least two of the past five years may you get the full benefit of the exclusion. Otherwise you will only be able to get part of the break.

Supplemental Security Income (SSI): The Safety Net

Many incorrect assumptions are made about people who receive benefits from welfare programs. Among them is the assumption that many who receive these benefits are not truly in need. The fact is that in 1996, 10.8 percent of people over the age of 65 lived below the poverty level. SSI is the program to which many of them turn as a last resort. Administered by the Social Security Administration, SSI is financed from general revenues.

Qualifications

SSI is the only federal program designed to provide monthly benefits to individuals who are at least 65 years of age, blind, and/or disabled, have very low incomes or none at all, and have very few assets.

Income, for SSI purposes, is not only money, earnings, and Social Security benefits and pensions. It also includes noncash items that you receive, such as free food and/or shelter. Depending on the state in which you live and whether or not you are employed, the amount of income you can have and still receive SSI differs.

Assets are everything you own. For a single person to qualify for an SSI benefit, assets may be worth no more than $2,000; for a couple, no more than $3,000. The value of a person's home and, in most cases, household furnishings and car are not included in the calculation.

Applying for Benefits

If you or someone you know is eligible for SSI, apply immediately. SSI benefits cannot be paid until the day you apply or the date you are eligible, whichever is later. You can apply at any Social Security office or you can call or write the Social Security Administration. You may also apply for someone else, who might be eligible, if that person is unable to apply on his or her own.

When applying for benefits, bring the following papers with you:

- Your Social Security card or number;
- Your birth certificate or oldest proof of age available;
- Information about the home in which you live. For example, if you own a home, bring documentation concerning your mortgage and a record of your property taxes. If you live in a rental property, bring your lease and the landlord's name;
- Tax returns, bankbooks, payroll slips, and other information about your income and resources;
- If you are applying for benefits based on a disability, bring your medical records and the names and addresses of your doctors.

As with Social Security benefits, apply even if you do not have all the specific papers listed above. The Social Security Administration staff will assist you to find appropriate substitutes for any missing documents.

Benefits

The basic Federal monthly SSI benefit is the same in all states. In 1998, it paid $494 per month for an individual and $741 per month for a couple. Some states also supplement the basic federal benefit for certain populations, such as those who are more than 65 years of age and living independently.

Estate Planning

If you want your assets distributed in a particular way after your death and if you want your beneficiaries to receive as much as possible, it is important that you have a will in which you state those preferences. If you die without a will, the court can distribute your property according to a formula established by the law in your state This distribution may or may not comply with your wish that Mary receive your sterling silver or John receive $10,000 so he can finish law school. Planning your estate and documenting your wishes is a way of ensuring that your wishes are carried out.

Wills

A will is a legal document in which you give directions about what you want to happen to your estate after you die. In most cases, a will must be written, signed, and witnessed according to your state's particular laws.

Although it is not a legal requirement that a lawyer draw up your will, it is probably advisable to work with a professional who knows estate law. Ask your friends if they have an attorney in whom they feel confident. Call several and ask for price estimates. Attorneys usually charge by the hour, but some will draw up a simple will for a set fee.

Your will should include as much or as little information as makes you feel comfortable. If, however, you have a large estate, it is probably better to be specific about your instructions. Do include reference to all your financial assets and to any particular bequests. For example, if you want your grandson to have your baseball autographed by Cal Ripkin, do not assume everyone will know that is what you wanted—write it in your will.

In addition to designating the distribution of your property, your will should name an executor—the person you want to be responsible for seeing that your wishes are carried out. This can be anyone you trust—an adult child, a close friend, or your attorney. Be sure that you and your lawyer, as well as another trusted individual, have copies of your will.

If you decide to change your will, do so, but do not just take it out of your desk drawer, scratch out one section, and pencil in another. When you die, it will not be clear what those scratches meant and a court may not recognize an inserted correction. Thus, if you want to make a change, consult a professional. Either draw up an entirely new will or have a codicil (addition) written that includes your changes.

Probate

Usually, before your estate can be distributed, it must go through probate, the process by which your property is inventoried, debts and taxes are paid, and the remainder is passed on to the beneficiaries. Probate can take up to a year to complete.

If your estate is not large or complicated and your local probate court is willing to help, your executor can probably handle a probate proceeding. If the executor runs into trouble, the probate court staff can help answer basic questions. If the proceeding becomes too difficult, an attorney can always be hired. Your executor can still handle some of the aspects of the process to keep the cost down.

Sometimes, probate is not necessary. For example, jointly owned property such as checking accounts with two names pass directly to the surviving owner. Life insurance or IRA proceeds pass directly to the named beneficiary. On the other hand, property and real estate that you solely owned will have to go to probate.

Trusts

A trust is an arrangement among you, the grantor, and the trustee who holds or manages your assets. It can be either revocable or irrevocable. A revocable trust is totally flexible. You are in control of the trust property and retain the right to revoke, change, or terminate the trust agreement at any time. This also means that you continue to be responsible for taxes on the property. An irrevocable trust means that you give up the control of the trust property. The advantage to this arrangement is the tax consequences. If you are no longer in control, you may save on income taxes. Remember that unless it is specifically an irrevocable Medicaid Qualifying Trust, generally trusts will not protect your assets from nursing home costs.

A Living Trust

Unlike a will that describes how your estate is to be distributed after your death, a living trust transfers your property to the trust and names a trustee (you can be your own trustee) to manage that property while you are still alive. When you die, the trustee you named will pay any bills and taxes from the trust funds and then distribute the rest to the trust's beneficiaries.

Some people choose a trust because it usually, but not always, does not have to go through probate. In addition, a trust is a private document, whereas a will becomes a public document as soon as it goes to probate. Finally, if you leave assets to your children in your will, they must receive it all at the age of majority, which in most states is age 18. In contrast, a trust allows you to designate at what age your grandson will receive his bequest (for example, not until he graduates from college).

Comparing Wills and Trusts

Either a will or a trust may be appropriate for you. Think about what you have and how you want it distributed. Talk with several attorneys and estate planners about the cost of writing a will and going through probate in contrast to the cost of creating and maintaining a trust.

Even if you decide on a trust for the lion's share of your estate, you should ask your attorney about a back-up or "pour-over will." This will compliment your trust by transferring to the trust any property (after probate) that was not placed in your trust.

A testamentary trust, which becomes effective at your death, is specified in your will. As part of your will, it has no effect on your property while you are still alive.

Gifts

If you have an estate worth more than $625,000 in 1998, Federal estate taxes (ranging from 37 to 55 percent, depending on the size of the estate) are currently assessed. Thus, if you have a large estate and do not plan carefully, your beneficiaries could end up having to sell some of your assets to pay taxes and get to keep only a fraction of your estate's value.

Giving gifts is one way to reduce the potential tax burden on your beneficiaries. Throughout your lifetime you may give up to $10,000 annually to anyone you wish. This both reduces your taxable estate and provides a tax-free gift to the donee. To maximize this option, you and your spouse, for example, could give $10,000 tax free every year to each of your children. You may, of course, give gifts of more than $10,000 annually, but the amount over $10,000 will be counted against your $625,000 lifetime exclusion. Although these $10,000 gifts help reduce large estate taxes, unless your child or other donee is a certified charitable organization, you may not deduct the gift as a charitable donation.

If your estate is worth less than $625,000, it can be passed on without the beneficiaries having to pay federal taxes. The 1997 Tax Act will incrementally increase this ceiling each year until it reaches $1,000,000 in 2006. However, state taxes, which can be substantial, must be paid. Be sure that, as you strategize about the distribution of your estate, you take these taxes into account.

Remember, as you are looking at estate planning choices with tax consequences for you and/or your beneficiaries, that you should speak with your financial planner, accountant, and/or lawyer, who can look at your specific needs and goals in conjunction with the laws in your state.

Planning with a Financial Planner

You may be doing just fine on your own—picking stocks, adjusting your portfolio as you grow older, increasing the amount you set aside as your income rises, and reviewing your insurance needs as the size of your family grows or your tax-deferred investments as your employment changes. On the other hand, you may feel uncertain about where to start or what to do now. If so, a financial planner may be just the person you need.

A financial planner can provide you with information that will help you achieve your financial goals by helping you make sense of the plethora of financial products, services, and terms currently available. As a result, you can stop worrying and start doing. An adviser can recommend adjustments to earlier investments so that they better suit your income and lifestyle. In addition, an adviser can help you anticipate the tax consequences of various investment choices and use the tax rules to make the best of your retirement savings.

A financial planner can offer useful information and advice. However, hiring a planner to make your decisions for you is irresponsible. Listen to the expert you have hired, but take the time to learn about the adviser's recommendations.

Selecting a Financial Adviser

In choosing an adviser, ask your friends for recommendations, but remember that your needs may be different from theirs. Talk with several planners. In addition to finding someone with solid credentials, you need to feel comfortable with this person and confident in the individual's abilities. Remember, this person is going to know that your checkbook is a mess or that you have left $5,000 in a passbook account for the last 20 years.

The major associations that represent professional financial planners (who have taken courses and passed tests) are the International Association for Financial Planning (IAFP), the Institute of Certified Financial Planners (ICFP) and the Chartered Financial Consultants (ChFC). If you write or call, they will provide a list of individuals near you who are certified by the organization. You can also check with the Better Business Bureau and the Securities and Exchange Commission to learn if there have been any complaints against against a planner whom you are considering.

Payments to the Financial Adviser

Some planners charge by the hour or by the job, while others charge a commission on the products they sell you, for example, insurance, mutual funds, or stocks. If a planner receives a bigger commission from one mutual fund than another, might the adviser find that is the fund with the "best prospects" or you? Not necessarily, but it is a scenario worth keeping in mind. Some planners operate on both fees and commissions. Whatever you decide, be sure you understand how your planner charges, and ask that the agreement and an estimate of the cost is put in writing.

In the end, your financial security is your responsibility. You must determine what makes sense for you. It is, after all, your money and your future.

Lawrence W. Lazarus, M.D., is a psychiatrist at the Rush–Presbyterian–St. Lukes Medical Center in Chicago, where he is Assistant Professor of Psychiatry and Director of the Geropsychiatric Fellowship Program. He is a specialist in geriatric psychiatry and has written extensively in the medical journals about his research in the field, especially on depression in the elderly. He has also served as editor of several professional books including *Comprehensive Review of Geriatric Psychiatry* and *Essentials of Geriatric Psychiatry: A Guide for Health Professionals.* When time permits, he relaxes by pursuing his love of American paintings—searching for an unrecognized treasure—and spending time with his family.

The Mind and Aging

Lawrence W. Lazarus

In addition to physical changes, aging brings certain normal psychological changes. This chapter explores these changes and offers suggestions for maintaining positive mental health. It also discusses specific mental problems that can occur, such as depression, hypochondriasis (a chronic exaggerated concern about one's physical health), anxiety, memory problems, and drug and alcohol abuse, and what one can actively do to overcome them.

Normal Psychological Changes with Aging

By understanding the normal psychological changes that occur with aging, one can better adapt to them and be able to distinguish normal from abnormal changes. As a result, one can more effectively decide when help is needed and how to obtain it.

Aging can be considered another phase in the life cycle. As such, it presents specific challenges, tasks, and goals. One of the most important is the need to maintain a positive self-image and healthy self-esteem despite the stresses, losses, and "slings and arrows of outrageous fortune" that almost inevitably occur.

In his description of the human life cycle, the psychoanalyst Erik H. Erikson identifies the tasks of later life as resolving the issues of generativity versus stagnation and ego integrity versus despair. Generativity is the capacity to become invested in establishing and guiding the next generation. Ego integrity involves the emotional integration of one's life experiences and acceptance of life as it has been lived. Achieving and maintaining ego integrity represents growth and maturation, because it enables the elderly individual to use a full lifetime of experience to come to terms with oneself and the world.

Most aspects of one's personality, self-image, and self-esteem remain constant as one ages. In fact, one's satisfaction with life, morale, positive self-image, and self acceptance remains stable from adulthood through the later years. In other words, one's self-perception does not change significantly after adulthood, especially if one is in relatively good physical and mental health.

Life Satisfaction

Satisfactory adjustment to changes during the later years depends on staying involved with friends, family, and social activities, and feeling that one can contribute to the welfare of others and society. Life satisfaction is also associated with overall good health, feeling emotionally and financially secure, coming to grips with age-related role changes, and maintaining a sense of continuity with one's past. This sense of continuity is partly accomplished by reminiscing in a positive way about significant, meaningful events, as well as interpersonal and occupational accomplishments during one's lifetime. Reminiscing makes one feel connected to the natural flow of a lifetime of experiences and enhances one's self-esteem.

Shift to an Inner World Orientation

During normal aging, one moves from more of a preoccupation with the outer world to an inner world orientation. This is expressed by becoming more philosophical, more concerned with one's security and safety, more conservative in one's political and other beliefs, and the desire to convey to one's children and grandchildren the wisdom achieved over a lifetime of experiences. Another aspect of this shift is a reorganization of values. Whereas in early and middle adulthood one focuses on such instrumental (means-to-an end) functions as success in the workplace, in later life one's priorities shift to a greater concern with emotional bonds with family and friends. For example, adult children tend to emphasize the assistance giving (instrumental) aspect of their relationship with their elderly parents, while the parents tend to emphasize the affectional aspects.

Maintaining Self-Esteem

Older people need to cope with the stresses and losses that can occur with aging, described by the sociologist Robert C. Atchley, and the negative stereotypes that society attributes to them. Among the techniques for maintaining self-esteem and a positive self-image are focusing on past successes, discounting messages that conflict with a positive view of self-image, refusing to apply general myths about aging to themselves, choosing to spend time with people who make them feel good, and selectively evaluating information from others. For example, many older people believe they will remain in good health, even while observing the onset of serious physical illness among others in their age group.

Sexual Expression

Normal, natural changes also occur in one's sexual life. Expressions of affection by the spoken word, by touching and holding often take on greater significance than genital sexuality. With continued good physical and mental health, men and women can and usually do remain sexually active well into their 70s, 80s, and even 90s.

The marital relationship is very important in the lives of older people, providing companionship and support amidst losses and changes. The majority of middle-aged and older adults perceive their marital relationship as improving with age.

Of fifty couples married an average of 55 years, in very good health and living independently, more than half reporting having been sexually active within the last five years. They described their marriages as companionship marriages and placed a high value on love and sex. The results of these studies challenge traditional myths that life for older adults is primarily problem oriented, that older people are rigidly fixed in traditional roles, and that they do not value love and sex.

Maintaining an active sexual life has been shown to contribute to a feeling of well being and to reduce the pain and discomfort of rheumatoid arthritis and other illnesses. When a young medical student asked his aging medical school professor what sex was like in later life, the professor answered with a twinkle in his eye, "Everything takes a little longer but it's time well spent."

Among the problems faced by the unmarried elderly is the unavailability of a partner or companion, given the greater proportion of elderly women than men. The elderly may inhibit their normal need for closeness and affection because of societal prohibitions regarding sexuality in later life and self-doubt and fear of having sexual problems (physical and emotional), even though such problems respond well to treatment. Unfortunately, sexual problems are underreported and are not treated because of shame and embarrassment or the mistaken belief that they are a normal expectation of later life.

Suggestions for Maintaining Positive Mental Health

By understanding these normal psychological changes, one can avoid feeling apprehensive and frightened about them. This understanding also helps one distinguish these normal changes from such pathological conditions as depressive and anxiety disorders. An older person should have regular medical checkups with a physician who is experienced in geriatrics, is knowledgeable about the special problems of aging, is familiar with the patient's medical and family history, and is a good listener. Thus, if anxiety, depression, or other symptoms of mental distress occur, the patient will have less of a tendency to falsely assume they are a normal part of aging or to allow old fashioned feelings of shame or embarrassment to dominate. The patient is thus likelier to seek professional help. Just as our awareness of the distinct problems of older people has grown, so have the resources for treating them. The American Association for Geriatric Psychiatry (AAGP) now has more than 1,000 psychiatrists members throughout the United States and Canada, with special interests and qualifications in treating such problems.

As one grows older, it is easier to slip into a less active lifestyle — one that increases boredom and feelings of isolation. Therefore, it is important to stay interested and involved with friends and family and to pursue hobbies and other activities. Instead of encouraging isolation, one can perceive of retirement as an opportunity to spend more quality time with family and friends, and for developing new interests for which there was "never enough time." Volunteering to help at a church, hospital, or community organization or at one's religious institution provides a good feeling of contributing to the welfare of others and enables the older person to develop new friendships with people in all age groups.

Friendships with people younger than oneself should be nurtured, so that one keeps in touch with the attitudes and

Searching For Things Past

While some memory loss is a fairly common part of aging, it should be put into perspective. After all, we have been forgetting things all our lives (it keeps the mind from becoming too cluttered). Recent medical and psychological studies in memory have produced some interesting facts that apply to many people.

- Memory slows down much as do the motor skills, such as walking. Do not always expect to summon up facts, names, or dates as quickly as when you were twenty-one.
- Memory loss may be a reversible condition caused by other conditions—alcoholism, depression, side effects of a medication, or hypertension.
- General health and fitness can affect memory. One more reason for exercise and good nutrition.
- Being engaged in social and intellectual activites can help maintain your mental edge.
- Memory has two aspects—the storage of something in the brain (psychoneurologists call it *encoding*) and recall. In many older people it is the encoding process that weakens. Some medical centers offer training to improve this part of memory.

concerns of the younger generation and has new relationships to enjoy if misfortune strikes older friends.

After retirement, think twice before moving to a completely new location. Familiarity with one's surroundings can be reassuring. Thus, staying in the same neighborhood where one has life long friends and family provides a solid support system and a sense of connectedness with the past. Under some circumstances, however, a new community can offer new stimulations. If one does move to another community, consider the same community where family and friends have relocated. This gives a base on which to build new relationships. Also, there are advantages to living in an age-integrated community where one has contact with people of varied ages, as opposed to a retirement community.

A more difficult aspect of aging is accepting, coping with, and finding restitution for physical and other limitations that can impinge on one's activities. It is a good idea to be realistic about what one can do and cannot do and to avoid self-recrimination and self-doubt. Denying or minimizing age-related changes can make one vulnerable to mishaps and injuries. For example, it may be more prudent to wait for the next bus than to run to catch one that is already leaving.

It can also be joyful and rewarding to accommodate oneself to new roles in life, such as that of grandparent or great-grandparent. Elders serve the important role of family historian in conveying to the next generation interesting tales and stories about the family, its traditions and values. Grandparents often help their adult children financially and often play a significant role in supporting and raising their grandchildren. Elderly parents can help their adult children understand these important roles. By accepting the normal changes that occur during this challenging stage of the life cycle one can use one's time in ways that are rewarding to oneself and others.

Depression in Late Life

Although periods of sadness and grief over losses are not unusual in later life, it is not normal to feel depressed and miserable. Grief and mourning are normal and run their course, whereas clinical depression is a psychiatric disorder that requires and is very responsive to treatment.

Normal Mourning

Although the later years offer opportunities, challenges, and potential for further emotional growth, the losses that sometimes occur lead to understandable sadness and grief. Grieving and mourning normally occur following the loss of a loved one, such as a spouse, or a close personal friend. There are feelings of sadness, repetitive thoughts about the loved one, sometimes a decrease in appetite, and difficulty sleeping. These normal reactions usually continue for a limited amount of time. The length of this grieving process depends partly on the nature and duration of the relationship. For example, if one has been married for 40 to 50 years, the mourning process is understandably longer than that following a briefer relationship. Emotional support from family and friends, the passage of time, and other interests will help the bereaved to adjust. For certain people, the mourning process may take considerably longer, but eventually mourner should be able to turn more attention to significant others, such as family and friends, and possibly consider finding another person with whom to form a close and special relationship.

Depression

A number of factors predispose some people to develop clinical depression. This is a treatable illness with a good prognosis. Sometimes there are a series of losses without sufficient time for the older person to recover from one loss before the onslaught of yet another. Other factors include the stress of medical illnesses and disability, retirement with its associated decrease in income and status, a history of depression in close relatives and the use of medications that have depression as a side effect. There are also biological changes that occur with aging that are characterized by the "slowing up" of one's physical and mental capacities, as well as changes in neurotransmitters in the brain that regulate mood.

Recognizing Depression

Although depression has both physical and psychological manifestations, one of the major symptoms is a pervasive feeling of extreme sadness and despair. This can be accompanied by physical symptoms, such as a decreasing of appetite, difficulty sleeping, and slowing down of one's bodily functions and movements. The psychological symptoms include feelings of hopelessness, helplessness, worthlessness; a loss of pleasure in activities that previously provided enjoyment; a lack of motivation; thoughts that life is not worth living; and even thoughts of suicide. The depressed person may harbor self-disparaging thoughts about himself and the world, sometimes feel confused, and have trouble making decisions. Some depressed patients are hypochondriacal, believing that they have a serious physical disease despite reassurance to the contrary.

Evaluating Depression

Most depressions have a good prognosis, especially if diagnosed and treated early. Because depression may sometimes be a symptom of an undiagnosed medical problem, the depressed person should first have a complete physical examination by his primary care physician. This should include appropriate laboratory tests and x-rays, as well as treatment of any acute and chronic medical problems. For example, medical illnesses such as hypothyroidism (insufficient functioning of the thyroid gland), electrolyte imbalance, vitamin deficiency, heart or lung disease, inadequately controlled diabetes mellitus, and a host of other medical conditions that may present symptoms that resemble depression. Patients should remember to bring to the physician's office all current medications, including over-the-counter medications. Such commonly used medications as diuretics, steroids, antihypertensives, minor or major tranquilizers, and drugs for Parkinson's disease can contribute to depression. If the initiation of a new medication preceded the depression, discontinuation of the offending medication under the supervision of one's physician or substituting another one may lead to improvement.

Evaluation should also include a detailed review of the patient's depression. When did it begin? What unusual stresses, if any, may have played a role? Is there a family history of depression, emotional problems, and/or alcoholism? If so, what was the response to treatment. Because the older depressed patient may have difficulty providing this information, the physician, with the patient's permission, should interview significant family members.

The diagnosis of clinical depression is based on an evaluation of the patient's symptoms. The physician will determine if these symptoms, when grouped together, meet the diagnostic criteria for depression established by the American Psychiatric Association in its Diagnostic and Statistical Manual of Mental Disorders (DSM-IV). There are a number of different mood disorders, including major depressive disorder, dysthymic disorder, manic-depressive disorder, and mood disorder caused by medical conditions. We will discuss major depressive disorder as one example.

Major Depressive Disorder

A physician will diagnose major depressive disorder when the patient exhibits five of the following nine symptoms or signs of depression nearly everyday over a two week period. In addition, this behavior should represent a change from a previous level of functioning. One of the five symptoms must be the loss of the capacity to experience pleasure or depressed mood. Other possible symptoms are significant weight loss or gain, insomnia or increased sleep, psychomotor slowing or agitation, loss of energy, feelings of worthlessness or guilt, a decreased ability to think or concentrate, and recurrent thoughts of death or suicide. Major depression is serious, is believed to have a medical or biological cause making it a bona fide medical illness, and is quite treatable. Thus, although there may be a precipitating stress such as the loss of a spouse, the extent of the depressive symptoms appears so out of proportion to the actual loss that there may be some biological, medical, or endogenous process occurring that accounts for some of the somatic symptoms mentioned above. The vast majority of patients who receive adequate treatment make a good recovery.

Treatment

Many elderly people are reluctant to seek treatment for depression because they were raised in an era when people felt ashamed and embarrassed about having a mental disorder. Some are hesitant to visit a mental health professional, such as a psychiatrist, because they feel they should be able to overcome the illness themselves and/or because of the old-fashioned belief that one has to be crazy to visit a psychiatrist. If the patient's family or physician suggests a psychiatric consultation, the older person may become angry and defensive. It is sometimes the depression itself, with its accompanying feelings of hopelessness, that deters people from seeking help.

The treatment of a major depression or other serious depression includes a combination of psychotherapy, antidepressant medication, and sometimes the use of a mild tranquilizer. Psychotherapy, or counseling, is one of the most crucial aspects of treatment because it helps the older person feel understood, hopeful, and trusting in his physician. The confidence that the patient has in his physician usually determines his level of cooperation with the treatment plan.

The psychotherapist is an attentive listener who communicates her understanding about how the patient feels in words the patient can understand. Depressed patients often feel misunderstood by, and find it difficult to talk with, family or friends because of concerns about becoming a burden on them. Therefore, psychotherapy often includes counseling for family members, so that they better understand the illness and interpret the patient's behavior properly. The psychiatrist can then enlist the family's help and support in carrying out the treatment plan.

The use of antidepressant medication is almost always necessary when treating a major depression; this is often not the case with milder depressions, which usually respond to psychotherapy alone. The standard medications used over the past 30 years are the so-called tricyclic antidepressants. They are effective in 60% to 70% of patients. When one type of antidepressant is not effective, another will often work. In the past seven or so years, a new group of antidepressants, known as selective serotonin reuptake inhibitors or the SSRIs, such as Prozac, Zoloft, or Paxil, have become more widely used. They are equally as effective as the tricyclic antidepressants but have fewer cardiac, anticholinergic, and other side effects. SSRIs are sometimes activating, so they are usually given in the morning rather than at night. Most antidepressants take between 3 to 7 weeks to fully work, although patients often experience relief from anxiety, insomnia, low energy, and other somatic symptoms before a lifting of the depressed mood. The prescribing physician begins with lower doses than those used for young adults and increases the dosage slowing while monitoring for improvement and possible side effects.

The tricycle antidepressants sometimes have anticholinergic side effects, such as dry mouth, constipation, and blurred vision, as well as lowering blood pressure, but these are usually transitory and can abate with time and/or reduction in dosage. Because most antidepressants are equally efficacious, the physician often chooses an antidepressant that is user friendly, having the least potential for side effects for that particular patient.

Because anxiety accompanies depression in approximately 30% to 40% of patients, a mild tranquilizer, such as a benzodiazepine, may help to reduce anxiety and improve sleep.

Patients who have psychotic symptoms, such as delusions, who are unresponsive to, or intolerant of, antidepressants combined with a major tranquilizer, or who are acutely suicidal or have given up often respond successfully and rapidly to electroconvulsive therapy (ECT). Contrary to public opinion regarding ECT—such as the distorted view portrayed in the movie *One Flew Over the Cuckoos Nest*, ECT is a very safe, humane treatment that sometimes has fewer side effects than treatment with a combination of medications. ECT is the treatment of choice for depressed patients with psychotic symptoms. It is effective in more than 80% of these patients, as compared with 40% for patients treated with an antidepressant and a major tranquilizer. Most older patients require about 8 to 12 treatments over a period of several weeks.

The following true story illustrates some of the above points. Mrs. Gambini was a delightful 78-year-old Italian woman who became depressed following her husband's three-year decline and eventual death from Alzheimer's disease. She singlehandedly cared for her husband at home during his last three years. She was too preoccupied caring for her husband to recognize her symptoms of depression (15 pound weight loss, insomnia, decreased energy and concentration, and social withdrawal). Despite her family's pleas, she refused to seek help for her depression.

After her husband died, she lost her role as caregiver and felt no reason to live. She was insulted and angry when her children and physician insisted she see a psychiatrist. She said she was not "crazy." For her family's sake, she finally agreed to see Dr. DeCostello. Fortunately, the psychiatrist was of Italian descent and Mrs. Gambini immediately felt comfortable and relieved when he reassured her that she "wasn't crazy" and that her referring physician fully intended to continue as her primary physician.

Over the next several sessions, she reminisced about her 50-year marriage and about feeling lonely and useless because she no longer had someone to take care of. Even though the psychiatrist, in consultation with her physician, discontinued a medication suspected of contributing to her depression and arranged a volunteer job for her at her church, the depression persisted. Dr. DeCostello decided she had a major depressive disorder rather than a prolonged reaction to grief. Mrs. Gambini began taking 50 milligrams of the antidepressant Zoloft every morning. In combination with psychotherapy, her depression completely resolved itself within four weeks. This enabled her to continue living independently. She continued in treatment over the ensuing two years without a recurrence of her depression.

It is sometimes difficult to distinguish a grief reaction from major depression. If intense depressive symptoms persist, as they did with Mrs. Gambini, despite a trial of psychotherapy and environment manipulation (for example, the job at her church), a depressive disorder may be the cause and may be very responsive to a combination of psychotherapy and an antidepressant.

In summary, depression is neither a normal part of aging nor a personal failing, but rather a diagnosable and treatable illness just as are hypertension and diabetes. Older people should avail themselves of the sophisticated treatments currently available. Feelings of shame, embarrassment, and hopelessness should not prevent the older person and his family from obtaining treatment. The physician treating the depressed patient should be skilled as a psychotherapist and as a pharmacotherapist, and should coordinate the patient's treatment with other health professionals and community resources.

Hypochondriasis

This disorder is characterized by a preoccupation with the fear of developing — or the belief that one has developed — a serious illness. Despite a thorough physical examination and a physician's reassurance that no physical illness exists, the belief persists. Hypochondriacal disorder is usually a chronic and disabling illness because patients focus most of their attention on their perceived illnesses, often change from one physician to another, and cause considerable distress to themselves and their families.

If the hypochondriacal symptoms are part of another treatable psychiatric disorder, such as an anxiety or depressive disorder, then treatment of the latter usually results in improvement of the former.

A patient with hypochondriacal disorder initially complains about a specific symptom or pain, but quickly moves on to the fear or conclusion that she has a serious disease. As time passes, the patient may believe that she has a different serious illness. The duration of the patient's fear may last for months, or even years. The patient actually experiences the symptoms reported; the patient does not consciously and willfully attempt to manipulate others or attract attention and sympathy.

Treatment of hypochondriacal disorder rests with the primary care physician, who should take the patient's complaints seriously, schedule regular brief appointments, avoid unnecessary laboratory and other tests, and try to refer selected amenable patients for psychiatric care. This is best framed in the context that their "real" medical illness has caused stress that requires special attention.

Anxiety Disorders

Although anxiety is ubiquitous in late twentieth-century America, disabling anxiety is not a normal component of aging. Anxiety disorders do, however, usually have a recognizable cause and are quite responsive to treatment.

Although community studies have shown that anxiety disorders are less frequent in persons over the age of 65, a common condition called generalized anxiety disorder occurs in 2% or fewer of persons in this age category. Women are affected more often than men. Although the majority of older people with an anxiety disorder had the problem when they were younger, phobic, generalized anxiety, and panic disorder often arise for the first time in late life.

Such anxiety occurring for the first time in late life may indicate a previously diagnosed or an unrecognized medical illness, a side effect of medication, an early sign of a dementing illness, or a component of another condition such as depression. Anxiety often results from the combination of psychological and social stresses faced by older persons. For example, anxiety rates increase for several years following the death of a spouse. This reflects the social isolation experienced by the bereaved. Other causes of anxiety include retirement, fears for personal safety if living in a bad neighborhood, caring for a disabled spouse, and financial worries.

Common Symptoms of Anxiety

The symptoms of anxiety are sometimes divided into two groups — cognitive (psychological) and somatic (bodily). Cognitive symptoms include fear, insecurity, and sometimes a feeling of impending doom. Somatic symptoms include shortness of breath, fast heart rate, sweating, tremulousness, and a magnification of the symptoms of the older person's medical problems. Because older people have more physical illnesses than younger persons, they may express their anxiety by focusing on bodily ailments.

Coexistence of Anxiety with Other Conditions

Anxiety is a frequent component of depression. In institutional settings, for example, 80% of depressed patients also suffer from anxiety disorder. Alcohol dependent patients have a high prevalence of anxiety, particularly panic disorder and social phobia. They may use alcohol to self-medicate anxiety or feelings of depression. An elderly person can also become anxious when experiencing early signs of dementia, such as failing memory and difficulty accomplishing tasks.

If a person experiences severe or protracted anxiety, a physician should review that patient's medical profile. Many medications used to treat medical and psychiatric illnesses, such as those for chronic lung conditions or Parkinson's disease, and even over-the-counter cold remedies, can sometimes cause or contribute to anxiety.

Evaluating Anxiety

When anxiety begins for the first time in late life, the physician searches for some underlying medical illness or medication that may be a contributing factor. Inquiry is made into possible alcohol and drug use, recent stresses, a history of psychiatric disorder, and a detailed account of situations that precipitate the anxiety. A common anxiety disorder, called adjustment disorder with anxious mood, is usually brought about by a specific stress and subsides when the stress subsides.

Treatment

Whenever possible, treatment other than psychiatric medications are tried first and are often successful. These include psychotherapy or counseling, relaxation techniques, reduction of current stress-creating situations, improving the environment to enhance a feeling of security, and providing education about situations that bring on the anxiety. For moderate to severe cases of anxiety that do not respond to the above measures, individual — and sometimes family — therapy can be combined for a short period of time with an antianxiety medication (mild tranquilizer), such as a benzodiazepine, like lorazepam, oxazepam, or clonazepam. Benzodiazepines that have a short half-life (remain for only a short time in the body), such as lorazepam, are preferable, because they do not accumulate in the patient's system. The starting dosage is one-fourth to one-half that used in younger patients and is slowly increased while the physician monitors the patient for side effects. The most common side effects of benzodiazepines and other antianxiety medications include sedation, a slowing down of motor performance, and, occasional impairment of cognitive functioning. These medications are best used only for a brief period of time until the stress is ameliorated. For long-time users of antianxiety medication, the dosage can be reduced under a physician's supervision to avoid withdrawal symptoms or a return of the anxiety.

As with other psychiatric conditions in the elderly, the prognosis for most anxiety disorders if properly treated is quite good, as is illustrated by the following patient's story.

Mrs. Smith had always prided herself on her perfection as a housewife, mother, and part-time accountant. After developing Parkinson's disease at age 67, she couldn't accept her increasing limitations and frequented the emergency room with palpitations, shortness of breath, and perspiration. After medical tests ruled out a medical cause of these anxiety attacked, she began treatment with Dr. Lazar, a psychiatrist. He encouraged her to talk about her frustration, disappointment, and feeling of rage that she couldn't live up to her goals and helped her find other constructive outlets for her need to help others (for example, volunteering at a local health facility). Using relaxation techniques, individual and family counseling, and a low dose of lorazepam, she recovered from her anxiety disorder. The medicine was gradually reduced over the ensuing six months.

Coping with Alzheimer's Disease and Other Dementias

Reports by the mass media have increased the public's awareness of—and anxiety over—changes in memory that sometimes accompany aging. As a result, older people tend to misinterpret normal, age-related memory changes with the onset of Alzheimer's disease. This, even though the two conditions are different. Normal, benign, age-associated forgetting is common in older people. Usually it does not progress to a dementing illness.

Nevertheless, dementing disorders are estimated to afflict from 5% to 10% of people over age 65, and as many as 40% to 50% of those over age 85. Alzheimer's disease alone accounts for approximately 60% of the dementias of late life. The essential features of dementia include memory impairment—usually first affecting short-term memory, impairment in at least one other cognitive domain, such as language skills, and disturbance in work or social functioning. The onset is gradual and progresses so slowly that even family members have difficulty estimating when the memory impairment first began. These patients have difficulty learning new information; later, long-term memory is also affected. Other cognitive areas, such as judgment, language skills and the ability to think abstractly, may show impairment. There is not, as yet, a cure for Alzheimer's disease, but there are many treatment approaches helpful to both patient and family.

The diagnostic evaluation includes a detailed history from the patient and a knowledgeable family member, a mental status examination, physical and neurological evaluation and laboratory and radiological exams. Easy-to-complete mental status exams help to quantify the presence and degree of cognitive impairment. Although Alzheimer's disease and multi-infarct or vascular dementia, the second most common dementia of late life, account for the vast majority (more than 80%) of dementias in late life, other treatable and reversible conditions that can cause memory impairment need to be first ruled out before either diagnosis is made. For example, certain vitamin deficiencies, dysfunction of the thyroid gland, heart and lung diseases, overuse of multiple medications, alcohol and drug abuse and even depression may resemble an irreversible dementia. In fact, these diseases, especially if identified early, can be successful treated. Many symptoms of depression, such as a general slowing down, decreased concentration, complaints of memory loss, and apathy, may be mistaken for a dementia whereas depression is treatable and reversible. Finally, approximately 30% of patients with a dementing illness experience significant depression. Treatment of the concomitant depression may improve overall functioning and quality of life.

Treatment

The physician's first step in assessing someone with memory impairment is to identify any underlying, potentially reversible illnesses that may be causing or contributing to memory impairment. Even if a patient has a dementing illness, such as Alzheimer's disease, she may have other, reversible medical illnesses that may contribute to the memory impairment and that can be successfully treated. If potentially reversible causes of memory impairment are ruled out and the presumptive diagnosis is Alzheimer's or multi-infarct dementia, a number of symptomatic treatments are available. These include the judicious use of psychiatric medications for depression, agitation, and delusions—all of which sometimes accompany dementia. Careful attention to the patient's living quarters and family support system of the afflicted person is another important component of treatment. Persons with cognitive impairment are sensitive to their surroundings and seem to function best in a tranquil, consistent setting. Daily routines increase a sense of security, and the use of clocks and calendars help to improve orientation. If the patient has to move to a new setting, it helps to bring familiar objects, such as furniture and pictures that provide a feeling of continuity with her past.

Education and counseling of family members helps them to understand the nature of the illness and alleviates their puzzlement at the oftentimes difficult-to-understand behavior of the afflicted person. The family also needs help in grieving over the loss of the afflicted family member as they once knew him. The Alzheimer's Association, which is a national organization with local chapters through out the United States, has been instrumental in providing educational and other support services for family members.

The above treatments are often extremely successful in alleviating the behavioral and emotional complications of a dementing illness and can help the family to better understand

Delirium

Many people, patients and family alike, are apt to think of all incidents of mental disorder in the elderly as a sign of permanent cognitive decline. One such frequently encountered condition is delirium. While dementias, such as Alzheimer's disease, can have delirious periods, delirium by itself is a very different problem.

Unlike dementia, which slowly develops over months and years, delirium has a rapid onset of days or hours and, unlike dementia which affects memory, delirium affects the state of consciousness with the sufferer being confused, having hallucinations, being hyperactive, or having trouble organizing thoughts. Most often delirium is treatable and reversible, but depending upon the underlying condition that causes it, delirium can be dangerous and sometimes fatal. Among the many types of delirium in the elderly are the following:

- **Polypharmacy.** Elderly patients take more drugs than younger patients and the greater the number of drugs, the greater the potential for their having adverse interactions.

- **Cerebral disease.** Stroke, tumor, and central nervous system infection are a few of the possibilities.

- **Concussion.** Older people are subject to more falls than other age groups and have a higher rate of injury from the falls they take.

- **Hypoglycemia.** This dangerous condition arises with diabetic patients who may have forgotten to take their insulin or other diabetic medications, or take the medicine but miss a meal.

- **Electrolyte imbalance.** This can be caused by a nutritional deficiency, liver or kidney disease, or dehydration in a summer heat spell.

- **Drug withdrawal.** Some drugs, such as barbiturates and benzodiazopines, can not be stopped abruptly. The patient must taper off over a period of time.

- **Alcohol or other drugs.** With aging alcohol tolerance can diminish and even small amounts can interact with medications to create a toxic condition.

what is happening and how they can help. The following patient illustrates these points.

Dr. Roberts had a distinguished career as chairman of the department of medicine until his failing memory led to retirement at age 72. He courageously continued his life-long hobby as a photographer by volunteering time at the hospital's audiovisual department. He was referred to psychiatrist Dr. Schwartz because of depression, manifested by weight loss, low self-esteem, self-deprecation, and frustration over difficulty expressing himself. His psychiatrist helped him minimize his anger by questioning why he persisted in trying to remember names of his physician colleagues and other less-important details of his everyday life. The patient, with the psychiatrist's and family's help, developed a list of names of the patient's colleagues that he could refer to when having lunch with them in the hospital cafeteria. When he could no longer live alone, a companion was hired who also drove him to the hospital. Supportive psychotherapy and an SSRI antidepressant helped him overcome his depression. This not only improved his overall functioning, but also helped his concentration and ability to express himself.

Alcohol Abuse

The elderly are at high risk for the development of alcohol abuse. The chances of alcohol dependence for people age 65 or older are 14% for men and 1.5% for women. The rates are much higher for those with medical and/or psychiatric illnesses.

Etiology

The same stresses that account for the development of depression and anxiety in late life can contribute to alcohol abuse. The risk for developing alcohol abuse increases if one's parents or other close relatives had problems with alcohol or depression.

Diagnosis

Alcohol abuse is often difficult to diagnose, because alcoholics deny or minimize the problem. It may be discovered by family, friends, or physicians, who observe its consequences, such as accidents, poor nutrition and self care, cirrhosis of the liver, periods of confusion and failing memory. This discovery may first occur when abrupt cessation or reduction of alcohol intake results in a delirium within a few days after the last drink. The delirium is characterized by hallucinations, agitation, confusion, and tremulousness, and can last from a few days to several weeks depending on when treatment begins.

How Much Is Too Much

Psychiatry defines two alcohol overuse problems—alcohol dependence and alcohol abuse. Alcohol dependence—whose sufferers are unable to control their drinking despite adverse consequences—is usually apparent to all close to the sufferer. Alcohol abuse, however, is a milder, less apparent problem. It too has adverse affects, but the sufferer still has some control over drinking patterns. When such behavior emerges for the first time in an elderly person, it is usually a sign of depression. Treatment is often delayed because denial is a part of the problem, but several screening tests are successful in revealing the problem to both physician and patient. The simplest one is probably the CAGE questionnaire (named for the acronym formed by the initial letters of significant words in the four questions that make up the questionnaire).

1. Have you ever felt you should **C**ut down on your drinking?
2. Have people **A**nnoyed you by criticizing your drinking?
3. Have you ever felt **G**uilty about your drinking?
4. Have you ever had a drink first thing in the morning to steady your nerves or get rid of a hangover (an **E**ye opener)?

Alcohol abusers are at much greater risk of dying from alcohol related medical and psychiatric illnesses, accidents, and even suicide. Alcohol can reduce suicidal inhibitions in depressed or anxious patients. If alcoholism is accompanied by poor nutrition, intellectual impairment can progress to Korsakoff's syndrome. This has an insidious onset, a long period of suffering, and profound impairment of recent and remote memory. Fortunately, some alcohol-related memory problems can improve with abstinence from alcohol, improved nutrition and good medical, and psychiatric care.

Treatment

For patients addicted to alcohol, hospitalization is often necessary for detoxification and treatment of related medical problems. After several weeks of abstinence, the physician can clarify whether or not coexisting psychiatric problems, such as depression and anxiety, exist. Treatment includes patient and family education, active involvement in Alcoholics Anonymous, psychotherapy, and sometimes medications for coexisting psychiatric problems. With aggressive treatment and acceptance by the patient of the problem, the prognosis for recovery is often quite good.

Drug Abuse

The elderly are the largest consumers of prescription medications. The average person over age 65 uses 4.5 prescription drugs and 3.4 over-the-counter medications daily. In one study, 50% of the elderly people interviewed misused medications, especially psychiatric drugs. The most commonly abused drugs were sleeping, antianxiety, and pain medications.

Older people are more prone to adverse drug reactions because they metabolize and excrete drugs more slowly, often take them incorrectly, and are at risk for the combined side effects of multiple medications. In addition, the brain is more sensitive to side effects as one ages. Another factor contributing to the high prevalence of drug abuse is the elderly's limited financial resources. This may lead to a greater use of over-the-counter medications in an attempt to self-treat potentially serious illnesses.

Diagnosis

Most physicians are highly suspicious when a patient exhibits such symptoms as confusional episodes, psychosis, or sundowning (confusion and agitation late in the day). The family is encouraged to bring to the physician's office all medications, including over-the-counter drugs, the older person is taking to identify possible drugs of abuse. In addition, urine and blood tests can verify the use of alcohol and drugs.

Older people who misuse drugs have more frequent hospitalizations, visits to the emergency room, accidents, confusional episodes, and drug related medical illnesses. Benzodiazepine abusers are at risk for withdrawal symptoms, accidents and overdoses resulting from impaired judgment.

Treatment

Treatment of drug abuse usually results in a positive outcome, particularly promptly diagnosed and treated. Patient's dependent on benzodiazepines can, under a physician's supervision, have the dosage reduced slowly and then discontinue the medication over a period of a few months. This will prevent uncomfortable withdrawal symptoms.

Education about the problem is provided to patient and family. For this purpose, self-help groups such as Narcotics Anonymous are essential. Psychotherapy plays a key role in the treatment because the patient's trust in the therapist facilitates compliance with the treatment program.

Physicians can discourage the misuse of drugs by carefully limiting and monitoring prescription drugs that have the potential for abuse, such as benzodiazepines and pain and sleep medications, and by staying in close contact with the patient's family and other physicians when drug abuse is suspected.

Summary

Aging is another developmental stage in the life cycle, with its own challenges and goals. Most older people achieve and maintain healthy self-esteem and a positive self-image. This enables them to cope with, and find compensation for, the losses and stresses that sometimes occur. Factors that facilitate healthy aging include staying involved with family and friends, pursuing various interests, contributing to the welfare of others, taking stock of one's assets and limitations with a focus on the positive, and taking pleasure in new and rewarding roles, such as family historian and the joyful role of grandparent or great-grandparent. Regular visits to one's physician, careful use of medications and proper diet and exercise contribute to a satisfactory adjustment.

Should the stresses, losses, and other "slings and arrows of outrageous fortune" cause one to experience persistent depression, anxiety or substance abuse, a physician should be consulted. The patient and family should not assume that this is a "normal" expectation of aging. Such conditions are bona fide illnesses, just like any other medical illness, that can be diagnosed and treated. One should not allow old fashioned notions, such as shame and embarrassment about having an emotional problem, prevent one from actively seeking help from a mental health professional. With early and active treatment, the vast majority of psychiatric illnesses have an excellent outcome.

Walter M. Bortz II, M.D., is a geriatrician at the Palo Alto Medical Center and Associate Professor of Medicine at the Stanford University School of Medicine. The son, son-in-law, nephew, and father of doctors, he has devoted both his professional and family lives to the investigation and pursuit of a healthy, vigorous lifestyle. His research, published in a number of medical journals and professional texts, has been in the areas of diet and exercise. He has also addressed a public audience in his books (*We Live Too Short and Die Too Long* and *Dare to Be 100*) and a newspaper column for the *Dallas Morning News*. Among his many professional activities, he has served as Co-Chairman of the American Medical Association–American Nurses Association Task Force on Aging and as President of the American Geriatrics Society. Running is an integral part of his daily life and, now in his late sixties, he still competes in marathons.

Aging and Activity

Walter M. Bortz II

For the young, physical exercise is an option. For the old, it is an imperative. A young person has seemingly endless reserves of vitality and endurance and as a result is able to withstand a variety of threats with casual indifference. This is not so with older people. When challenged, persons in their 70s and beyond are simply at greater risk for harm, which earlier would have been easily avoided. Until recently this greater vulnerability has been held to be an inevitable consequence of aging, and therefore not amenable to active intervention. New information has created a major change in this impression. A variety of studies have clearly linked a great proportion of the susceptibility to the disease and fraility of older people to lack of physical exercise.

Dr. Steve Blair, director of research at the Cooper Institute for Aerobics Research in Dallas, looked at the records of thousands of attendees, all of whom had fitness evaluations. Not surprisingly, he found that the fittest survived, a lesson that has been handed down to us from Darwin and his colleagues. But of greater interest was his finding that the survival benefit that physical fitness confers increases as the person grows older. In those over 70 the difference between those least fit and most fit was in the range of six-fold.

Reflecting on this reveals that this should be the case. For young people the major threats to well-being — violence, accidents, and infections — do not appear likely to be affected by one's fitness level. But for the old the principal threats to well-being — heart disease, stroke, and skeletal fragility — are clearly inversely related to the individual's vitality.

Simply observing youngsters often makes a person tired. They appear to be perpetual motion machines. In contrast, persons at the other end of the age spectrum usually appear to be fixed to their chairs, or worse, their beds. Life seems to reveal a pattern that starts out at double speed, but near the end moves in slow motion. This pattern presents itself so persistently that it appears to be the rule. But there are enough exceptions—persons in their 70s and beyond still running marathons or leading orchestras or nations—that it is important to ask whether indolence and inactivity are hard coded into the lives of old people, or instead, are merely options that can be addressed and converted to activity and independence. Is typical aging inactive, and successful aging active? Can the lives of old people, like the grandfather's clock that runs down, be wound up again?

Historical Perspectives

In nature, survival for the animals in the trees, on the plains, or in the seas and lakes is sternly coded to their ability to move. Imagine a hawk or robin, wildebeest or bear, or shark or trout that loses its ability to move. For the rest of the animals the ability to move is in turn tightly tied to food, either in the ability to find and capture it, or in avoiding being found and eaten. Throughout nature the cause of death for most animals is starvation, predominantly as a result of the animal no longer being able to move.

Is it any different for us? A major truth holds that we are the only animal species that has uncoupled the need to move from the need to eat. We uniquely no longer are required to expend any effort to fill our bellies. All we need now is a telephone call or a car trip. It was not always so.

I spent my fifty-first birthday with the Bushmen of the Kalahari. My wife and I visited there as part of an effort to trace the importance of physical exercise to our evolutionary history. Four to five million years ago our genetic line split from our closest cousins, the chimpanzees, when we left the shelter of the jungle, went out into the Serengeti Plain, and started to walk upright. This was surely the most important journey in the history of our species, and it occurred 200,000 generations ago. Our earliest ancestors, like Lucy (the early humanoid whose skeleton was found in 1980), probably retained some tree climbing ability, but fundamentally adapted the lifestyle of the hunter–gatherer with an upright two-footed gait. Somewhere along the way we lost most of our body hair and developed the prodigious capacity to sweat (quantitatively unsurpassed in the animal kingdom). These adaptations further facilitated our active lifestyle. Not coincidentally, the growth of our brain rose from the 500 cc capacity of the chimp and Lucy to the 1200 to 1500 cc current volume. This may be a reflection of the increased use and complexity of our central nervous system required by the new environment. Stephen Jay Gould observes that predators have larger brains than prey — they move more.

I recall awakening on my birthday morning at dawn to find that a bush buck had come through camp that night and the Bushmen were already on the move. Various studies reveal that the Bushmen move on average 8 to 20 miles each day. They search the horizons for the clouds, which is where the animals, their food, are. They chase the animals, which chase the rain.

This is the lifestyle our ancestors followed for over 99.9% of our species' time on Earth. Then, 10,000 years ago, only 500 generations back, our ancestors largely abandoned the lifestyle of the hunter–gatherer and became farmers and agriculturalists. No longer did they chase their food or were chased for food. They stayed home and grew it. This was the Agricultural Revolution. The present life of a farmer, while still vigorous, is not so active as his forebears'. Our great-great- . . . -grandparents lived as farmers until 200 years ago — 10 generations ago, a mere eyeblink of evolutionary time — when they entered the Industrial Revolution, and since then, relatively speaking, we stopped moving altogether.

Anthropologists have a doctrine called the Principle of Least Effort. It is a simple principle that asserts directly that any creature when faced with several ways of performing a task will select that way that requires *the least effort*. No one could fault the simplicity and economy of this observation. If a beaver chooses to build a new dam, it will select the building materials from his personal valley rather than from a valley two ridges away. If a hummingbird is going to fly from the Keys to Honduras, it will navigate a straight course (allowing for the winds) and not a sightseeing jagged route. Present-day humans have, however, perfected the Principle of Least Effort to its highest form. We no longer have to walk between floors of a building or between golf shots, we ride. We don't even have to use much energy to carve the turkey or scrub our teeth. We

The Race Is Not Always to the Swift

One of the joys of becoming a runner is race day. That is when you have the chance to measure your progress.

You pin a race number on your T-shirt, show up at the starting line, and wait for the signal to begin the race. Friends and a few strangers wish you luck. You are a little nervous (you have retied your shoelaces three times this morning), but, at the same time, confident that you have improved over the past few months. The signal is given, the spectators are cheering you all on, the race has begun.

"But wait a minute," you say, "I can't compete against all those lean twentysomething kids with legs that seem to go on forever." Of course not. For you (and most people in the middle and back of the pack) it is a two person race—the you of today, race day, against the you of a few weeks or months ago. Finishing the race, perhaps setting a new personal record for that particular distance, may not bring a trophy, but it will bring a personal victory. That is what all the cheering and applause from the crowd (many of whom are runners themselves who are not racing today) is about.

However, if you feel reluctant to enter what you think is such a serious event at first, you might search out some of the more lighthearted races that are run in many parts of the country:

- **Halloween or New Year's Eve run.** Usually a wacky affair with not too many runners concerned with much other than having a good time. Many of the runners are in costume.

- **Prediction run.** No watches allowed. No visible clock at the finish line. Every runner before the race predicts his or her finishing time; the prediction is recorded. The person finishing closest to his or her predicted time wins. This is one race where it really pays to know yourself.

- **Poker race.** This is usually a five-mile fun run with race officials handing a playing card to each runner at the each intermediate mile and the finish line. The winner is the one with the best poker hand.

Whichever type of race you choose, try to get some fun with your fitness.

have electric carving knives and toothbrushes to do it for us. Our muscles thereby seemingly become vestigial organs of no particular utilitarian value to us. We are all now like zoo animals, born free and active in East Africa, but now caged, confined in highrises with little purpose remaining for our musculoskeletal system that once served us so well. We have become domesticated, and as any vet can testify, domesticated animals, zoo animals, must be tended with particular care. They become prey to novel conditions.

Are we paying a price for our flight toward sedentism? Certainly much of our biology was shaped during our hunter–gatherer era. Severe selection pressures chose who lived and who died. Simple inspection of world population figures reveals the tenuous hold our earlier relatives had on living. Until the Agricultural Revolution the number of humans on Earth was less than 1 million. Five hundred generations of having enough to eat has generated a world population of nearly 6 billion, and climbing, fulfilling Malthus's law. But the point is the severe restraint that food scarcity placed on who lived and who died, and the ability to eat was synonymous with the ability to move. Another governing law used by anthropologists is called the Principle of the Least. This means that when tracing the life history of any species it is important to examine not the gentle environmental circumstances that prevail usually, but instead the harshest and most threatening, because it is those periods of severe drought, heat, or cold in which survival was at greatest risk. Only those who could squeeze through the narrow aperture of the "least" condition survived to pass their genes on down the line. For our hunter–gatherer ancestors this meant that one year in 100 or 1,000 when the ability to move enough to catch the last wildebeest determined who lived.

For all these reasons and more, it is obvious that the biologic heritage of our species is a physically active one, and one that we have now abandoned. What have we lost? What is normal? The structure and function of our present-day biologically atrophied selves, or those of the hunter–gatherers? What is a normal cholesterol value—250, 200, or 77, which is what the Bushmen reveal? What is a normal bone, our own crumbly type or that of our ancestors, which could outlive a sledgehammer that assaulted it? Several books report that "primitive" aboriginal people have no heart disease, hypertension, diabetes, or obesity. Bushmen die of infectious diseases, but numerous sources project that infection too was rare in early cultures. So what did our early ancestors die from? It was starvation, much like the situation for animals in the wild.

The Disuse Syndrome

Just as Dr. Hans Selye fifty years ago described those adverse conditions that occur when the living organism is confronted with too much energetic input, as with stress (ulcer, hypertension, diabetes, and arthritis) the Disuse Syndrome represents those situations seen so commonly in the doctor's office and hospitals of today which are the direct results of our collective physical inactivity. The six components of the Disuse Syndrome are: (1) cardiovascular vulnerability, (2) musculoskeletal fragility, (3) immunologic susceptibility, (4) obesity, (5) depression, and (6) premature aging. These features are commonly found particularly in older people, and are byproducts nearly exclusively of lack of physical exercise.

Any survey of what a body does reveals that most of our anatomy is geared to movement. On a mass basis alone, the bones and muscles comprise most of our body mass. So, too, when we move blood and nutrients are directed to the moving parts. The gut, the excretory, and reproductive organs are largely excluded. Only the brain is spared this diversion. It is predictable that when the primary function is defaulted bad things happen.

Today the principal cause of death is cardiovascular disease, which translates to narrow, clogged arteries. Numerous features contribute to this epidemic, and all of them are results of physical inactivity. Elevated blood cholesterol has been mentioned previously, but there is even more to this story than the level itself, and this concerns the subtypes of cholesterol. High density lipoprotein cholesterol (HDL) has been repeatedly observed to correlate negatively with heart disease. HDL has been called "the good cholesterol," since the higher its value, the lower is the risk of heart problems, probably because this is the part of the cholesterol pool that is on its way out of the body. Dr. Peter Wood showed that physical activity is, along with genetic factors, the principal determinant of HDL levels. The more active we are, the higher the good level of HDL cholesterol.

High blood pressure is favorably affected by exercise. Any bout of exertion expands the vascular bed and thereby lowers the pressure inside the blood vessels. The thickness of the blood determines its tendency to clot, and once again physical activity lowers coagulability. Finally, exercise enlarges the size of the arteries themselves. A Stanford University Medical School study performed coronary arteriograms on a group of ultramarathoners and found that their arteries were substantially larger than those of inactive persons. Pouiselle's law asserts that the flow through any tube varies with the radius of the tube raised to the fourth power, therefore any slight increase or decrease in artery size has an enormous effect on the flow through that vessel. Cardiovascular vulnerability is the first component of the Disuse Syndrome, the result of the various negative effects of physical activity just listed.

Dr. Maria Fiatarone and her colleagues at the U.S.D.A. Human Nutrition Research Center on Aging in Boston selected the most vulnerable population they could find, 90-year-old nursing home residents. They measured the muscle mass, muscle strength, and tendency to fall. The muscles of these individuals were weak and frail, a condition that Dr. Bill Evans of Penn State has called "sarcopenia" (deficiency of the flesh). The important issue arises as to whether such weak muscles are the inevitable result of being 90 years old, or could be instead the result of decades of disuse. The research workers thereby enlisted the residents in a muscle building program of weight lifting. Within 6 weeks of their "pumping iron" protocol, the ninety-year-olds' muscles were bigger, stronger, and the tendency to fall decreased significantly. This study, more than any other, has shown that most of the frailty of older persons is not inevitable, and can be prevented and reversed. Much emphasis has been placed on the weak bones of older people being the cause of one million spine, hip, and other fractures that crowd the orthopedic floors of hospitals. But more likely it is the weak muscles, as the result of disuse, that cause such instability as to bring about the fall in the first place. Also the weaker, small muscles do not offer much in the way of a shock absorber upon impact.

But weak bones, the result of osteoporosis, are a coconspirator. Wolff's law asserts that the robustness of any bone is in direct proportion to the physical forces working on that bone. Years of couch sitting and riding in automobiles washes the calcium crystals out of bones and makes them weak. Even several weeks of the weightlessness of space results in the astronauts' entering a markedly negative calcium balance. This observation has led to the use of a variety of exercises to counteract this effect. Osteoporosis is one of the commonest findings in older people. Is this aging or disuse? Can the weak bones of old people regain some of the strength with an exercise program? Some early experiments indicate that this too may be possible. But it is clear that exercise retards further loss of calcium. A regular program of exercise together with an adequate dietary calcium intake and hormone replacement therapy for women represents the best overall strategy to avoid the epidemic of broken bones that old people suffer.

The third component of the Disuse Syndrome is immunologic susceptibility. On any list of changes in body function found with aging is a loss of immune competence. Old people simply seem to be more prone to infection than are young people. But is this proneness a feature of being old, or could it be due to the fact that the individuals are unfit? There is an accumulating fund of knowledge indicating that fit people exhibit a number of changes in their abilities to fight infection, which seems to protect them from getting sick. Runners, for example, get fewer colds than the average population unless, and this is an important exception, they are pushing their training schedule very hard, at which time they are conversely more susceptible to infection. The rule seems to be, therefore, physical conditioning improves your resistance, but don't overdo it.

This protection comes in various forms. Levels of the types of white blood cells that protect against infection are increased in fit people. Also the levels of the different blood proteins, the immunoglobulins, that act to neutralize bacterial and viral infections are higher in those with an active lifestyle.

Several histories report that the early civilizations had much lower rates of infection than do our contemporary ones, and this is attributed to the effect of crowding on rates of infectious illness. But it seems logical that the physical inactivity that accompanied crowding may be closer to the real cause. To avoid infections, move.

Every survey of the American population demonstrates the high prevalence of obesity. The numbers seem to be getting progressively worse. The seats in Yankee Stadium were replaced with wider ones. So too, analyses of old people reveal among the most common features an increase in total body fat and a decrease in lean body tissue. Is this due to richer diets, or to lessened physical activity, or aging?

The experiment that best explains these findings was performed by Dr. Jean Mayer when he was at the Harvard School of Public Health. His group took laboratory rats and exercised them by specific amounts more than normal: 20%, 50%, 150%. Throughout this range of increased activity the rats ate exactly the amount of food necessary to sustain the energy expenditure, and their weights stayed stable over the entire range of exercise load. This demonstration showed the wonderful integrating effect of eating behavior and exercise need. The crucial part of the experiment, however, concerned the findings when the rats were confined to a small space, and prohibited from moving. They then continued to eat the same amount that they did when they were active and as a result became fat.

The extension of this finding to the human condition is direct. Our eating centers in the hypothalamus of the brain were programmed during the millions of years of our hunter–gatherer era. We were then very physically active, and the caloric supply and demand were in balance. There was no obesity in primitive people, just like there is no obesity in wild animals. But domestication changed that. Now we suffer from an epidemic of fat, which carries with it the health risks of hypertension, osteoarthritis, and adult-onset diabetes—all because of physical inactivity.

The fifth component of the Disuse Syndrome is depression. Textbooks of psychiatry include physical exercise as a treatment modality for depression. That exercise should help the blues is not surprising when you consider the chemical changes that accompany any physical exertion. The compound that causes the heart to pump, the blood vessels to dilate, the sweat to flow, the blood sugar and fat to rise, and the senses to sharpen during exercise is adrenalin. It is in this regard that Dr. Robert Dustman of the V. A. Medical Center in Salt Lake City has shown that a conditioning program provided to old people increased their IQs. Adrenalin is also decreased in the nervous system of people with depression. Giving antidepressant medicine to a depressed person restores the normal level, which is analogous to giving insulin to a diabetic person or dopamine to a patient with Parkinsonism. The physiologic, nonpharmacologic equivalent of antidepressant medicine is exercise. The natural high exercise gives has been shown to be related to the release of endorphins, the natural pain modulators. Exercise is not only good for you, but makes you feel good too. Depression is noted too often in older people. An appropriate prescription for this debility is exercise. Dr. Anita Stewart has encouraged a group of 85 year olds to walk. She found their sense of self-worth, self-esteem, and independence was markedly improved, even with a relatively modest level of activity.

The sixth and last component of the Disuse Syndrome is precocious aging. Someone observed, "If you're going to grow old, you might as well grow as old as you can." Said in another way, "There is no sense growing older any faster than is necessary." For all the above reasons it is clear that physical inactivity causes a host of problems that hasten the course of aging. The single most vital body function is oxygen transport. When one surveys all the functions the body fulfills it is clear that the most critical is how we transfer oxygen from the atmosphere through the many transport steps eventually to the mitochondria of our cells where it is used for energy generation. We can live whole lifetimes without thinking (some people seem to), whole lifetimes without sex (if we absolutely had to), weeks without food, days without fluid, but only four precious minutes without oxygen. Like a candle under glass we extinguish quickly without oxygen.

Exercise physiologists measure our ability to transport oxygen by a test called VO_2 max. Drs. Fred Kasch and John Boyer of San Diego State University have followed a group of physically fit men for over 22 years. Their VO_2 max deteriorates over time at the rate of 0.5% per year. In contrast, unfit persons' VO_2 max decreases at a rate of 2% per year. Over a period of time this difference becomes magnified to such a degree that it is possible to calculate that physical fitness confers an age advantage in oxygen transport, our most important function, of 30 to 40 years. Said in another way, a fit person of 70 is like an unfit person of 30 to 40. Disuse seems to accelerate aging.

Vitality and Aging

All of nature is constructed in such ways as to exhibit extra capacity. This is very similar to the design specifications of an industrial engineer. The airplane wing, the bridge, and the skyscraper all have built-in safety margins in case of extraordinary demands. We are the same. This redundance is evident in our having two eyes, two ears, two lungs, two kidneys, two testes or two ovaries, when only one would serve us admirably. This means that we can start with 100% capacity, usually around age 30, and give away 50% with no apparent fall-off in effectiveness. We can lose another 10 percent of maximal vitality with still no failure of function. After another 10% loss down to 30% of starting maximum, we start to note some symptoms—shortness of breath, decreased hearing, etc. Another 10% loss down to 20% of original function leads to death. It is this range of 20 to 30% of starting vitality that is responsible for all doctors' visits, hospitalizations, and medical costs. It is a narrow margin.

The analogy to the bank account is direct. When the checking account balance shows $100,000 in reserve a high-risk lifestyle seems safe. When there is only $20 left one must be very careful how big a check is written. The problem is that we all have a much firmer handle on how much is in our checking account than is in our health audit. Too often, too quickly, we find ourselves with only 30% of maximum function remaining and medical attention is sought. Sadly, the reparative capacity of Medicine is seldom up to the tasks of restoring the lost reserve.

The term "biomarker," (the title of Bill Evans's book) signifies a determination about an individual which allows an observer to detect something about that individual without asking. The search for a biomarker for aging has been intense. Many papers and books have been written, and conferences held exploring the topic of how can you tell how old a creature *really* is. The calendar has always been found to be deficient as a biomarker. Many young people appear old. Many old people appear young.

In an effort to address this question physician and athlete son Walter and I surveyed the world records by age of a number of running, rowing, and swimming events. We reasoned that for a person to run a marathon, for instance, all the parts of that person's anatomy and function must be working optimally. Therefore any fall-off in performance over time would be rate limited by that single organ or action that deteriorates fastest. Further, we reasoned that no feature can degrade faster than the performance itself. When we plotted these record athletic performances against age, they all closely approximated a fall-off of 0.5% per year, much like the VO_2 max decline in fit persons noted above. When we surveyed a host of other age-related changes, nail growth, bone calcium loss, maximum pulse rate, levels of a key enzyme (telomerase), rate of cell division, etc. we again found 0.5 percent per year decline. It is our contention, therefore, that this 0.5% per year represents a key basic biomarker for aging, and that rates of decline faster than this are not due to aging per se, but to other, modifiable, processes, notably disuse.

Successful aging therefore proceeds at a stately pace of 0.5% per year whereas typical, standard aging proceeds at 2% plus per year. It is important to note that the difference between typical and successful is only 1.5% per year, which is scarcely discernible at any given moment, but when this difference is multiplied by decades of difference the effect is pronounced. If we are at our biologic maximum vitality function, 100%, around age 30, and we give up 0.5% per year, by age 70 we will have lost only 20% of max. In contrast, if at age 30 we commence losing 2% of vitality per year, by age 70 we will have lost 80% of original function and survival is in doubt. This seems to mimic what is currently occurring. The reports from persons involved in the Framingham Heart Study, which has been tracking a group of several thousand people since 1948, reported that a large percent of older people cannot climb stairs, arise from a chair unaided, or lift ten pounds. Is this aging or disuse?

How Nature Works

The world is rediscovering the work of a Scottish biologist, D'Arcy Wentworth Thompson. His major book, published in 1917, *Growth and Form*, is a brilliant assembly of examples of how the varied shapes and forms of nature are not random structures, but are instead precisely related to construction principles that maximize economy of function. Earlier Sir Isaac Newton observed "Nature is well pleased with simplicity — nothing in vain when less will serve." Forms as diverse as the beehive, the shell of the chambered nautilus, the leopard's spots and intertwined double helix of DNA are not constructed for the aesthetic pleasure of humans, but rather fulfill natural design laws, and conform to the most functional basic spatial arrangements. Thompson calls such design "diagrams of forces." It appears that organisms become what they do.

This intimate relationship between form and function is graphically observed in plants. Plants, after all, do not have the luxury of moving their location in response to change in environment like animals do. It has been shown that within a very few minutes of touching or sprinkling on the stem or leaves of a plant the messenger RNA content goes up 50-fold. Such stimulation thereby sets in motion the process wherein the structure conforms itself to the energetic stimulus. The famous cypress tree on the 17 Mile Drive in Carmel, California featured in innumerable calendars and postal cards because of its wind-shaped form, derived its shape because the antennae on its trunk and branches captured the mechanical energy of the westerly winds and the tree bent sternly to the east, precisely reflecting its environment. The intricacy of a tropical rainforest is in reality a precise solution to the complex interplay of rain, sunlight, and wind.

Every cell of every living thing has on its surface myriads of receptacles, called by scientists receptor sites. These receptor sites are like satellite dishes, into which are projected various forms and amounts of energy. Some receptor sites receive mechanical energy, some collect radiant, or acoustical, or thermal, or biochemical energy. Once the cell has received its hit of energy, it internalizes it, like a satellite dish, and the cell changes the form of the energy to another form with which it can do its work. In such a fashion the cells of a plant leaf receive solar energy, which it uses to unite carbon dioxide and water to form glucose. $CO_2 + H_2O$ + sunlight energy yields $C_6H_{12}O_6$ (glucose). But the cells of the leaf also use the energy from the sun to alter their genetic constitution to be more receptive to the next packet of energy for the cell, a process termed "forward feedback control."

In just the same way the receptor sites on the surface of a muscle cell will receive a packet of mechanical energy from activities such as lifting a weight. The mechanical energy becomes internalized, which does two things: it generates the energy usually found as the high energy compound adenosine triphosphate (ATP) which allows the muscle cell to contract, and it uses some of the energy to stimulate more of the protein of the cell, through expression of the genetic machinery, to make the cell stronger and thus better able to perform the work for which it is intended.

The details of this biochemical mechanism were unknown to D'Arcy Thompson 100 years ago, but his intuition of how nature works to integrate function and form was as true then as today, and as it will be tomorrow. Nature works in such ways as to become what it does.

But what if, over time, we stop doing? What if, as we age, we allow our muscles, our bones, our arteries, our brain cells to wither? It follows, then, if what we do is who we are, when we do not we are not. What if we disengage from active involvement with our environment in the mistaken notion that changes we note within ourselves are secondary to the passage of time, rather than to the dereliction of disuse? The Second Law of Thermodynamics dictates that any isolated system goes inevitably to greater disorder—entropy. This law is among the most powerful in the entire universe. Nothing can escape it. But life is not an isolated system. Living creatures can extract energy from outside sources, indeed it requires such an importing of energy to operate at all. The famous experiment in which the gases of the primordial atmosphere, carbon dioxide, methane, and ammonia, were mixed together and then energized by an electric spark, similar to a lightning bolt, and the resulting amino acids of life thereby created, could not have worked without the energy provided by the electric spark. The gases would have remained just that, gases, without form or complexity, without the externally applied energy. In just such a fashion life emerged from inert matter, and order evolved from chaos.

The benefit of physical exercise to persons of all ages, but particularly to older persons, derives therefore according to evolutionary principles. Exercise is a survival fact of life, the benefits of which have become obscured by the progressive affirmation of the sedentary way of living. Success in contemporary society seems to accompany financial gain, but the contribution of physical exertion to this is minimal if any. The conditions seen in our nation's doctors' offices and hospitals however are the byproduct of too much energetic input to our nervous system, as stress, and too little input to our musculoskeletal and vascular systems, as with disuse. The receptor sites of our cells are simultaneously bombarded by the event density of such an existence and underloaded by the sedentism of our desk-bound, golf cart, elevator, electric toothbrush existences. These simple lessons need to be relearned if we are to exploit our true biogenetic potentials.

A New Medical Model

The new understanding of the effect of a modulated energy flow on all aspects of our lives, coupled with the recognition that we have the biologic potential to live truly long lives, leads to a new conceptual framework for Medicine. All human ailments can now be confined to one of four basic causations: (1) blueprint error; (2) "lightning"; (3) "dissonance"; and (4) time. Blueprint error contains those tragic results of genetic miscombinations. Examples are cystic fibrosis and sickle cell anemia. These conditions result from a failure of the basic design. Fortunately these are relatively rare. Most of the malunions never have a chance to develop in utero. The genetic category is important to address when it comes to aging, because far too much fatalistic projecting has been done concerning the effect of heredity on lifespan. Many studies now indicate that genetics contributes only 20% to how long a person may live. In other words, it's not the cards you are dealt that matters—it's how you play your hand.

The second category of ailments is termed "lightning" to indicate those conditions in which the person is suddenly struck by an external agency with a bad result. Lightning conditions include infections, malignancies, injuries, and poisoning. With these occasions the stricken individual is usually

Warm Weather Wisdom

While you should maintain a program of physical activity all year around, the summer months require special caution. This applies to people of all ages but especially to older people, whose thermoregulatory system is not as resilient as in the young. When you exercise during the summer, please exercise common sense as well and be sure to:

- **Drink plenty of liquids.** Water and fruit juices are the best choices. Avoid carbonated beverages and very cold liquids; they often produce stomach cramps. Alcoholic beverages should also be avoided, since they cause you to lose even more fluid. If you are on a reduced-fluid diet, talk to your doctor about what and how much to drink to balance your exercise.

- **Replenish salt and minerals.** Heavy sweating causes heavier-than-usual loss of these important substances, so fruit juices, fresh fruits, and vegetables should make up an even greater proportion of your diet in these months. If you are on a salt-restricted diet, check with your doctor before changing your diet and before using any of the sports beverages.

- **Dress appropriately.** Your clothing should be light-colored and loose-fitting. Wear shorts and a T-shirt or tank-top—this is not the time to worry about covering up wrinkles. Wear a hat for protection against the sun. This is a rule for everyone, but bald men should especially follow it.

- **Use a sunscreen.** Sunburn is not only painful, but interferes with the body's ability to regulate heat. Use a preparation with an SPF of 15 or higher, put it on 30 minutes before going out, and replenish it according to the directions.

- **Pace yourself.** Adjust the level of your activity your activity to the weather—the more it gets hot, the more you should not.

- **Schedule wisely.** Use the cooler parts of the day—early morning and late evening—for exercise.

- **Use a buddy system.** Exercise with a friend and watch each other for possible early signs of heat exhaustion or sun stroke.

Finally, on the hottest days,

- **Stay cool indoors.** When temperature and humidity are too high, it is a good time to do stretches and light calisthenics in an air-conditioned room at home or just take a long walk inside an air-conditioned shopping mall.

an innocent bystander, and the damage occurs out of the blue. "Lightning" conditions have been the major preoccupation of the medical profession. At the start of this century eight of the top ten killers were of the "lightning" category. In these situations time plays little role, cure is often possible, and the patient may, after treatment, be restored to his or her original health status.

Unfortunately, the major category of conditions that we now suffer is not so susceptible to cure. Heart attacks, stroke, cirrhosis, emphysema, and arthritis are treatable, but not curable. The third category of illness, those due to "dissonance," results from an inappropriate interfacing of the individual with his or her environment, either too intense a relationship, as with stress and its associated byproducts, or with disuse, as in the conditions of the Disuse Syndrome. Dissonance conditions have an inherently large time component, and are essentially behavioral in nature. The ideal therapy therefore involves preventive strategies that emphasize a rebalancing of energetic throughput with the ideal structural and functional outcomes.

The fourth source of ailment is time, aging. But as stated above, the ravages that are truly due to the inevitable side effects of time are far fewer than earlier guessed. To date no one has found the cure for aging. The antioxidants provide a theoretical approach to slowing the aging process, but their use and value has not been adequately demonstrated.

This simple framework acknowledges the new appreciation of the interplay between structure and form and function and energy throughput. It is an optimistic projection because of the four categories, the two major causes of difficulty, lightning and dissonance, are open to active strategies of prevention and reversal.

The Exercise Prescription

To conserve energy and minimize effort our species falls prey to a lifestyle that is hazardous to our health. We have defaulted to a way of living that escapes evolutionary pressures, and consequently live the last, post-reproductive parts of our lives with frailty and a lessened capacity to adapt and endure. The theoretical background for an advocacy for a life of physical fitness is well established. The issue arises of how to implement the operation of an exercise need. Through prior history we returned from work to rest. Now we need to return from work to exercise. How do we do it? This is where details are lacking. Enough is known of the basic types of exercise but not nearly enough about how much, how long, and how intense it should be. One type of such and such form may be ideal for one function, say blood pressure control, but may be different for another need such as weight control or depression. The shapes, sizes, and amounts of exercises for longevity, therefore, are likely to be byproducts of all of the subthemes. Sometimes resorting to an anthropologic model can illuminate. Exercise physiologists have correctly shown that exercise of sufficient intensity to make the heart thump, and the skin to sweat for three times per week for a half hour or more each time results in a training effect that builds oxygen carrying capacity. It seems not merely coincidental, therefore, that the hunting frequency of the Bushmen necessary to provide sufficient calories for the family is three times per week. This ancient pattern of movement has been inscribed onto our genetic structure. It represents itself now in the need to go to the gym or walking trail or swimming pool to satisfy the requirement.

In medicine research workers seek drugs to correct problems. Can there be a drug for exercise deficiency? Can we still watch TV eight hours a day and pop a pill and make everything okay? Billions of dollars are being spent in such an effort, but common sense reveals that there cannot be a pharmacologic answer to a basic problem of physics. There is no surrogate for energy.

In approaching exercise deficiency, we can at least use some of the techniques that pharmacologists employ . When designing a new drug, research workers define what is known as a dose–response curve—how much of the new remedy is necessary, and at what times, to receive the sought-for benefit? How much and how often is penicillin required to kill the strep bugs in your throat?

Before going through this process, however, it is necessary to define the components of the prescription. Exercise needs for older people have been grouped into four separate but obviously connected categories: aerobics, muscle strengthening, flexibility, and balance training. It appears that to live a full long life of extended vitality, each of these four categories of exercise must be included. It would be ideal if the simple acts of daily living would confer sufficient quantities of each to fill the need, but this is rarely the case. Therefore an identified protocol that addresses the four categories is advisable.

Aerobics

Earlier in this chapter the fundamental role played by oxygen transport was described. To accomplish this most of the body systems must be involved, but the trigger is movement of the bones and muscle. The two adjectives that describe the form aerobic exercise must take are rhythmic and sustained. The types of such movements are many, including walking, jogging, swimming, biking, rowing, calisthenics, and square dancing. Other athletic activities such as most team sports, racquet sports, and golf depend on the manner in which the sport is played. For example, it is possible for an experienced tennis player to be quite successful while scarcely moving at all or breaking into a sweat. Also, some star athletes may be strong as a brute, but yet be in terrible shape aerobically.

To achieve aerobic fitness it is necessary to exercise three or more times per week in such a fashion as to increase the pulse rate to a target range. This range is generally considered to be approximately 70% of maximal pulse rate, which is calculated by subtracting your age from 220 (220 − 70 years, for example, = 150 × 70% = 105 beats per minute = target pulse). This pulse should be sustained for 30 minutes. The question of duration is being currently debated. Some feel that it is necessary to maintain the pulse at the rate for 30 consecutive minutes. Others feel that three 10-minute periods are equally advantageous. My current reconciliation of these opinions is to do whatever sequence is most convenient, but be sure that it gets done. For me the one-half hour period is an easier and more natural routine than three separate smaller ones, but others are surely different. How often is probably not so important as the fact that it gets done.

Muscle Strengthening

The advantages to being strong are less evident than in the past, but are no less real, particularly as we age. To achieve and maintain muscle strength in late years it is necessary to ensure that each of the major muscle groups is challenged in a regular and sustained way. Innumerable varieties exist. Some involve sophisticated machines, but actually no equipment is necessary. Household items such as canned foods, broom handles, and elastic bands can be employed in such ways as to provide good workouts. Some people prefer to exercise alone, others with other people. To each his or her own, but do it. Your life, both quality and quantity, depends on it.

Each particular muscle group should be worked in such fashion as to be exhausted at the end of a series of repetitions.

One method of achieving this is to measure the amount of weights that can be moved with one maximum effort. Then, back down to 90% of this amount, and do that effort eight times in a row. This completes what has become known as a "set." Three such sets within several minutes with several minutes' rest in between constitutes the workout for that set of muscles for that day. The maximum single lift step can be neglected, and the weight that can be lifted in such a series estimated directly. Recognizing that with practice a person becomes stronger, the work load will need to be gradually increased as well. The repetition should be done slowly, under control, and without breath holding. Each muscle group should be put through its full range of motion, as restricted motion ranges lead to one becoming "muscle bound."

With such a strengthening program frailty is offset, and independence of later life assured. Too much institutionalization is the direct outcome of lack of muscle strength. Drs. Bill Evans and Maria Fiatarone, mentioned above, and leaders of the "longer better life through better strength" school of thought teach too that muscle strengthening has the added value of providing major side benefits to the other three types of exercise training, aerobics, flexibility, and balance. None of the other forms themselves convey such beneficial auxiliary yields.

Flexibility Exercises

A major caricature of aging is the little stooped individual, so bent that he or she cannot even look straight ahead. Contractures and rigidity are the end results of inactivity. They seem to be too frequent side effects of aging. But they are not aging. They are the results of lack of use and thereby can be prevented with a specific program of flexibility training. Some loss of elastic tissue is probably a true biomarker of aging, the result of chemical cross-linking of the fibers of connective tissue. The longer time it takes the skin of the back of your hand to reshape itself after a pinch is a reflection of such loss of elasticity.

But what if the connective tissue of all the tendons and ligaments similarly loses its resiliency? The ability to bend, stoop, reach, twist, turn, stretch, and extend is threatened by loss of flexibility. The loss of flexibility is usually slow and insidious. Increased difficulty in tying one's shoes, or pulling on pants, or reaching the top shelf or bottom drawers may be simply a nuisance, but could become a substantial disability.

Independence of movement means that the joints are just that, flexible junctures, and not rigid stems.

Accumulated injuries, large and small, over the life span leads to a collection of scar tissues in the fingers, ankles, knees, and elsewhere. Yet it is the effect of decades of failure to stretch the joints repeatedly that is the commonest cause of freezing of the joints late in life. Obviously the best approach is to avoid it in the first place, because once a joint is frozen it is often difficult and painful to unfreeze it. But it is never too late to start a flexibility program. Usually in conjunction with a strengthening session a set of joint stretches is studiously created and followed.

The American College of Sports Medicine recommends that a steady stretch that lasts 10 to 30 seconds in a series of three to five repetitions for each joint be undertaken a minimum of three times per week. These stretches should include every major joint in the body (neck, shoulders, trunk, hips, and knees). Recognize that the stretches should be over the full range of motion and in both directions. The stretches should always be smooth and only within the usual range of motion. Bouncing or forcing joints beyond the usual arc are hazardous. Avoid discomfort. If it hurts, it is too much.

Maintenance of flexibility in the late years must be worked at. It does not happen automatically. But the yields provided by the above flexibility exercises will go a long way to assuring an active life habit until the end of one's days.

Balance Exercising

Lastly, the fourth exercise form for older persons addresses the issue of decreased balance in late life. Over a million fractures occur each year in America, mostly in older persons, and mostly because of poor balance. The precise cause of poor balance is often difficult or impossible to determine, since it likely results from a combination of factors including circulatory, inner ear, position sense, muscle strength, and vision features. Each of these should be addressed individually for specific benefit, but even with this effort imbalance often remains. Therefore, targeted balance exercises are advised.

The first recommendation is the flamingo stand, in which the individual practices standing on one leg and then the other for a count of 30 each for a total of 5 minutes twice a day, every day. If a person cannot accomplish this, then hold on to the back of a chair while doing the one-legged stands with two hands if necessary, then one hand, next one finger, and progressing to the no-hold-on state. The gold standard is to be able to do the flamingo stand with the eyes closed. If this can truly be mastered, the risk of falling is minimum.

There are of course other methods of balance training. Standing 6 to 10 inches away from a wall and leaning toward it without support in each direction helps to develop balance. Similarly, the heel to toe walk, forward and backward, helps to restore unsteadiness and limit falls.

Taking a fall early in life is usually considered a trivial event, but after 70 years of age new caution is appropriate. Although falls are rarely directly fatal, the resulting immobility and loss of muscle strength and conditioning often leads to bad outcomes. Falls are to be avoided by attention to balance training.

Cautions

The ancient Greeks taught us "Everything in moderation." This admonition certainly applies to an exercise program for older persons. Physical exercise for older persons, even those with substantial health problems, is extremely safe. Dr. Paul Thompson of the University of Pittsburgh is the authority regarding exercise-associated medical problems. He has calculated that the exercisers suffer much fewer problems than the spectators. Every study of which I am aware concerning exercise protocols with people over 70 years of age has remarked on the lack of injuries and side effects suffered by the participants.

But moderation remains a proper cautionary advice. Particularly to be avoided is any sudden impulse to replicate some physical feat last attempted 40 years ago. Such adventurism is just plain dangerous.

For an inactive person, age 70, for example, to decide to embark on an exercise lifestyle modeled after the above guidelines, certain considerations appear. If the person has one or more "risk factors" for heart disease such as smoking, high cholesterol, hypertension, or a family history of heart trouble, a thorough physical examination by a physician including a stress electrocardiogram is appropriate — acknowledging that in the absence of these risk factors everyone over the age of 70 should have an annual physical exam. Successful completion of this is sufficient assurance to start to exercise.

If during or after exercise a chest, throat, or arm pain develops; or the heart goes into an irregular rhythm, too fast or too slow, or faintness occurs, then medical attention should be sought promptly. If after exercise muscles or joints remain persistently inflamed, or if shortness of breath, rapid pulse, or fatigue remain for more than a reasonable period of a day or two, a physician should be consulted before exercise is commenced again. For most exercise-related symptoms, however, good judgment is all that is required. Reducing the intensity and/or time of the exercise periods, then resumption of low levels or times solves most problems. Judicious use of acetaminophen, aspirin, or ibuprofen, with or without ice, manages most muscle aches. The body is meant to be moved. Just do it.

Barriers to Exercise

The mountains of evidence that continue to build about the many benefits a physically active lifestyle confers, not only in longevity but more importantly in life quality, are overwhelming. There simply is no further doubt about the categorical affirmative answer to the question, "Is exercise good for an older person?" If the answer is so obvious, the next question immediately arises, "Then why aren't more people doing it?" Until now science has lacked a cohesive way of addressing this issue, and as a result efforts to encourage or induce older persons to exercise were random and lacked a conceptual framework. Largely as the result of the experimental base provided by the work of renowned psychologist Albert Bandura, several research workers are now looking at the barriers to exercise.

Of course there are as many excuses offered up as to why exercise was avoided as the imagination can conjure. Among the most common ones are fear of injury, lack of opportunity, poor weather, lack of time, boredom, slowness of progress, self-consciousness, and lack of family support. Unfortunately exercise for many connotes competition, and not winning is almost un-American. This emphasis on being first is certainly a substantial disincentive. In fact competition itself is a disincentive for most older people. The reason to exercise is to exercise and not to win. Life has enough time urgencies without applying a stop watch to an exercise performance.

There is increasing awareness that the belief in one's ability, one's self-efficacy, is the single major determinant in changing behavior. Self-efficacy is of course a major issue in all aspects of aging, but particularly in regard to initiating a physical activity program. The four ingredients in building self-efficacy according to Bandura are: (1) small steps of mastery; (2) peer examples; (3) social persuasion; and (4) diminishment of cues of failure. Small steps of mastery means

A Thousand and One Ways to Keep Fit

Dr. David Satcher, the United States Surgeon General, has said "physical activity is not something that you need a gymnasium for or membership in a club that costs $1000 a year." There are literally hundreds of activities—not all of them sports—that will help keep you fit and reduce your risk of coronary artery disease, stroke, colon cancer, diabetes, hypertension, and osteoporosis. A good vigorous exercise program, as recommended in this chapter is the best way to get the most benefit from physical activity, but you can find many other activities to supplement the program. Or, if your doctor recommends against a vigorous program for you, some of these other activities might be an acceptable substitute.

You can take long walks, go dancing, bicycle, take up gardening, take the stairs instead of the elevator, push a grandchild in a stroller around the neighborhood, go for a swim, wash the windows, clean and wax the car, jump rope, paint the fence, have a snowball fight, rearrange the closets, or actively play with a young child. Possibilities for activity can be found all around you. If the local museum or art society offers an architectural walking tour, take it. Volunteer to help serve food or run the coat check at a church function.

A 1996 U.S. Surgeon General's report, *Physical Activity and Health*, recommends for all Americans at least a moderate amount of physical activity every day. The report defines a moderate amount as enough activity to use approximately 150 Calories (kcal). That is not a lot of time or energy—twenty minutes of swimming laps or forty-five minutes of gardening, for example—but the rewards are great. Just get out of that chair and get moving.

encouraging the inactive person to begin slowly by taking short walks, or avoiding the elevator or escalator. Ride only when you must. Start with low expectations and build up. Peer example is easy in these days when older individuals are increasingly demolishing the stereotypes about what older people cannot do. Social persuasion simply means the mustering of the hosts of scientific evidence and indications for benefit that exercise provides. Diminishment of cues of failure means taking a hot bath after a long walk, or using aspirin in anticipation of a workout, or documenting that being short of breath while exercising is expected and not a danger sign.

When initiating an exercise program, awareness of these four elements in building a positive belief system has a higher chance for success. How do you motivate someone to exercise? By building a program with these ingredients. An enthusiastic, attractive instructor helps build and sustain motivation. Intimidation is out.

A derivative technique called "stages of change" was derived for smoking cessation programs. Use of this approach acknowledges that all persons fall into groups that differ in their receptivity to change in behavior. Some are eager and ready, while others are resistant and even ornery. To classify these groups a six level scale was suggested: (1) precontemplation, "I'm not even thinking about it;" (2) contemplation, "I'm considering it, but I haven't yet started;" (3) preparation, "I'm getting ready" or "I've just started;" (4) active, "I've really begun;" (5) maintenance, "I'm well under way;" and (6) relapse, "I did, but I'm not doing it now." By separating these stages, different types and intensity of intervention strategies are planned. Certain cue words or phrases can reliably place a prospect into the appropriate group and the motivating effort specifically targeted. All stages require reinforcing efforts. No one is ever secure; however, there has been a suggestion that once well underway exercise has an addicting potential by its elaboration of endorphins, the natural pain modulators and mood enhancers.

It is recognized that there may be only a small gap between denial and insight. The weight of respect and authority conveyed by a physician helps to bring to the arena of encouragement an older person needs to exercise cannot be overstated. Dr. Anita Stewart has found that a physician's endorsement is a strong incentive for many. With this in mind, Dr. James Sallis and his colleagues in San Diego have developed the PACE program (Physician-based Assessment and Curriculum for Exercise) and report good early results with its use. Establishment and maintenance of morale and enthusiasm are central issues.

Summary

Risk of institutionalization is a huge issue to persons confronting the last of years life. Emphasis has been placed on maintenance of independence of action, behavior, economy, thought, and belief. The term "active life expectancy" (ALE) has been introduced to emphasize that portion of life in which personal freedoms are maximum. In contrast inactive life expectancy (ILE) is the fragile end segment of too many persons' lives. Compression of this inactive portion to the smallest time span is ideal. A seldom identified major benefit of physical activity is its increased likelihood of avoiding a prolonged dying process. Living actively decreases what René Dubos called "medicated survival."

There is no disputing the effects of time on all our lives, but involvement is a more potent determinant of how we will live the late segment of life. Paul Baltes of the Max Planck Institute in Germany measures memory. A young person can remember eight words from a list, but an old person six. But when you train the old person he or she can recall 30 words. If you train a younger person the youngster will recall 40 words. Therefore the youngster, trained or untrained, will always outperform the older person in memory challenges. But the differences between young and old are really small as contrasted to the difference between trained and untrained persons of whatever age.

The same illustration holds with regard to physical vitality. The youth will outperform the older person, but the differences will be much smaller than the effect of training. A fit older person will outperform an unfit younger person. The message is clear. If we hope to escape the sequence of "the child won't, the parent doesn't, and the grandparent can't," a lifelong effort at increasing physical fitness appears as a high personal and national urgency. The present and future well-being of each of us separately and as a member of the larger community depends upon it.

Life is the one race we win by finishing last.

Lou Glasse, M.S.W., became a medical social worker after putting aside her girlhood dreams of becoming a professional dancer. In the course of her work she found an entrenched institutional bias against older people, especially women. Speaking out against this bias launched her on a new career as an advocate for the rights of aging women. She has served as Director of the New York Center for Policy on Aging in New York City; Director of the New York State Office for the Aging; member of the National Advisory Committee on Research on Women's Health of the National Institutes of Health; speaker at the 1985 UN Decade for Women Conference held in Nairobi, Kenya and the 1995 NGO World Forum held in Beijing; member of the Advisory Committe to the 1995 and President of the Older Women's League. She currently serves as the Chair of the Geriatric Society of America's Task Force on Women and as a member of the editorial board of the *Women and Aging Letter.* Also she finds time for active participation in local church and civic activities, and for cooking for her family and friends at home in the Hudson River valley, where she lives with her husband, a retired professor at Vassar College.

Making the Most of the Gift of Time

Lou Glasse

The current generation of older Americans is pioneering the use of additional years of life. Only recently has it been possible for so many people to realistically expect to retire. Longer life expectancy, supported by Social Security and pension plans, have enabled millions to move from the labor force into retirement, or semiretirement.

Although most people talk about their desire to retire, few realize how long that retirement might last. Of course, no one can predict exactly how long he or she will live, but most of us will have many years in retirement. At age 65 today, life expectancy extends another 17.5 years. The Social Security Administration estimates that in the year 2000, nearly 76,000 persons will be 100 years of age or older. As Eubie Blake, the famous jazz pianist, said at age 96, "If I had known I would live this long, I would have taken better care of myself."

These additional years provide older persons nearing retirement with time to consider new activities, develop new skills, explore new fields of learning, or even to begin new careers. Or, they can now devote time to a long-held interest or deepening the bonds to loved ones. Some persons never develop interests outside of their work. These people may find retirement is a major adjustment. In contrast, homemakers may find little change; their responsibilities simply continue.

Some people have clear goals for retirement and happily pursue activities that lead to those goals. Others begin retirement just longing for the leisure time to linger over breakfast coffee and the morning newspaper. Another group may be eager to play golf or tennis or go fishing, hunting, and camping. But many people tire of unending leisure and yearn for a sense of purpose or just to be needed. One perceptive wordsmith observed that "more people rust out than wear out."

Gerontologists point out that growing older has a unique place in the life cycle. If these additional years are to be satisfying and rich, we need to give thought to which dreams are left unfilled or actions are still undone.

If you are financially secure and your health is good, retirement can provide great freedom and opportunities. Even when income is reduced and some infirmities afflict the body, these may not be barriers to a successful retirement. With good planning, impediments may be overcome. Equally important, retirement usually brings time for reflection, even if movement and action are restricted. To draw from Viktor E. Frankl's powerful book, *Man's Search for Meaning*, we each have the inner freedom to choose one's attitude toward life. Time spent in intellectual and spiritual development can provide growth, satisfaction, and enrichment of the quality of life. In large measure, what we do with our retirement depends on what we make of it. Good luck in using well this gift of time.

Retirement: Chosen or Involuntary

After World War II, when eligibility for pensions and Social Security became more widespread, a greater number of workers began to take early retirement. Today, nine out of ten persons over 65 years of age are no longer in the labor market. According to the American Association of Retired Persons, this trend may have slowed. From 1985 to 1995, the 65-plus workforce increased 31%. Nonetheless, older workers still represent only 2.9% of the total labor force.

Although millions of workers elect to retire early, some are pushed out of employment before they are ready. Mandatory retirement is no longer legal, but employers in both the public and private sectors have followed practices that reduce the number of older workers among their employees. Reductions in the workforce and changes in technology have displaced many able people who want or need to continue to work. Sometimes this takes the form of layoffs; other times the employer offers an attractive early retirement package to older—and usually more expensive—employees.

Studies have shown that some workers who had not intended to retire as early as they do have a harder time adjusting to retirement. Such workers may feel that they have "been put out to pasture." These involuntary retirees may face ten to fifteen years before they are eligible for Social Security and pensions. Financial need may push them to seek other employment. Some find they are restless and unhappy without paid employment. They love their work and value the structure and purpose that a job provides.

Leaves of Absence

Some people consider retirement because they feel "burned out." Without enthusiasm and energy for their work, retirement seems to be the only solution. However, other solutions should be considered, such as reducing the number of hours worked, transferring to a different section within your corporation or business, a leave of absence, or temporary out-placement to another location.

One insightful manager of a transportation company reported that when a valued employee reports feeling "burned out," he has found that a three to six month leave of absence provides the answer. Many employees need occasions to change their schedules and free their minds to consider new ideas. This manager believes that more corporations should use this practice to revive employees' flagging interest in their work.

A leave of absence, with or without pay, is an option more frequently available to college or university faculty. Usually, the faculty member must have an educational purpose and plan for the leave. Time away from the demands of teaching and from campus responsibilities can provide the change so vital to continued productivity.

In addition, an increasing number of opportunities are available for people in other professions to work temporarily in another part of the United States or even in another country. For example, medical journals advertise both temporary and full-time opportunities for health professionals. These temporary positions can provide an opportunity to test an idea about changing jobs and moving to a new location. Other national trade organizations and journals print similar employment offerings. Check with the associations and journals in your field for such opportunities.

Second Careers

Remember, if your health is good, you may still have many years ahead of productive activity. If paid employment is

Employment Alternatives to Consider

- Employment in the same field, but with a different company.

- Part-time employment or contract work with your old firm.

- Job sharing with another worker who wishes to reduce his/her hours of work.

- Developing a hobby or long-held interest into an income-producing activity.

important for current and retirement income, for your own self-esteem or because it contributes to your quality of life, you have several alternatives to consider.

First decide if you wish to continue the same work or are eager to try something different. Do you want to continue working, but reduce the number of hours you spend on the job? Whatever your circumstances, specialists in employment encourage the job seeker to take the time to think about your goals, evaluate your skills, and consider the local job market.

In a self-assessment, list all of the skills you have developed throughout your life, not just those you used on your last job. Most of us perform many activities in the home and in volunteer work that we forget about when applying for jobs. To learn more about employment opportunities for "older workers," contact the American Association of Retired Persons and visit your local library for suggested readings.

There are many examples of persons who have begun successful second careers after reaching the traditional time for retirement. One of the best known is Colonel Sanders, founder of Kentucky Fried Chicken. When Sanders was 64 years of age, a new highway was built that bypassed his fried chicken restaurant. When his local business began to decline, he decided to franchise the name and method of preparing the chicken. Ten years later, he had 638 franchises across the country.

Merrilyn Belgum, retired after 41 years as a social worker, started a new career as a stand-up comedienne. A white-haired matron, whose bearing conveys dignity, she stimulates laughter and applause when she appears wearing a bright pink sequined sheath, a dozen long strands of beads, and a feathered boa. She talks about the most mundane facts of life that everyone experiences. Yet, her humorous phrasing and comic view of life are delightful, and her audiences laugh with self-recognition.

James, a clergyman, eased into retirement. After leaving a full-time administrative position, he was invited to become an interim pastor for a church while its congregation sought a new full-time minister. James discovered that he liked this new role. Because he had years of experience, he was able to recognize problems quickly and to develop solutions with confidence and skill. Because these assignments extended for only one to two years, and with few family responsibilities tying him to one section of the country, James was able to become acquainted with new cities in different sections of the country. After serving in a half dozen such churches, he decided to develop a long-held interest in woodworking. The networking skills he had honed throughout his career helped him meet other skilled craftsmen, from whom he learned more about woodworking, design, and marketing. James now has the joy of turning and selling his beautiful creations.

Duane has just begun his third career at 65 years of age — he has entered politics. Duane began his career as a minister and served in that capacity for 16 years. Then, he became a college professor of sociology and earned a Ph.D. along the way. As he neared retirement from teaching, Duane ran successfully for supervisor of a small town in upstate New York. Although each position he has held differed from the other, he was always concerned about people and public policy. It was these interests that propelled him to his new career.

Public Service

One of the most fulfilling activities of retirement may be public service. Most people take pride in their community and gain satisfaction when able to contribute to it. Few, however, can really appreciate the various ways that they can help.

These opportunities extend from mundane filing, licking stamps, and stuffing envelopes to the more intellectually challenging mentoring, serving in an advisory capacity to government programs, churches, small businesses, schools, and community organizations. Or the service may be physically demanding work with the environment, small maintenance work for persons who are homebound, or the heartwarming work of helping people in need. Even persons who are not mobile may serve through their crafts or in programs that need telephone callers.

Volunteering to help neighbors and communities has been a unique characteristic of Americans for centuries. Alexis de Tocqueville, a nineteenth-century French observer of the United States, marveled at the way Americans organized associations and worked together to achieve a common good, even "sacrifice[ing] a portion of his private interest to preserve the rest."

Some people call retirees the greatest untapped resource in America. Others suggest that older adults are greedy and only interested in personal pleasure. A more accurate description may lie somewhere between these two extremes.

Clearly, without the necessity for employment, retirees have an unusual opportunity to contribute to their communities. Most of us are grateful for the benefits we have received during our lifetimes. This period of greater freedom from daily, demanding jobs is a time when we can help our communities, our nation, and even our world by giving of our wisdom, our skills, and our creativity.

Communities across the country are in need of mature counsel and leadership. The problems within our communities include high illiteracy and school dropout rates; teenage pregnancy; drug and alcohol abuse among the young; crime on the streets and violence in homes. Poverty and homelessness confront every community.

Some communities are finding it difficult to attract volunteers. Increasingly, both husbands and wives are employed; they sometimes travel great distances to their jobs. More families are headed by single parents, who have little time to volunteer for Girl Scouts, the volunteer fire department, the Red Cross, or other needed programs. Because retirees are more likely to be available during the hours needed by community service organizations, program survival may depend on the availability of dedicated senior volunteers.

Our communities would be less desirable places if not for the services and benefits provided by public and private institutions. On the other hand, most not-for-profit organizations and public institutions are understaffed and are struggling with budget difficulties. Without volunteers, programs would be curtailed and life would become bleak for many persons of all ages.

A lifetime of experience can make the older person a valuable volunteer. That experience can come from work or be the result of a hobby or interest. Often, the personal warmth and caring of a volunteer may be essential to a frightened child or to a lonely, homebound older person.

Whether your experience was gained when raising a family, managing a business, teaching school, directing an agency, or through some other activity, your knowledge and skills may be important to your community. Some place in your community your contributions are needed.

Personal Benefits of Volunteering Your Services

By helping others, you are likely to be helping yourself. In addition to making you feel good, studies have shown that there are real physical and psychological benefits to volunteering. Some scientists have even linked increased life expectancy to helping others.

If we are to thrive, social relationships are important. Volunteering provides a way of staying connected to people and maintaining your own self-esteem. When people move out of the labor force, day-to-day interactions with colleagues are usually lost. Surveys have shown that retirees spend from 18 to 25 hours a week watching television and doing housework. According to a Louis Harris poll, 55% of older respondents expressed a loss of usefulness after retirement. While 20 to 30% of older Americans are involved in volunteering, another 15% said they would like to be volunteers.

As expressed by the late Erik Erikson, psychoanalyst and author, "service can meet a deeper need . . ., satisfying the impulse toward generativity, the instinctual drive to pass on to the next generation what an individual has learned from life." "The final challenge of life," Erikson states simply, "involves coming to terms with the notion, 'I am what survives of me.'" Theodore Roosevelt put it another way, "What we do for ourselves dies with us. What we do for our community lives long after we are gone."

Volunteering in Your Home Community

There is great diversity in volunteer sites. The public is generally aware of the volunteer needs of churches, schools, nursing homes, meal programs for the homebound and the poor, and both adult and child day care centers. Environmental programs, parks, and historic sites also use volunteers. Even small businesses may welcome volunteers. Volunteers carry out many functions and activities. Some organizations are especially successful at matching the skills of the volunteer with the appropriate activity. There may be hundreds of opportunities to serve within your community.

Voluntary Action Centers, the United Way, Area Agencies on Aging, children's organizations, and youth centers are good places to explore opportunities for public service. They are likely to know of community needs and are probably listed in your telephone directory.

Two national organizations that may have many local operations specialize in placing volunteers in needed locations. Voluntary Action Centers and Retired and Seniors Volunteer Program (RSVP) recruit, orient, and place volunteers. They also screen the site to determine if it is safe and to clarify the reason for the volunteer.

Some programs offer stipends or pay expenses. The Senior Companion and Foster Grandparent Programs, both part of the National Senior Service Corps programs, provide a small stipend and are aimed at low-income older persons.

Studies show that one half of all volunteer work is through religious organizations. Local congregations provide opportunities for teaching, serving on committees, participating in music programs or clubs, and helping with office work or maintenance. Many religious organizations also call on members to participate in mission programs that focus on the poor and homeless. For example, some active churches in metropolitan New York organize nightly trips to bring food, clothing, and blankets to locations where the homeless gather. Others volunteer in prisons, at soup kitchens, and in shelters for abused women and their children.

Many religious organizations offer the opportunity to volunteer in other parts of the United States, as well as abroad. The programs may run from a few months to several years. Some financial aid may be available. Thus, if you are affiliated with a religious group and wish to consider volunteer work outside of your home community, ask your local clergy or contact the regional or national office for information. Church, synagogue, or temple publications may list telephone numbers to call for more information about volunteer activities.

Retired Business Leaders

One unusual and successful program designed to assist small businesses is called the Service Corps of Retired Executives Association (SCORE). Drawing on experts from virtually every area of business management, SCORE provides volunteer counselors free for one-on-one management sessions, as well as low-cost workshops on a wide variety of business topics. SCORE has approximately 800 counseling locations across the country. Most of their volunteers are retired.

An overseas opportunity for volunteer business executives may be found through the International Executive Service Corps. This not-for-profit organization, based in Stamford, Connecticut, places U.S. executives with management and technical expertise in businesses in developing countries where they can help local businesspeople increase their productivity, upgrade management skills, and improve basic technologies. With a 30-year track record of assisting free enterprise in developing countries, IESC proudly states, "We don't offer a hand out. We provide a hand-up."

Local, state, and national parks, environmental programs, and historic sites use volunteers in many capacities. Some on-site activities include tours, lectures, office work, land maintenance, monitoring of borders, and even research. Sometimes, off-site services, such as bird counting or measuring rain or snow, are also needed. Some of the many organizations using volunteers for environmental work are the Nature Conservancy, the Sierra Club, the Environmental Defense Fund, the National Audubon Society, and the World Wildlife Fund.

A good way to learn about such opportunities is through organizational newsletters to members. The local newspaper and library may include information about volunteer opportunities. You can also contact the offices of the organizations directly.

Alice, a recently retired schoolteacher, is now coordinating an educational program for schoolchildren at a local park. Though she felt drained and discouraged when she retired, she is excited by her new "job." She has been able to combine her knowledge of science and teaching with her interest in nature and the environment. She is delighted with this opportunity.

In 1974, Julian began a hobby of checking and logging on a daily basis the weather at his home in Oklahoma. He monitors the wind's speed and direction, precipitation, barometric readings, and the temperature. Because of his personal interest in weather changes and his careful recordkeeping, he was asked to provide certain information to the National Weather Bureau. This is another example of public service that is helpful to others and adds interest and purpose to the volunteer's life.

Time to Speak Out

Although retirement is indeed a period of life that each of us must shape for ourselves, it comes with responsibilities. A democracy needs the involvement of people. Freedom from job responsibilities does not free citizens from the responsibility to support and contribute to their communities, state, and nation. And, retirees are in a unique position. No one will reduce your retirement income if you speak up for important services or policies.

Some gerontologists have referred to this "third age" as an opportunity for "radical freedom." Retirees are fortunate that they are no longer bound by the restraints of daily employment, the demands of a growing family, or the fear of saying or doing something that might displease an employer. You have spent your life proving who you are, and what you can do. You risk little and gain much if you use your years of experience to speak up for services and policies to promote healthy families and communities.

Maggie Kuhn, the feisty founder of the Grey Panthers, spoke up when the policies of her employer forced her to retire. Angered by the assumption that persons 65 years of age and older were obsolete and no longer valued employees, Maggie mobilized people of all ages to work for changes in society. From 1970 until her death in 1995, Maggie was an outspoken and vigorous leader for social justice and environmental conservation and against the proliferation of nuclear weapons. This diminutive woman asserted, "We are not senior citizens or golden-agers. We are the elders, the experienced ones; we are maturing, growing adults responsible for the survival of our society. We are not wrinkled babies, succumbing to trivial, purposeless waste of our years and our time."

Tish Sommers and Laurie Shields were 66 and 55 years of age respectively when they founded the national Older Women's League. They organized this grassroots membership organization to promote reforms when they learned that millions of women shared their problems: no health insurance, difficulty in finding employment, and unrelieved caregiving.

Few of us will organize a national association when we enter retirement, but there are many other examples of retirees who initiated action to correct a community problem. When businessman Sam Sadin retired, he decided to devote his attention to promoting legal services for the poor elderly. Although not a lawyer, he knew it was important for older people to know their legal rights and entitlements when facing eviction, the denial of pension or social security benefits, or other problems. With support from Hunter College of the City University of New York and its Brookdale Center on Aging, he organized the Institute on Law and Rights of

Older Adults. It became an important resource throughout metropolitan New York.

Healthy communities depend on the well-being of people of all ages: the health and education of children, families that are financially secure and able to nurture their young and support their older members. Although we are a nation that values individual independence, our country was founded by pioneers who helped neighbors and worked together to build strong communities. With growing numbers of people living longer, we must look to elders to provide leadership in facing the challenges of today.

Travel

More and more Americans, including older Americans, are traveling to unfamiliar places, both in the United States and abroad. Travel is one of the privileges of living in the late twentieth century. Few of our grandparents and great grandparents had the opportunity to travel for pleasure. If they did, going more than a few hundred miles from home was considered a long distance.

Retirees of the current generation can now see for themselves what the rest of the world looks like and how people of other nations live. We need not rely solely on the media or picture books.

But vacation travel is still considered a luxury, and most people need to budget for unusual trips. Many can only make one trip in a lifetime to Asia or Africa or other faraway places. Whether going to exotic places in other countries, which have different traditions and cultures, or exploring the beautiful United States, veteran travelers report that careful planning will help you make the most of your trip.

Begin by learning about the area you will visit and the significance of the sights you will see. Otherwise, you may see only the popular tourist spots and miss places that are of special interest or importance to you. A recently retired neighbor reported that "half the fun of a trip is the planning that comes first. After our trip to England, we decided to include only two or three grand houses in our trip to Ireland. When we see too many, the homes begin to blur in our memories."

If you want to go beyond the usual tourist attractions, experienced travelers advise that a sense of adventure is essential. Leave your schedule open, so you can do things or see places that were not a planned part of your trip. Some of the best experiences come from such surprises. That is why some regular globetrotters arrange hotel accommodations for the first night only, and rely on finding the next bed and breakfast as their trip develops.

Where to Begin

Deciding where to go will sometimes make you feel like a child in an ice cream or candy store. Everything looks so good that it is hard to decide. Newspapers, magazines, and television offer glimpses of places to visit. Travel agents provide descriptions of tours, as well as things to do and see on your own. Associations to which you belong may offer participation in a tour. Sorting this all out takes some time.

After you have decided where to go, decide what interests you—the people and their history, the terrain, the wildlife, the customs, the arts? A young female friend, who takes frequent trips abroad, sometimes travels alone. For travel information, she recommends *International Travel Network*; for people whose budgets permit better hotels and restaurants, consult *International Living*. She also enjoys armchair traveling; *National Geographic* is a regular item on her Christmas list. She writes, "When I plan a trip . . .

- "I usually buy a travel book that covers the areas I'm planning to visit. I generally browse a good travel book section in a library or bookshop before choosing the one that fits the type of travel I want to do. Often guidebooks provide specialized information about subjects within the country: for example, antiques, ceramics, churches, old mansions, and animals.

- "I talk to my friends who have been to that area— particularly friends who have a similar philosophy on travel.

- "I start a file with article clippings or whatever I can find about an area I'm interested in.

- "I contact any friends in the area I'll be visiting. Seeing an area with people who actually live there is one of the best ways to see it.

- "To get some ideas, one time I attended a slide show presented by a company that organizes group tours to an area that interested me. Occasionally, lectures at museums and universities about the country of interest will be available.

- "When I'm traveling alone, I try to stay at places where I'll be likely to meet people with whom I might like to travel. Sometimes, I get ideas from travel books or from other travelers. A lot of budget type places have central meeting areas, coffee shops, etc., and these are generally good meeting places."

My friend observed that some persons advertise for a travel companion, but that has risks. These risks may be minimized by conversations and references. *International Living* is one publication that prints such advertisements.

If you prefer to travel with a tour group, many choices are available and the descriptions often sound exciting. Some are led by specialists in the area to be visited. Museums and universities frequently offer such opportunities. Religious associations sometimes organize tours to sites important in their history. Professional organizations may arrange trips to visit their counterparts in other countries. For example, U.S. health professionals have traveled together to visit health centers in China. Similar programs are available for gerontologists, social workers, and other professionals.

Travel agencies, both local and national, are the more typical organizers of tours. The cost and the travel plan will be affected by the sponsor. Most tour operators are undoubtedly reliable, but a word of caution is advisable. Because there are occasional reports of tourists being stranded in foreign cities or left without the accommodations they expected, it is wise to take some precautions. To select a reliable travel or tour agent, follow these guidelines:

- Find out if the company or agent has a good track record. Get the names of others who have been on tours with this agent and talk with them.

- Get plan in writing, along with specific information about the places you will stay.

- Find out about refunds or travel company insurance in case they cancel or change tour plans.

- Buy travel insurance to protect yourself against disruptive events or the possibility that you might have to cancel the trip.

Low-Budget Vacations

Camping, walking tours, trips with local nature groups, and visits to museums, historic sites, festivals, and national and state parks provide opportunities for low-cost vacations. And, they offer fun, the occasion to meet new people, and the opportunity to see and learn about your surroundings.

Walking tours are organized for small groups (approximately 25 persons) both in the United States and abroad. One organization plans trips lasting two weeks. The group usually walks seven or eight miles a day, stopping for local sights and lunch. The group may use three or four hotels while touring. Some people plan their own walking tours, consulting guidebooks to find routes and trails that are particularly scenic or historic.

State and national parks often have very good camping facilities. Information can usually be obtained from your local library, state tourist information service, or American Automobile Association. Some popular campgrounds require reservations. To avoid disappointment, check with the park service about your travel plans.

Environmental Vacations

The Sierra Club, one of our oldest environmental organizations, was instrumental in the creation of the National Park Service and the National Forest Service, and in the designation of several national parks. Fortunately, we now have many state and national parks, as well as an increasing number of environmental groups. Many of them organize trips to view and learn about conservation and wildlife. They publicize these trips and other activities through their membership materials.

A friend who is a "birder" reports that trips for bird watching are held in many local as well as distant places. Organized trips are usually led by an expert who is knowledgeable about the particular birds in the vicinity. Activities continue year round, with lectures, slides of birds, and participation in the annual bird census. Information about such bird watching is usually announced in membership materials and is often listed in the local newspaper.

Housing Options for Extended Trips

Some people are not satisfied with staying only few days in one location. They prefer to extend their travel for weeks, or even months. The annual migration of older adults from northern states to the south during the winter months is the largest example of this phenomenon. Some of these "snow birds" return to the same location winter after winter.

An option selected by millions of people is to invest in a recreational vehicle (RV). Traveling turtlelike (carrying their

Planning a Vacation: Questions to Ask Yourself

Obvious questions are what places will you visit and where will you stay. However, other important questions include:

- What is my budget? Am I going economy class? How long can I afford to say? Are there discounts if I travel on certain days, through the American Association of Retired Persons or other associations?

- Should I fly, rent a car, or travel by train? Should I buy a rail pass?

- Will the currency exchange rate be an advantage or will it increase the price of the trip?

- Am I more comfortable traveling with a group, for which activities are planned and structured.

- How important are modern conveniences to me? If physical comforts are really essential and I do not enjoy changes in food or customs, perhaps my travel should be limited to the United States.

home with them), retirees strike out across the country in search of the right temperature in interesting locations. This type of travel enables the wanderer to visit national and state parks, as well as friends and relatives, without the anxiety of needing a place to stay.

Rentals of apartments and homes in other cities and in other countries also provide opportunities for staying in other locations for a longer period of time. Exchanging homes for several months with someone from a different country or another part of this country is yet another option. Proposals for house swapping are often listed in college or university publications. Of course, personal knowledge or references provide some protection that you will be satisfied with the swap.

Extending the Trip

The pleasure and excitement of travel can extend beyond the trip itself. After seeing whales in Alaska or elephants in Africa, you may appreciate even more the nature reports on television. Or, travel may help answer questions raised by reports of volcanoes, earthquakes, floods, or thousands of other events around the world. News accounts of another country take on greater meaning if you have traveled there. It may be as simple as understanding what the underground train system is like when reading of a terrorist gas attack in Japan.

Community groups are often interested in seeing slides or photographs of unusual travel. Some travelers accompany their slides with a narrative that describes the trip more fully. By sharing travel interests with friends or at meetings of church groups, senior centers, and schoolchildren, the pleasure of the trip is kept alive.

Most of us wish to purchase some remembrance of the trip. Sometimes, travelers are tempted to search for an item that is less expensive than back home. Others search for an item that is not seen where they live. My young friend reports that the "memory of how I got it brings me pleasure."

Travel provides an opportunity to see one's state and nation from the perspective of others. We may return home with new ideas gleaned from seeing the way another part of the world lives. We may return home with greater appreciation for our home, friends, state, and nation. In either case, travel can enrich our lives.

Lifelong Education

Retirees have an opportunity that was seldom available to their parents and grandparents—the chance to go back to school. This may sound like a crazy idea to some folks. They ask may, why get more education just at the time when you are leaving the workplace? What value does it have? Here are some of the many answers.

- To carry out a dream. Many adults had to interrupt their education in their younger years because of family responsibilities or to earn a living. Even with the passing years, the dream has not died. Now they can pursue the goal they set out to achieve many years ago.

- To have a greater understanding of the way the world works. Science has brought us a long way since the days when most of us studied chemistry, geology, and astronomy. Extraordinary discoveries have been made about the universe, the world, and its first inhabitants. In addition, international issues draw our attention to other countries and people. Education can help us keep informed about world events and understand the underlying causes of wars, national upheavals, and changing policies.

- To develop a skill. It is rapidly becoming essential that we know how to use new technologies in business and in our social lives. Every office, big and small, is relying more and more on electronic means to carry out its work. To guard our own interests, it helps to understand these new procedures.

Information about Educational Opportunities

Admissions offices are good places to find information about college and university offerings and policies. The annual university catalog will list courses of study and entrance requirements. A good local library will probably have the catalogs from schools in your area. Many of them offer reduced rates to older adults, but sometimes this just entitles you to audit the course.

Community Colleges

Community colleges are usually low-cost, accessible, and open to the "nontraditional student." These two-year programs offer a wide variety of courses from the usual liberal arts to training in computers, nursing, engineering, and other skills.

Many faculty members welcome the older student, whose maturity can improve the level of class discussion. Although some older adults admit feeling a bit out of place at first, most report that they enjoy the younger students and are accepted by them.

Many colleges offer practical, short-term courses aimed at the older student, such as financial and estate planning, caregiving, and gerontology, as well as courses in areas of special interest, such as film, creative writing, and jewelry making.

Elderhostel

One of the more interesting educational opportunities for persons over 55 years of age is Elderhostel. This not-for-profit organization offers low-cost, short-term academic experiences in areas ranging from the arts to wildlife. More than 2,000 colleges, universities, museums, national parks, educational facilities, and environmental centers organize and host programs that are diverse in both content and settings. Described as an educational adventure for older adults, Elderhostel programs build on the purpose of the sponsoring institution and are located in every state and in 70 countries.

Whether studying classical art and literature or Native American culture, Elderhostel offers informal opportunities for learning with persons from many parts of the country. Most of the programs last five to six days. Through a comprehensive catalogue with listings by state and country, people can select the programs of interest to them. The sites offer differences in physical activity and various levels of knowledge or skill in the chosen subject.

Why is Elderhostel so successful? It combines a number of characteristics desirable to retired people. It joins travel with the opportunity to learn in a setting that encourages give and take with the faculty and other students. The field activities provide a change from the classroom and an opportunity to see some of the surroundings. Also, participants can make new friends and singles need not feel out of place.

Elderhostel Service Programs

Elderhostel also sponsors service programs, in which hostelers provide volunteer service to worthy causes around the world in cooperation with such well-established organizations as Global Volunteers, Heifer Project International, and Habitat for Humanity.

Elderhostel Institute Network

A variation on the short-term academic programs described above is the Elderhostel Institute Network. This expanding association is a year-round program aimed at local retirees; it combines an interest in learning with socializing and travel. In some locations, other activities are included that are similar to those found in the better senior centers. Marist College for Life Time Studies is an institute in Poughkeepsie, New York, that provides educational programs for older adults in the Hudson Valley. It began with two people—Joan and Jonah Sherman—and was patterned after a Center in Asheville, North Carolina.

The Shermans wished to memorialize a favorite deceased aunt. Sensitive to the loneliness and the lack of mental stimulation that she sometimes experienced, they sought to find ways to enrich the lives of older persons who live in the Hudson Valley. After talking with a number of community leaders, the Shermans invited a small group of retirees, who served as a planning committee to organize an ongoing educational program.

Drawing on an extensive mailing list, they invited older adults from the Hudson Valley to a reception and presentation of the plan. According to organizers, they expected forty persons to come. Instead, nearly 400 appeared. The Shermans approached a local college to be the sponsoring institution. Now operating with a part-time secretary and with classes taught by volunteers, the program is in its sixth year, with more than three hundred enrollees and a long waiting list.

A Time to Create

Did you ever say to yourself, "When I retire I want to learn to draw? to sculpt? to become a potter?" At some point in our lives, many of us have had a desire to carry out some creative urge. However, with the pressures of employment and family responsibilities, the majority of people push aside such urges or simply become dabblers.

It is not too late. Creativity is not limited to a particular age. people do not cease being creative when they reach 60 years of age or older. Although studies show that "the peak of creative productivity occurs in young or middle adulthood," this is by no means universal.

Some artists continue to be creative throughout their lives. The history of art includes many examples of artists, such as J. S. Bach and Beethoven, who have a burst of creativity even when they are nearing the end of life. Other artists developed different art forms in their later years: Martha Graham will be remembered especially for her creative and powerful choreography of modern dance, which she turned to when she was no longer able to dance. Henri Matisse, the great painter, created wonderful paper cutouts and collages when his health would no longer permit him to stand. These collages are considered among his finest works of art.

Some people discover artistic talents after they reach their older years. Grandma Moses, the well-known primitive artist, first turned to embroidery to fight the depression she experienced after her husband died. She began to paint when her arthritis became too severe to do needlework. Elizabeth Layton, who battled mental illness, began to paint when she was 68 years of age. Her bold and vivid pictures, which have been widely exhibited, are insightful and penetrating.

A fifty-year study of folk art determined that one half of African-American folk art has been created by older persons, one out of five of whom is more than 85 years of age. According to Gene Cohen, the former director of the National Institute on Aging, folk art is dominated by older adults.

When you are retired may be the time to indulge that desire to express yourself on canvas, in clay, on film, on paper, or on the stage. Although few of us will be recognized as great artists by the public, part of living life to its fullest is to develop our talents and pursue our passions.

Many community centers offer classes for people of all ages. Classes in your particular art or craft may also be available in a nearby college. Your region may have theater and music groups that involve older adults. Some innovative senior centers may also provide programs in the creative arts.

New York City is home to several organizations that tap the artistic talents of retirees. Seniors Share the Arts was established to transfer people's life experiences into dance, theater, poetry, visual arts, life books, and writing. This organization offers both model projects and training programs to promote its work.

Albert Einstein wrote, "every individual should have the opportunity to develop the gifts which may be latent in him." Actor/film director John Cassavetes observed, "No matter how old you get, if you can keep the desire to be creative, you're keeping the man-child alive."

Who Am I?

Who were my ancestors? Where did they come from? Were they rich? poor? farmers? in business? doctors? When did they come to this country? What were their lives like? These are a few of the questions that prompt some retirees to begin a fascinating search to learn about their family histories. It is surprising how little most of us know about our parents, grandparents, and their forbearers.

On the other hand, most of us have some records that provide leads to begin the search. The first step is to collect what you do have: old letters, photographs, or a family bible that has notes about the family. There may still be some older relatives or other "old timers" from whom you can learn more. Most libraries and Mormon church centers have genealogical information or even records that are available to outsiders. By initiating correspondence with distant cousins and reading back issues of hometown newspapers, you may add to your knowledge. The Internet may also be an excellent resource.

But knowing about your ancestors will only tell you where you came from. It will not tell you who you have become or where you are going. In an effort to understand the meaning of their lives, some retirees begin a review of their own life experiences. making sense of the steps and twists that your life has taken can aid in self-understanding. What does my life add up to? What have I achieved for my family, in work, or in the community? What kind of person have I become? This reflection may help you recall those transforming moments of life—whether glorious music, a view of magnificent scenery, the exultant joy of love, the overwhelming tenderness and devotion in holding a new baby, or your sense of the presence of God. "It is," as Stendahl said in writing of love, "the past brought alive again."

One way to start such a life review is by keeping a journal or diary. Some people find that this provides an opportunity to reflect on experiences and consider their meaning. Sometimes such a journal is maintained with a group, where each person shares his or her writing. More and more community programs are designed to assist the older adult in putting these reflections on paper or describing them in a drama or storytelling activity.

Whether in a group or in private, questions can help probe your memories to search for understanding. Gerontologists observe that this is part of the work of growing older. It should not be surprising that so many autobiographies are written by people in this third stage of life.

Storytelling

Storytelling has often been the way that family histories have been passed to succeeding generations. Native Americans have kept alive much of their history this way. Gifted speakers will often draw on stories as one of the most effective ways to communicate an idea. Abraham Lincoln was known for his homey and meaningful stories.

Each of us has a story. Most people enjoy telling friends and family about their personal experiences. These personal memories enrich the lives of others and advance the review of one's own life. Shared memories are often precious to children and grandchildren, and in some instances, to the larger world.

At 80 years of age, Elsie Howard enrolled in a correspondence course for writers. Her formal education had ended in the tenth grade, the highest level available in her small town in Oklahoma in the early part of this century. Despite this, for most of her adult life, Elsie wrote skits, poems, and stories for her own pleasure or to use in her activities with Girl Scouts, Eastern Star, and her church. Now she wanted to take on a more ambitious project. She wanted to write down her memories of her childhood and her pioneer parents. She wanted to preserve these remembrances for her children and grandchildren.

The registration charge of a few hundred dollars seemed like a lot of money to Elsie. She felt uneasy about this expenditure and hesitated to tell her adult children. However, as the course proceeded, she began to develop her story. On completion of her manuscript, Elsie presented a copy to each of her delighted children. Her description of family life in the early days of Oklahoma's statehood is a valued family history and a link between siblings and cousins who now live thousands of miles apart.

Elsie's next project was a history of her hometown. As part of the town's National Bicentennial celebration, the local newspaper published this lively history in a series of articles. Elsie's good memory and delightful way of expressing herself has provided her hometown with historic information that otherwise would have been lost.

Retirement: A Problem or an Opportunity?

What do you want to do with the rest of your life? What do you want to see, or learn? What kind of person do you want to be? Although each of us will answer this question differently, we deserve to consider the question and to be intentional in our response.

The retirement years offer opportunities that can be interesting, fulfilling, and even exciting. Now that we are likely to be freer from a growing family and employment responsibilities, our options may be limited only by our imaginations. Increasingly, older adults are discovering the pleasures of going back to school, participating in sports, mentoring younger persons, volunteering to help those in need, developing a skill, craft, or art, traveling, and participating in other activities. May we each use this time well.

Ernest Hemingway observed that "retirement is the ugliest word in the language." Pablo Casals, the famed cellist who performed well into his nineties, shared that opinion. He said, "To retire is the beginning of death."

But, this opinion is not shared by all. Seneca the Younger, who lived from 3 B.C. to A.D. 65, held that "the gradually declining years are the sweetest in a man's life." Cicero described leisure thus, "If the soul has food for study and learning, nothing is more delightful than an old age of leisure. . . . Leisure consists in all those virtuous activities by which a man grows morally, intellectually, and spiritually. It is that which makes a life worth living."

Whether retirement is a curse or a time of adventure, freedom, and renewal will largely depend on you!

Judith L. Howe, Ph.D., is Assistant Professor of geriatrics at the Henry L. Schartz Department of Geriatrics and Adult Development and in the Department of Community and Preventive Medicine of the Mount Sinai School of Medicine. She also serves as Chairman of the Board of Directors of the Project Linkage Housing Fund Development Corporation. After college she entered graduate school, where she was awarded a traineeship in gerontology with the U.S. Department of Health, Education, and Welfare. This experience initiated a career in aging services which has included staff positions at the U.S. House of Representatives and the U.S. Senate, the National Institute on Aging, and her present position at Mount Sinai. She also managed to earn two master's degrees, in sociology and public administration, and a doctorate in social work. She lives with her husband and young daughter near New York City. In her free time, she loves travel and winter sports, particularly skiing and skating, and arts and crafts projects.

Living Arrangements

Judith L. Howe

Introduction

One of the most complex decisions facing people as they grow older is where to live. A home is much more than four walls—it represents security, memories, family, and the possibilities of the future. When thinking about the retirement years, some people consider moving to a new home, perhaps in a different region of the country, but most desire to remain in the same home, or at least community. Although an increasing number of retirement housing options are available, the decision is complicated by confusing terms and overlapping definitions. This chapter presents an overview, definitions, concepts, and principles regarding retirement housing as a guide to decision making. The various choices and issues surrounding living arrangements in the later years are considered, with an emphasis on how one can remain in one's own home. The role of community-based and in-home services and programs is discussed, as well as various measures, such as home adaptations and financial incentives, enabling older adults to stay in their homes.

The 1995 White House Conference on Aging invited public comments regarding themes and issues that should be highlighted at the Conference. After health, long-term care, and income security and other benefits, housing and social and community services were identified as the most important issues facing older people. Several resolutions on housing were passed by the delegates. They call for continued and new governmental initiatives promoting the independence of persons in their homes through a variety of measures, such as linkages with supportive services and tax credits. This reflects concern about the ability to "age in place," which is the preference of most older people, and the need to develop more options enabling older people to remain in their homes as they grow older.

In general, governmental support of affordable housing and incentives to remain in one's home remain quite limited, and there are often weak linkages between provision of services and housing. This has resulted in older people living in inadequate, and sometimes unsafe, housing, and having no alternative but to move from the community to assisted living or nursing home facilities because of unavailable health and social services. For middle and upper income retirees, however, in response to market demands, there has been an upswing in the development of housing options, such as continuing care retirement communities and assisted living facilities.

In the future, the most significant change in housing arrangements for older Americans will be in the number of people living alone. Between 1960 and 1984, the percentage of older adults living on their own increased from 20 percent to approximately 35 percent. Most of these people have been women over the age of 75, with almost half of all elderly over the age of 85 living alone. Most older women living alone are widows, who on average have fewer economic resources.

Overview of Housing for Older Americans

An American Association for Retired Persons (AARP) survey on housing for older adults found that three-fourths of older Americans live in single-family detached homes, 12 percent live in multi-unit buildings, six percent live in semidetached homes, and six percent live in mobile homes. More than 80 percent of people 55 and older either own or are in the process of buying their current homes. While 35 percent of older people do live alone, 49 percent say that they would like to.

According to the AARP, 80 percent of older people in the United States prefer living in a neighborhood comprised of people of all ages. In fact, just six percent of older Americans live in housing designed specifically for older adults. If they were to move, the majority would prefer to live in a small town, the country, or the suburbs, with only 12 percent choosing to live in the city.

Recent data indicate that most older adults prefer to remain in their own homes for as long as possible. In a 1992 national AARP Survey of Americans aged 55 and older, 85 percent said they wanted to stay in their homes and never move. In fact, more than half of older people have modified their homes to make it easier to remain there as they get older. For those wanting to move, the most common reason is to be closer to family. Over 50 percent of those surveyed had not made any plans for future housing arrangements, with the majority of these individuals representing the most vulnerable groups of the older population, such as women, lower income people, and minorities.

Key Concepts

Aging in Place

The ability to remain in one's home as one grows older is referred to as "aging in place." It is dependent on a variety of factors, including the availability of assistance from an informal support system of family and friends and access to and the economic resources to purchase formal services to supplement or substitute for informal care. In addition, the immediate and larger environment must be compatible with changing physical and sensory capabilities. Remaining in one's home can be made possible with various home modifications as well as living in a community that is "elder friendly" in terms of services, programs, and the physical environment.

The Continuum of Care

The continuum of care spans services for healthy and independent older adults to those whose chronic or acute health and other conditions necessitate a higher level of service. For example, the most independent older persons might live in their own houses or apartments with little or no need for assistance. At the other end of this continuum, a highly dependent older individual would require the services of a skilled nursing facility. In between these two extremes are various congregate and shared housing and assisted living programs as well as community-based and in-home services enabling older people to remain in their homes.

Age-Segregated versus Age-Integrated Housing

Both age-segregated and age-integrated housing have advantages and disadvantages. Studies indicate that the majority of older adults prefer age-integrated settings. On the other hand, residents of age-segregated projects and communities report a preference for this arrangement. An age mix of younger and older residents may bring advantages in terms of the formation of support networks, resident participation in management, and the extent of integration into the larger community. However, the potential for conflict already inherent in a non-self-selected mix of cultures can be exacerbated by age differences. In housing built specifically for older adults, such as Linkage House, subsidized rental housing for the elderly that is discussed later in this chapter, people of different ages can be brought together through intergenerational programs. This allows for interaction among the generations in a more limited, yet productive, way.

Health Status

Health is often a basic criterion in determining who is qualified to move into a particular housing setting. In the United States the level of assistance is generally tied to housing type. In most retirement communities, shared housing, and multiunit rental housing, new residents are expected to be healthy and active on arrival. The minimum expectation for most is that new residents can take care of themselves and their rooms or apartments. However, the level of ability and health status often changes over time for residents, and remaining in these living arrangements depends on the availability of community-based and in-home services enabling "aging in place." Since this often proves to be impossible or complicated, residents may choose or be forced to move into another type of housing, such as an assisted living facility, which provides a range of health, social, and housekeeping services.

Privacy and Interaction

A key consideration when choosing retirement housing is the balance between privacy and opportunities for social interaction with others. While the ability to have privacy is key to well-being, the availability of a setting for social relationships is necessary as well. Finding the appropriate balance in a residential setting for older adults can be difficult. Research has shown that satisfaction and well-being are higher for those older people who feel they are in control in deciding when to be with others and when to be alone. In fact, having a sense of control often compensates for other shortcomings in the housing setting. The housing options discussed below offer different levels of privacy and opportunities for social interaction. While remaining in one's home certainly provides a great deal of privacy, the opportunities for social interaction and participation may be more limited than in a planned retirement community.

Range of Housing Types

Introduction

There is an increasing variety of housing options for older adults in the United States that fall somewhere on the continuum of care between independent living and requiring skilled nursing care. Housing for the elderly is often categorized into "independent living" and "assisted living" arrangements. However, this is not an entirely accurate characterization since individuals can remain in one setting, such as the home, and live either independently or with assistance. The housing options listed here, with the exception of assisted living facilities and nursing homes, are generally suitable for older adults needing no assistance and those needing limited services.

- Remaining in one's present home, with or without modifications;
- Shared and cooperative housing;
- Age-segregated retirement communities, including continuing care retirement communities;
- Congregate housing;
- Government subsidized rental housing for older persons;
- ECHO or manufactured housing and accessory apartments;
- Board and care facilities;
- Assisted living facilities; and
- Nursing homes.

Remaining in One's Home

While many older adults wish to remain in their homes as they grow older, this can prove to be difficult because of physical, financial, and service considerations. Increasingly, however, a larger number of measures are becoming available that make staying in one's home a feasible option.   These include:

- Home modifications;
- A community that is "elder friendly";
- Various forms of financial incentives to keep one's home, such as tax credits;
- Formal and informal services;
- Care coordination by a professional; and
- Shared and cooperative housing arrangements.

Home Modifications

Many steps can be taken to adapt one's home or apartment to facilitate "aging in place." As we age normal changes occur in our strength, dexterity, and senses, including vision and hearing. There is, of course, variability among individuals with regard to the extent of these changes. For those older adults who desire to remain in their homes or apartments, it makes sense to modify the existing environment to accommodate changing needs. It should be noted that home adaptations can be made incrementally, in other words, with modifications occurring as the need arises, or, alternatively, homes can be totally retrofitted in anticipation of future needs. The latter can be quite expensive, however, and is not a practical option for most.

There is increasing interest among designers, architects, and consumers in what is called "universal" or "transgenerational" design. In this approach, environments and products are designed to accommodate people of all ages and ranges of ability. Universal design, if applied in all settings, would obviate the need in the future for modifying or retrofitting existing homes and communities by creating environments suitable for individuals of all levels of independence and disability, regardless of age. The 1990 Americans with Disabilities Act heightened awareness of the importance of accessible environments among planners, designers, architects, and consumers. However, presently, there is still limited application of universal design principles and most environments must be modified to accommodate changing needs of individuals as they age.

Most home modifications are quite simple, "low tech" adjustments such as installing European style lever door handles, grab bars in the bathroom, non-skid rugs, higher wattage light bulbs, and handrails by stairs. These are just a few

Making the Old Kitchen Elder-Friendly

The kitchen is, for most of us, the room where the most physical work gets done and where a good share of accidents take place. While a total remodeling with aging residents in mind is the ideal solution to reduce both accidents and strain on the residents, a lot can be done with limited funds. Among the things that can be of help are:

- Rearrange uppper cabinet use so that frequently used items can be reached without excessive stretching or the use of stepstools. Try to arrange as much as possible at eye level and reserve the topmost shelves for special occasion or holiday items when friends and family will be over to help.
- Under-the-counter cabinets can be inexpensively fitted with wire racks with pull out draws that make it easier to get to many more items.
- If a new refrigerator-freezer is needed, consider one with the freezer on the bottom.
- A microwave oven can be a great help in defrosting and heating leftovers and can significantly reduce the number of pots and pans to clean up.
- If the cookware was originally bought for a large family, most of whom have since grown up and moved away, a few new, smaller pots and pans for everday use might be better.
- Some kitchen chores—chopping, slicing, mixing—can be done while sitting. Create a work area where this can be done. Removing one under-the-counter cabinet, installing a drop-down or pull-out shelf, or using a table (if there is room) are a few ways to ease the burden of standing. Be sure the chair or stool is matched to the work surface height and is convenient to use.
- Invest in a few age-friendly tools. Bottle and jar openers and paring knives and vegetable peelers with larger, softer handles are just a few examples. There are dozens available.

of many examples of home adaptations that can be made. The majority of these modifications can be made by home owners themselves, family members, or hired workers. In addition, many local, state, federal, and voluntary organizations provide funding for home maintenance and repairs for older homeowners. Also, in some localities home assessment teams will visit one's home and make recommendations for alterations. Alternatively, arrangements can be made with an occupational therapist to visit the home to give advice.

A more comprehensive and expensive approach is to totally retrofit an existing house in accordance with universal design principles to prepare for all eventualities as the homeowner grows older. This involves modifications such as widening doors to make room for wheelchairs, lowering cabinets so they can be easily reached, installation of an emergency response system, and installation of a walk-in bathtub/shower unit. In addition, a house can be remodeled to include a one-bedroom suite that can be used by a caretaker in the event one is needed. The AARP publishes several excellent guides regarding home modifications, including tips, products and information, and funding suggestions. The Hartford House, a full-scale transportable model home, incorporates universal design features illustrating modifications that enhance independence for older adults. An excellent booklet is available that gives advice about home modifications as well as a listing of products found in the Hartford House. Please refer to the Resource Guide at the end of this book for further information.

The Community

Another important consideration in a housing decision, beyond the home itself, is the larger community. Some environments are more "elder friendly" than others, and this should be considered carefully when choosing where to live. For example, many suburbs were designed for younger families and often lack features needed to promote safety and comfort for older people. A number of measures can make communities more accommodating for the elderly. For instance, it is essential that sidewalks be in good condition since many older people conduct their errands on foot. Changes in traffic lights should be spaced so as to allow sufficient time to cross the street, and major thoroughfares should have pedestrian overpasses. A comprehensive public transportation system is another important consideration for older people. Signs should be large and readable, waiting areas should be well lit, crime-free, and provide cover and seating, and fares should be reduced for older adults during off-peak hours. Further, some communities are more supportive of innovative living arrangements for seniors than others. Zoning laws often prohibit and neighbors may oppose shared housing or board and care facilities for the aged, accessory apartments, ECHO or manufactured housing, and multiunit senior housing projects.

But, beyond these considerations, a hospitable community is one that provides a stimulating and pleasant overall atmosphere for older residents. For some, this can be found in a planned community geared to older adults, many of which offer leisure activities such as golf or tennis. While these planned communities have traditionally been built in the Sun Belt states, such as Florida, Arizona, and California, there is a marked increase in the number of retirement communities being developed in the mid-Atlantic and Northeastern states, in part because of a desire among retirees to be closer to family. In fact, after spending their earlier retirement years in the Sun Belt, an increasing number of retirees are moving back to the more northern regions.

There is also a trend among retirees to move to college towns and cities because of their concentration of educational, cultural, and recreational opportunities, as well as quality health care. For those choosing to move to a rural area, a college town, such as Ithaca, New York, provides not only a lower cost of living for those on a retirement income, but also benefits not generally found in rural areas. For those wanting to live in an urban center, a university city, such as Raleigh, North Carolina or Burlington, Vermont, offers both urban and university-related amenities. In recent years, developers have targeted many of these university locales for senior housing projects.

Financial Incentives

For older homeowners on fixed incomes, maintaining a house can be financially cumbersome. There are programs that provide assistance with housing costs, including a variety of home equity conversions plans. These include deferred payment loans, reverse mortgages, and sale/leaseback arrangements (in the latter, the older homeowner sells his home, usually to a family member, and then leases it back). The most widely available type of home equity conversion is property tax relief, offered by some state and local governments, whereby a loan is made to the older homeowner against the equity of the house. The loan is repaid when the homeowner moves or dies.

Formal and Informal Services

Services enabling older people to remain in their homes can come from the formal, or paid, system of care and the informal care system. The importance of the informal system of care, consisting of family, friends, and neighbors, cannot be underestimated. Research has found that family members, particularly children, are the preferred source of support among older people. Children are often the "bridge" between the informal and formal systems of care, accessing formal services, such as home care and medical services, when these are needed by their parents. This underscores the importance of older adults living relatively close to family members.

There are a variety of paid or formal services that help older people to remain at home or to "age in place." These include the following:

- In-home services;
- Home maintenance and repair programs;
- Community-based programs, such as senior centers, recreation programs, meals-on-wheels programs, and transportation services;
- Services that monitor older people in their homes;
- Care coordination and information and referral services.

In-Home Services

These services include home health and medical care during chronic illnesses or recovery from an acute condition such as a hip fracture. For example, after discharge from a hospital older people often require rehabilitation services. Provision of physical, occupational, and/or speech and hearing therapy in the home allows older people to leave the hospital sooner and may prevent nursing home placement. Nonmedical care for assistance with activities of daily living, such as toileting and dressing, is also important for older people recently discharged from the hospital, as well as those with chronic conditions such as heart disease and diabetes.

There are also a number of "chore" service groups, often in rural areas, that provide a volunteer for an hour or two every week or so to help with difficult home maintenance tasks.

Community-Based Services

For a great many older people living in their homes the key to continued independence and well-being is access to community-based services. These programs include congregate meals, adult day care, and senior centers providing recreation and opportunities for socializing. Special transportation services operated by government agencies are particularly important for older people not able to drive or walk. Transportation services are the "glue" of the social and health care delivery system for older adults and their importance in enabling optimal "aging in place"cannot be underestimated. Supportive living arrangements for the elderly, regardless of the setting, rely on efficient transportation services for older people needing to access community services as well as caregivers traveling to the homes of older people to provide informal and formal services.

Professional Care Coordination

A relatively new development is care coordination for older people and their families. Professionals who provide this service, usually social workers or nurses, assess the client's needs and develop a plan for care. Depending on the older person's situation, the care plan might include medical services, community-based programs such as senior centers or day care, in-home services such as home care or housekeeping, and counseling or support groups. The care plan is monitored by the professional care coordinator and periodically revised as the client's needs change. Care coordination is particularly useful for families with adult children in different regions of the country. It is one more way to assist older adults to age in place.

Shared and Cooperative Housing

During the last 15 years, shared and cooperative housing has gained increasing attention as an innovative approach to meeting the housing needs of older adults. It has become a recognized alternative to traditional housing arrangements by planners and consumers because of its economic, social, and practical advantages. Shared housing can be considered by both older people who own homes and those in need of housing. It is also an attractive option for those interested in age-integrated living environments.

Shared and cooperative housing are attractive choices for the elderly, their families, younger people, and society as a whole. For older people, they are affordable alternatives that allow independence in a setting conducive to companionship, privacy, self-determination, and security. For the families of older people, these arrangements can prevent or forestall other more costly and inconvenient arrangements such as institutionalization or having an older family member live with the family.

There are two general kinds of formalized shared housing programs: match-up and agency-sponsored programs. In the

Linkage House

The Mount Sinai Medical Center in New York City and three community-based organizations—the Union Settlement Association, Greater Emmanuel Baptist Church, and the Community Association of the East Harlem Triangle—have developed a residence for older adults to address a broad spectrum of needs of low-income elderly in the city's East Harlem neighborhood. Linkage House, a 70-unit senior citizen residence, funded by a grant of over $7 million from the U.S. Department of Housing and Urban Development, opened its doors in May, 1997.

Inherent in the Project Linkage vision are five goals:

- To create informal helping networks;
- To promote a sense of productivity;
- To foster autonomy, independence, and self-determination;
- To successfully bridge informal and formal support systems;
- To promote positive interactions among the generations.

The building is designed to facilitate communal living and the formation of friendship and support networks, while maintaining residents' privacy. Each one-bedroom apartment has its own living room and kitchenette and on each floor five apartments are grouped around shared living space. The intent of this design is to eliminate isolation and promote interaction and socialization among neighbors.

The ground floor has greater common space than typical HUD section 202 buildings to provide for larger group activities and an intergenerational after-school program for children. This space is designed to serve as a center for community activities and programs that promote expansion of networks beyond the residence walls. The floor also includes space for building management, social service, and health program coordination. Two medical examination and consultation rooms are used for health screening and education. Mount Sinai is coordinating some on-site health programs and overseeing the overall health care needs of the residents, referring residents to outpatient and hospital services at Mount Sinai Hospital as needed.

Linkage House has been designed to meet the changing needs of residents as they grow older. A social worker assesses residents' needs and links them with community-based and in-home services as needed. While many of the design features were created for flexibility to allow residents to age in place, the level of services offered is not extensive enough for seriously ill or impaired residents. The on-site social worker assists in locating a more appropriate living environment, such as an assisted living facility or nursing home.

match-up type, a non-profit group matches all the homeowners with unrelated individuals. While arrangements of this source have always occurred on an informal basis, there are an increasing number of more structured matching programs throughout the country. In the second type of arrangement, a nonprofit agency develops and sponsors a group-shared residence. These residences house an average of eight individuals, and services such as cooking, cleaning, and laundry are generally provided.

Many homesharers are unmarried, usually because of widowhood, and tend to live in urban areas. Despite the obvious advantages of homesharing, older adults are often reluctant to enter into these situations because of cultural norms that encourage independence and reticence about sharing homes with nonrelatives. Further, it is also difficult to design matches that complement the personalities and lifestyles of the individuals involved. These obstacles are exacerbated by the fact that governmental programs, statutes, and zoning advances have not always been supportive of shared housing arrangements. Nonetheless, some have overcome their reticence to discover the rewards in homesharing. For example, a retired widow who lived near a university rented rooms to a few carefully-screened students. She earned a little money, but more importantly for her, she enjoyed cooking for them on occasion, got some convenient help with household chores, and found her boarders to be intellectually stimulating.

Despite the obstacles, it seems clear that shared housing will become an increasingly popular housing option for older adults for several reasons. The extremely large number of "baby boomers" will necessitate the development of an array of creative living situations in an era of multiple and pressing resource demands. Further, culturally this group is likely to be more accepting of homesharing arrangements than today's older population.

Senior cooperative housing, with its roots in the rural midwest, is an increasingly popular option for middle and lower income elders. Like shared housing, co-op housing can provide an affordable environment promoting independence, autonomy, and self-control. Elders purchase their apartments and pay a monthly bill to cover expenses such as taxes and maintainance.

"Naturally occurring retirement communities," or NORCs, are part of the senior cooperative living movement. These are communities, including apartment buildings, that were not originally intended for older people, but that over a number of years have evolved such that more than half of their residents are over the age of 60. NORCs can enable a continued sense of independence in a familiar setting and a greater concentration of services and programs geared to older adults. In New York City, for instance, ten NORCs have organized services, generally in cooperative apartment buildings. However, these formalized programs serve just a fraction of the estimated 300,000 New York City elderly living in NORCs.

Retirement Communities

There are a number of retirement communities, also referred to as "leisure" or "lifestyle" communities. These are usually age-segregated, planned communities with limited services geared to healthy, independent older adults. Some focus on recreational pursuits such as golf.

Continuing Care Retirement Communities

Continuing care retirement communities (CCRCs), also referred to as life care communities, are planned housing developments that provide a spectrum of living arrangements and services for older people ranging from independent living units to assisted living facilities to skilled nursing units. Residents enter into a contract with the operator to receive services over a period of time, generally for the remainder of their lives. When the resident either moves from the CCRC or dies, some or all of the up-front fee is refunded. Most life care communities cater to the more affluent elderly because of relatively high one-time entrance fees and monthly fees that cover in advance some or all of the services that may be needed in the resident's later years. In other CCRC programs, residents pay for services as they need them.

Life care communities have many advantages to offer because the full continuum of care available provides insurance against future disability. However, there are potential pitfalls, including the loss of some autonomy since the facility may have the ability to shift residents from one level of care to another. Additionally, residents must turn over substantial assets when entering the CCRC, so a great deal of trust must be put into management. In light of past fiscal solvency problems in some life care communities, a decision to enter a CCRC must be very carefully researched and considered.

Congregate Housing

This type of housing offers individual units and common areas for dining, recreation, and socialization in a residential environment with varying levels of supportive services. Generally one main meal a day is offered in a large dining area, as well as other services such as housekeeping. These services may be included as part of the rent or available for an extra charge. These facilities typically have a professional staff with expertise in aging services responsible for recreational and social activities. Ideally, congregate housing should have ties to community-based programs such as physicians, hospitals, and transportation programs, but this varies from site to site. However, congregate care facilities do not provide ongoing monitoring or care, so are not suitable for the more frail elderly.

Subsidized Rental Housing

Federal and state governments subsidize rental housing for lower income older people through subsidies for apartments in senior citizen and family buildings. In addition, the federal government issues housing vouchers for use in non-subsidized buildings. There are age and income guidelines; those who qualify pay 30 percent of their incomes for rental.

The federal government also gives grants to not-for-profit organizations to build housing for lower income older people, with rent subsidies provided for tenants. An example of this kind of housing is described on the opposite page.

ECHO or Manufactured Housing and Accessory Apartments

ECHO is an acronym for "Elder Cottage Housing Opportunity," and is also referred to as manufactured housing. These are small, self-contained housing units that can be temporarily placed in the yard of an older adult's relative or friend if the lot is of suitable size. The concept originated in Australia, where these units are called "granny flats." There are many obvious advantages to ECHO units because of their relatively low cost and ease of installation and removal. They allow an older adult to maintain privacy, yet live in close proximity to a relative or friend, thereby providing opportunities for interaction.

Another low-cost and innovative solution for elder housing is the accessory apartment. Added to a single family home, an accessory apartment has separate living quarters, including a kitchen and a bathroom. An older person can live with a family member or an unrelated individual in an accessory apartment or, alternatively, an older homeowner who is "overhoused" can create an accessory apartment with the rent helping to defray housing expenses. In some cases, rent is reduced in exchange for the renter helping with chores, yard work, or shopping. Like ECHO housing, accessory apartments provide an optimal balance between privacy and social interaction.

Increasingly, communities are changing zoning ordinances which have in the past restricted housing arrangements other than single family residences to allow for creative solutions such as ECHO units and accessory apartments, as well as group shared homes. Often, there are stipulations such as removing the ECHO unit once it is no longer occupied by the older person and ensuring that the unit blends in with the character of the neighborhood.

Board and Care Facilities

Board and care facilities are also referred to as personal care homes, rest homes, domiciliary homes, and group homes, among other names, depending on the state. These residences, which are typically quite small and operated for profit by individuals or organizations, are suitable for older adults who need a good deal of assistance. Housekeeping, meals, and some oversight are provided in board and care facilities. There is great diversity in board and care homes, with some catering to lower income elderly and others to affluent older adults. Because of the great variation among these facilities it is important to gain as much information as possible before entering one.

Assisted Living Facilities

The newest innovation in housing for older adults is assisted living, which can be broadly defined as residential care for disabled older persons. Unfortunately, there is a lack of consensus in the use of the term "assisted living," making a choice among facilities more difficult for older consumers and their families when looking at these facilities. On the continuum of care, assisted living falls between independent living in one's home and a skilled nursing facility. Assisted living settings may be board and care homes with additional services, residential care units adjacent to nursing homes, congregate housing settings with added supportive services, or the middle level of continuing care retirement communities.

While not a nursing home, an assisted living facility provides a certain level of personal care to older adults needing assistance with the activities of daily living. These services in addition to meals and housekeeping, include personal care such as assistance with dressing and bathing, accessing medical care, and being "on call."

Nursing Homes

Despite the prevailing impression, only five percent of people age 65 and older live in nursing homes, also referred to as skilled nursing facilities. The nursing home provides a medical environment for individuals requiring intensive, ongoing medical supervision and is an unavoidable living arrangement in some instances.

Because most admissions to a nursing home result in a stay of less than six months, the nursing home is not always a long term arrangement. It may be a transitional facility, for instance, after a hip fracture, between the hospital and the home. Increasingly, efforts are being made to provide the medical services traditionally found in a nursing home in the older person's home, although this is not always feasible.

Housing Checklist

The decision about whether to move from one's home, and, if so, where, is a complicated one. Generally, the consumer needs to think about these three broad questions:

- Where do you want to live?
- With whom do you want to live?
- How do you want to live?

Beyond these general questions, there are a number of important considerations when making a decision about housing. While it is beyond the scope of this chapter to provide a comprehensive guide, the following points might be considered:

- Availability of health, community, social, and transportation services;
- Access to cultural, recreational, and educational programs and facilities;
- Proximity to family and friends;
- Provisions for more intensive services in the future;
- Whether the setting is age-integrated or age-segregated;

- Cost of living, including taxes;
- Weather and geographical considerations;
- Individual health considerations;
- Desired balance between privacy and social interaction.

It is necessary to carefully plan for future living arrangements well in advance, keeping in mind that needs might change with time. Of course, options regarding retirement housing depend to some extent on factors such as retirement income and health considerations. When looking at planned communities, congregate care facilities, and group residences it is important to interview management, tour the facility, and speak with current residents in order to make certain that needed and anticipated services are offered and the financial arrangements are clear.

Sometimes the best-planned move may prove to be disappointing. A small but significant number of retirees who move to a new community come to regret their decision. This is most commonly found where the move is a considerable one—to a different region of the country or to a community that is less varied in the ages of its residents. The very differences that made the new community seem so attractive—appearing to be like a permanent vacation—can prevent it from ever feeling like home.

But by the time this is realized, a return to the old community is sometimes not economically possible. To protect against such disappointment, you should investigate whether a trial is possible—leasing your current home for six months or a year while you rent a place in the new community.

Conclusion

Most older adults wish to remain in their own homes as they grow older. While there is an increasing emphasis on "aging in place" among planners, policymakers, and consumers, and the development of new options enabling this, there remains a great need for more home- and community-based services. A substantial number of older people also wish to move from their homes for a variety of reasons, including being relieved from the burden of home maintenance, realizing the profits from a home sale, a desire to live closer to family, or wanting to live in a different geographical area. And, for some older people, it becomes necessary to move from the home to an environment that allows for more supportive services. While these settings exist in the form of assisted living facilities, for instance, they are out of the financial reach of many older people. Although the more affluent elderly likely will have the resources to choose among an increasing number of housing options developed by the private sector, the needs of those with more limited means are not being adequately addressed.

Judith C. Ahronheim, M.D., is Chief of the Eileen E. Anderson Section of Geriatric Medicine at St. Vincent's Hospital and Medical Center of New York. Among the many positions she has held are membership on the Biomedical Ethics Committee at the Bellevue Hospital Center in New York, membership on the Ethics Committee of the American Geriatrics Society, Deputy Executive Director of Choice in Dying, President of the New York Metropolitan Area Geriatrics Society, and faculty member of New York University School of Medicine and Mount Sinai School of Medicine. She has published works on a number of geriatric topics in the professional literature and has authored several books, including *Handbook of Prescribing Medications for Geriatric Patients* and *Ethics in Clinical Practice.* She lives in New York City with her husband.

Medical Ethics

Judith C. Ahronheim

Patient Autonomy

Until recently, the approach to medicine was largely paternalistic. When treating medical problems, the physician's recommendation was rarely questioned. One assumed that the physician acted ethically and in keeping with the patient's best interests.

Then, in the second half of the twentieth century, developments in medical knowledge and capabilities raised new and more complex ethical issues that were not so easily defined by the moral principles of right and wrong. Questions of euthanasia, genetic engineering, organ transplantation, and the definition of death itself have led to the study of bioethics, which explores the ethical implications of developments in medicine on the quality and value of health care and human life. This is further compounded by a renewed emphasis on individual rights, and the problems faced by medical practitioners in balancing quality care with the new demands of many HMOs that limit physicians' choices in an effort to reduce costs. Thus, medical ethics now involves medical practitioners, patients, families, theologians, philosphers, and lawyers.

For the patient, the change has been from a paternalistic approach to medicine to one of personal autonomy (also called "self-determination"), which is a fundamental right in American society. In health care, autonomy means the right of an adult patient to make his or her own decisions about medical treatment; patients are encouraged to become informed and assume a responsible role in treatment decisions. A physician has no right to treat you against your will, withhold needed treatment that you would like, or withhold information about your treatment options. These rights are protected by law. Patient autonomy does not mean the physician gives you complete reponsibility for decisions concerning your medical care. Your physician is still responsible for guiding you, answering your questions, making recommendations, presenting your options, and assisting you in the final decision-making process.

Informed Consent

One of the requirements for autonomy is informed consent, which means that the patient has been given adequate information on which to base a decision to agree to a test or treatment. To make a decision and before giving your consent to proceed, you need to be informed of the risks, benefits, and alternatives. For example, if the doctor is advising surgery for back pain, you need to know the chances of improvement with and without surgery, the chance of complications, and whether acceptable nonsurgical alternatives are available, such as medication or physical therapy. Once you have this information, you will be able to make a choice about treatment. A physician is obligated to provide you with this information and to answer any questions you might have about your condition.

In addition, a decision to undergo or refuse treatment must be voluntary. No one—not your doctor, your friends, or your family—can coerce you. Although you may wish to discuss complex medical decisions with family or other trusted individuals, or to seek further medical advice, the final decision belongs to you. Some people want others to decide for them, but giving this authority to others should be the patient's decision alone.

Your right to refuse any and all treatment includes treatment that could save your life. Although some people do so for religious reasons—for example, Jehovah's Witnesses, who are not permitted to receive transfusions—the right to consent or refuse any particular treatment is not based on membership in a particular group and does not require explanation to your physician. For example, if your physician recommended an urgent blood transfusion because of serious internal bleeding, he cannot force you to receive this treatment. This applies even if your refusal costs you your health or your life. Of course, you should seriously consider the risks involved in your refusal, ask questions about the consequences of refusing treatment, and weigh the impact of your decision on others. And your physician will want to question you so that he or she is assured that your denial (refusal of treatment) is informed. In a few specific situations, your autonomy can be challenged.

Challenges to Autonomy

Autonomy, the foundation of patients' rights, may be challenged during medical emergencies, when a patient is unable to handle the responsibility of autonomy, when family members, doctors, and others try to "protect" the patient from negative information, and when the patient has a disability that prevents a clear understanding of the situation and thus, the conveying of a decision about treatment.

Medical Emergencies

A physician can act without your explicit permission in only a few situations. One is an emergency, during which the physician must act promptly and there may not be time to ask your permission. For example, if you were in a serious accident and required urgent surgery, but were unconscious and unable to give consent, surgery would proceed. If your heart stopped beating or you stopped breathing (a "cardiopulmonary arrest"), a doctor or other qualified professional would take immediate action to save your life by performing cardiopulmonary resuscitation (CPR). In an emergency situation, health professionals operate under the assumption that a person would consent to needed treatment unless reliable information to the contrary is presented to them.

Some life-threatening situations can be anticipated, and treatment can be refused in advance. For example, someone who is terminally ill might wish to be allowed to die naturally and avoid uncomfortable treatments that merely prolong the dying process. Even emergency procedures, such as CPR, can be refused as long as the request is made in advance. In the case of CPR, terminal patients or their families can authorize the physician to write a "do-not-resuscitate" (DNR) order, instructing health professionals not to perform CPR.

Therapeutic Exception

Other exceptions to the rule that patients must always be fully informed occur in rare situations. One is if the physician has strong reason to believe that providing the information or imposing the stress of decision making might harm the patient. Under such circumstances, the physician can postpone or withhold information. This situation is referred to as the "therapeutic exception" to informed consent. Examples include someone with serious psychiatric illness or depression, for whom frightening information might lead to suicide, or someone with an unstable heart condition, for whom stress might bring on a heart attack. However, even in these unusual situations, the physician must be prepared to provide the information sensitively and as soon as the patient seems capable of handling it. In all situations the physician must work closely with family members or others who have intimate knowledge of the person's wishes and values.

"Protecting" a Patient

In contrast to the therapeutic exception to informed consent, physicians sometimes withhold information inappropriately. This often arises when the patient is elderly or frail or when family members, usually with beneficient motives, request the patient be "protected" from negative information. In these cases, the real obstacle may well be the doctor's or the family's anxiety about the situation, or their discomfort over breaking bad news to the patient, rather than the patient's unwillingness to hear the information. For example, relatives sometimes implore the doctor not to inform the patient of a cancer diagnosis because the information "will kill her." However, if the patient is fully competent and capable of making her own decisions, she—not the family—has the right to know the diagnosis and consent to—or refuse—treatment options. In fact, the patient must authorize the doctor to inform the family. Sometimes the family's concerns are based on relevant knowledge about the patient, such as a history of severe depression, that the doctor should take into consideration. When the physician informs the patient directly about her condition, the family's disclosure may affect the manner in which the news is given, as well as how much and how fast.

Keeping information from someone is likely to cause more harm than good. If you had a serious illness, you would find out sooner or later, as the illness progressed. To be told "everything is all right" when obviously it is not, can be confusing, cruel, and counterproductive. It can prevent a person from selecting activities and treatments that might alleviate symptoms, planning appropriately for the future, setting one's affairs in order, participating in fulfilling activities that one might put off under other circumstances, and, if a terminal disease is involved, saying one's goodbyes.

It is not necessary for a physician to convey negative information immediately — or all at once. The information can be broken down into smaller pieces and presented sensitively. However, you have a right to receive all information about your condition, so that you can ultimately be in control of your care, regardless of your age. This does not mean you *must* receive this information; your have a right not to know. Most people are anxious about receiving bad news, and many have said, "I don't want to know if I have cancer (AIDS, etc.)." However, when considering the option of not knowing, remember that in the long run, you may well know, and it is probably better to be involved in decisions along the way so that care can proceed as you would prefer.

Decisional Incapacity

"Decisional capacity" refers to a person's ability to make decisions — to understand the nature of the treatment being proposed, weigh the options presented, and make and communicate decisions. Unfortunately, not everyone has the mental capacity to fully comprehend a situation and make an informed decision. One example would be people with severe mental retardation, who have lacked this capacity all their lives. But adults who are able to participate in treatment decisions should be given the opportunity to do so, regardless of their age. Although age alone does not determine whether an adult has the ability to make health care decisions, the chance that a person will experience mental incapacity either temporarily or permanently increases with advancing age.

Temporary decisional incapacity is usually the result of serious medical illness. In addition, people with psychiatric illness may have periods of severe impairment interspersed with normal periods. Permanent incapacity in late life is usually the result of Alzheimer's disease, severe stroke, or other forms of brain disease. Although loss of the capacity to make decisions is not a part of normal aging, Alzheimer's disease and other forms of dementia (once grouped together under the catchword "senility") are common and may impair a person's ability to make medical decisions.

However, even people with limited brain disease may still have the ability to make certain decisions. For example, in the early stages of Alzheimer's disease a person becomes forgetful, but may still retain sufficient intellectual abilities to discuss and make decisions about certain treatments, especially ones that are relatively simple. In such situations, doctors and family members should make an effort to directly involve the person, to the extent possible, in decisions about care. Only when a person clearly lacks these mental abilities should others make all choices for them. Even when it is obvious that a person cannot discuss the complexities of a treatment option, their response to it—for example, agitation when an uncomfortable medical procedure is performed—can be taken into consideration when deciding whether treatment should continue.

Mental incapacity does not necessarily mean a loss of autonomy. Your wishes can still be honored, if you made them known in advance in discussions with your doctor, family, and other trusted individuals. Your doctor and others are obliged to honor the wishes you have conveyed in conversations, but it is better to put them in writing by executing a living will or by appointing someone to speak for you if you are unable to speak for yourself. A living will specifies the kinds of treatment you would or would not want in the event of an incurable illness. A personal appointment for health care decisions is called a durable power of attorney for health care (or a medical power of attorney or a proxy appointment). These "advance directives" are to be used *only* in the event that you are incapacitated. If you can still make decisions for yourself, you are entitled to be the decision maker.

Because one cannot anticipate the array of treatment options that doctors might propose in the case of future illness, no living will or conversations with individuals will cover all possibilities. Certainly someone who has been diagnosed with a specific illness, such as cancer, will have a better idea of what to expect and can discuss specific possibilities in advance with the doctor. If you are healthy, be sure to inform family members or close friends about your health values. Let them know, for example, whether length of life is more important than "quality of life," or vice versa, and what you consider to be a quality of life that is acceptable to you.

Most disputes about treatments at the end of a person's life involve decisions about respirators, tube feeding, and antibiotics for life-threatening infections. Therefore, you should become informed about the benefits and burdens of each of these options and then express your feelings about these specific treatments, including treatment preferences, to those involved in your care.

Autonomy in the Managed Care Era

While your autonomy in deciding medical treatment is a right, it is a right that you may agree to surrender to some degree by contract. With the recent growth in managed care, many more patients have been discovering that some aspects of their autonomy are relinquished to insurance companies or HMOs upon enrolling in a particular plan. Some of these restrictions in autonomy are apparent to the patient from the outset, such as the limitations in choosing a physician or place of treatment. Many others have taken the form of quiet, behind-the-scenes changes in the physician's freedom to prescribe for and treat his or her patients as the physician sees best. This is a significant departure from the traditional unfettered relationship between doctor and patient that most of us have enjoyed through our lifetimes. Some of the plan-imposed restrictions have included:

- **Formulary restrictions.** For any particular ailment, a physician may choose from a number of medications. Under most managed care plans, the physician is restricted to a list drawn up by the plan administrators.
- **Gag rules.** Some plans restricted physicians from telling patients about some treatment options that the plan considered too expensive.
- **Limitations on therapy.** Rehabilitation therapy is severly limited under a number of plans.
- **Limitations on length of hospital stays.** Most plans have a maximum stay period for each reason for hospitalization.
- **How a particular surgical procedure will be performed.** It is the plan that specifies whether a procedure is to be done on an outpatient or inpatient basis.
- **Approval rights to referrals.** Any referral by your physician can be questioned and overruled by the plan administrators.

Occasionally, the physician might request an exception to one of these limitations, but it is a time-consuming process that might mean delay in treatment.

There has been a backlash against some of these restrictions in recent years, resulting in new regulations to control some of these practices in several states. Some of the practices listed above might no longer be allowed where you live, but it varies from state to state. In any event, it is important that you read and understand all the details of any plan before you enroll and keep abreast of any updates or changes to the plan thereafter (read everything you receive about the plan very carefully). If you are unsure of any of the details, your attorney or accountant might be of help.

Our society considers autonomy so important that elaborate legal procedures have evolved to protect this fundamental right. It is important to emphasize that these legal means are designed to protect you—the patient—and not the doctor or the hospital administration. They are not required by a hospital, nursing home, or by the government.

Confidentiality

For a physician to accurately assess your situation and recommend the treatment you need, he or she needs accurate information about your condition. What symptoms do you have? How long have you had them? What brings them on? Makes them better? Have you had any contact with someone else with these symptoms? Have you been taking any medications? Drugs? Alcohol? And so on. For you to provide information, you need to be able to go to your physician with your questions and discuss all problems freely. For this reason, your interview and the results of all tests should be held in strict confidence. Without this guarantee of confidentiality, you might be reluctant to speak up.

The physician and everyone in the physician's office is obligated to keep any and all information strictly confidential. Although important information will be recorded in the medical record (chart), no one can read or photocopy your chart without your explicit permission—not a family member, your employer or a prospective employer, or any government agency. With very few exceptions, the information in your medical record can be withheld from others.

Such strict confidentiality is required so that you feel free to convey to your physician all information that is vital to your health care. If, for example, you abused illegal substances, but were afraid that your physician would tell your employer, your family, or the authorities, you might avoid seeking needed medical attention and rehabilitation.

A few limited exceptions exist to the confidentiality of your medical records. For example, unless you choose to pay for your own medical care, your insurance company has the right to receive information from your medical record. Under many plans, your doctor may be asked to supply complete information not only for current conditions and treatments, but for your entire chart for several years back. In fact, without such access to your records, the company might refuse to pay for treatment. Another exception is when the well-being of others is at stake. For example, if you contracted an infectious disease, such as tuberculosis, while living in a closed community, such as a nursing home or a senior care complex, appropriate personnel would be informed so that others with whom you had contact before your treatment began, could be informed and tested to determine if they also need treatment. In short, when the health of others is involved, your situation may no longer remain completely private. However, confidentiality is seen as so important, that even in these situations, strict limits are put on who can be informed and how.

More difficult conflicts can arise, however. For example, a married person developed a sexually transmitted disease as a result of a relationship outside of marriage. That person asks the doctor not to inform the spouse, even though the spouse may be at risk. In such circumstances, the doctor might feel morally obliged to inform the spouse himself, if he or she cannot convince the patient of this need. In fact, the laboratory involved in testing an infected patient might be obliged by law to report the disease evidence to a health department which, in turn, would do "contact tracing"—that is, to identify and notify any people who might have been infected in order to prevent further spread of the disease. This process might include notifying or treating the spouse. Concern over this disclosure prevents some patients from seeking treatment or encourages them to seek treatment under an assumed name.

Another serious conflict arises when a psychiatric patient discusses violent feelings about a specific individual with a psychiatrist or other psychotherapist. If the patient indicated a specific plan to harm that person, this might create an untenable conflict in which the therapist feels the need to inform the person who was in danger, and, in fact, would probably be legally obliged to do so.

Limits to Autonomy

Just as the guarantee of confidentiality has limits, so does personal autonomy. Although you cannot be forced to undergo unwanted treatment for yourself, your refusal of treatment cannot extend to others, such as a child. For example, as a member of a religious group, you can refuse certain medical treatments for yourself, but you cannot refuse for your child or grandchild, if avoiding the treatment puts the child at substantial risk. The reason is that a young child does not yet have the maturity to form opinions of his own and may, in time, reject your views entirely.

Limits to your own personal autonomy may be imposed in a variety of circumstances, particularly if your decision would adversely affect the health or well-being of others, or if you were to demand treatment that is illegal, unethical, unnecessary, or "futile."

The Well-Being of Others

Autonomous choices may not be honored if they are likely to affect the health of others. If you developed tuberculosis, but were careless about taking medication to control it, you could be overruled. Older people are more likely to develop tuberculosis, for example, than younger people, because of a decline in immunity that occurs with advancing age, as a result of certain illnesses that are more common in late life.

Tuberculosis, for example, is spread through casual rather than intimate contact. If the patient does not take the required medication on a daily basis for the months involved and visit the doctor regularly, the disease can easily spread to other people who are unaware that they are near an infected person. Although most people comply with their medication regimen, some are carelessness, misunderstand the risks and benefits of treatment, or are forgetful. To allow a person maximum freedom during this treatment period, but to ensure that the public is protected, "directly observed therapy" is given to certain patients as an alternative to months of isolation. With direct observation, health care workers visit these patients at home on a regular basis to observe them taking their medication. These visits continue until the patient is free of the disease and no longer harmful to others.

Another group whose autonomy may be limited by society is impaired drivers, who are a danger to both themselves and others. Clearly, people who drive while impaired by alcohol may be incarcerated and lose their driving privileges. But other problems may also limit a person's driving ability, including hearing or visual impairments, cognitive problems, diminished reaction time, or other difficulties that are particularly common in late life. Despite such impairments and the risks they bring to themselves and others, many people continue to drive. Although some people may not recognize how significant their impairments have become, for others it reflects the need to maintain one's independence. In most American communities, the decision to giving up driving permanently can severely alter a person's lifestyle, making it difficult to shop and perform other important tasks. As a result, it can lead to social isolation, loneliness, and depression.

When it becomes obvious to others that an elderly driver "should no longer be driving," family, friends, or a physician generally advise the person to stop or severely limit driving to ideal conditions (for example, during daylight hours and in good weather), at slower speeds, and in familiar places. As a result, if an accident occurs, it is at a slower speed and causes less damage than accidents involving younger drivers. In stark contrast to young males, who cause by far the highest total number of accidents, older drivers appear to drive relatively safely. However, older drivers cause more accidents per mile driven, and when involved in automobile accidents have a higher fatality rate.

Although an impaired driver might harm others, the physician is usually not legally required to report such a person to the authorities. Only in a very few states and for a very small number of medical conditions is a physician required to report a specific impairment to the department of health or the motor vehicle bureau. This is in keeping with the principle of confidentiality, which is intended to enable someone who is unwell to feel free to seek a physician's help. The decision to report medical impairments to the motor vehicle bureau are almost always left up to the driver. Many states even allow drivers to renew their licenses by mail, without even appearing for a vision test. Even when renewal requires a repeat vision test, the test is simple and does not include an evaluation of night vision, perception of movement ("dynamic visual acuity"), or reaction time, all of which are often impaired in older drivers who still have adequate visual acuity to pass the vision test.

It is essential for impaired people or their families to find alternatives to driving, such as public transportation, local pickup services, delivery of groceries and other goods, and the helpful resources of community volunteers and agencies. A local senior resource center or office on aging can usually provide information.

Unnecessary or "Futile" Treatment

Another limit to autonomy is that a physician is not required to render treatment that is not medically indicated or necessary. For example, if you believed you needed a certain medication or operation, but your physician disagreed, the physician is not required to follow your wishes. You have the right to obtain another physician's opinion, but if there were no need for the treatment, you would probably not receive it (and probably ought not to) even if you demanded it.

A more complex issue is "medical futility." A physician is not required to render treatment that he or she considers medically futile, although not everyone agrees on the definition of futility. For example, a patient or family might demand that the physician "do everything" for someone who is dying. This might include artificial life support, such as mechanical ventilation (a breathing machine) even if it could never restore the patient's ability to breathe on his or her own. One side argues that this treatment is futile because it not only fails to cure the patient, but fails to even relieve the symptoms or restore function. Others argue that as long as a treatment does something — for example, even to just keep the person alive for a few more days, then it is doing what it was designed to do — support breathing and maintain life. The precise definition of futility is partly a philosophical issue, but it has important practical implications. Without agreement on the definition, there can be only limited guidelines on how far technology should be permitted to go. When requests for life-sustaining treatment seem extreme, physicians generally comply. They do so not because they necessarily agree with the request, but because under the law, life is generally prolonged unless evidence exists that the patient would want it otherwise. However, the longer the treatment continues, or the more extreme the request, the more the "futility" argument makes sense in the minds of health care providers. For example, a demand for continued respirator treatment in a patient expected to die from a terminal illness within a few weeks might seem less extreme than if the demand were made for a patient in an irreversable coma, for whom treatment might continue for a year or more. Increasingly, in the climate of skepticism over the limits of technology and the need to limit excessive expenditures for health care, these kinds of extreme requests are being carefully reviewed. A new development is that health providers rather than patients are now going to court to stop treatment.

Demands for "futile" treatment comprise a small minority of disagreements between patients and their health care providers. Most disagreements at the end of life involve the patient (or family's) wish to terminate life-sustaining treatment against the doctor or hospital's desire to continue it. The majority of Americans, according to numerous studies and public opinion polls, do not wish to continue treatments that prolong the dying process without alleviating discomfort.

Illegal or Deemed Unethical Treatment

Another limitation to autonomy is in the realm of unethical or illegal treatments. For example, a person cannot expect to obtain an unlimited supply of drugs, such as narcotics or stimulants, if he or she does not have a disease that requires such medication. Nor can a person expect assistance in performing suicide or euthanasia, even if he or she is suffering from an incurable illness.

"Assisted suicide" is the process of providing the means to help another person kill himself or herself. This may mean, for instance, the acquisition of a prescription for a legal dose of medication. Euthanasia (sometimes called "active" euthanasia) is a word derived from Greek, that means "good death." It is a process in which an individual, such as a physician, takes direct action to produce death painlessly, for example, by lethal injection. Euthanasia, which is currently illegal in the United States and most other countries, is treated as homicide under the law, even when requested by the patient. The United States Supreme Court recently held that terminally ill patients have no constitutional right to physician-assisted suicide and returned the issue of assisted dying to the States. Assisted suicide is technically illegal in the overwhelming majority of states, but even in those few jurisdictions where no law governs assisted suicide, physicians and others are reluctant to openly participate in this practice because they fear legal repercussions or because of personal moral opposition.

Great—often emotional—debate occurs over the practices of assisted suicide and active euthanasia (collectively referred to as "assisted dying"). Many people feel that the physician is obligated to relieve suffering by available means, including actively ending someone's life. They argue that it is not always possible to provide complete relief from pain and suffering. Others argue that pain and other symptoms can always be relieved and that cases of intractable pain and suffering that cannot be relieved by ordinary means can be alleviated by producing a general state of anesthesia with high doses of morphine or potent sedatives. However, many people find oversedation unacceptable; they contend that the patient, not doctors or the government, should determine the time and conditions of death. Moreover, the argument continues, little or no difference exists between producing anesthesia in the dying and using a slightly higher dose to actively cause death. The difference, however, may be one of intent, and this difference is important and fundamental to many people. Another argument often presented against assisted dying is that it would lead down a "slippery slope," which would end in involuntary euthanasia of people who were very old, physically disabled, mentally retarded, or were members of some other vulnerable group. The counterargument to this states that stringent safeguards could be adopted to allow euthanasia only for people who request it repeatedly after all other means have failed to cure or relieve suffering. Others argue simply that assisted dying is morally wrong.

Regardless of one's point of view, the law and the moral opposition that physicians and others feel place limits on the patient's autonomy when it comes to certain requests.

Forgoing Life-Sustaining Treatment

Whereas assisted suicide and active euthanasia are highly controversial and generally illegal, far less controversy exists about allowing a person to die of natural causes by withholding or withdrawing artificial life support (sometimes called "passive euthanasia"). For example, if someone has advanced, incurable cancer and is being kept alive on a respirator, this person (or a family member or other person authorized to make this decision) can request that the respirator be turned off so that death can occur naturally. In fact, it is considered unethical and illegal for a doctor or institution to continue treatment against a person's wishes in this circumstance. This holds for virtually any medical treatment, including surgery, artificial nutrition or hydration (feeding tubes or intravenous lines), and antibiotics.

Maximum Pain Control

Another situation that differs from assisted suicide and active euthanasia is the treatment of terminally ill persons with high and potentially dangerous doses of sedatives or pain medication to relieve suffering. People who are near death may be very sensitive to these medications, and in a few situations, the amounts required for comfort may decrease blood pressure or impair breathing to the extent that death could be hastened, though only by minutes or hours. In such situations, however, withholding pain-relieving medication might result in intolerable suffering. There is a consensus among medical ethicists and within the legal system that the theoretical hastening of death, when death is imminent, is an acceptable risk, because the purpose of the medication is to comfort and not to kill. This is the principle of "double effect," in which the intended effect (comfort) has an unintended second effect (hastening death). Moreover, it is difficult and perhaps impossible to know in these circumstances if it is the disease or the medication that is responsible for the precise moment of death, and when doses are given carefully and increased gradually, most patients are not in danger from the medication itself.

The moral arguments surrounding end-of-life treatments have been debated for many years, and although there is a consensus, there is not unanimity. Some people, including some physicians, are opposed to withholding and withdrawing life-sustaining treatments, considering every moment of life precious and the prolongation of life fundamental, regardless of "quality of life" or the burdens imposed by the treatment. Some might consider foregoing one type of treatment acceptable (for example, respirator treatment in advanced lung cancer) but not another (for example, artificial nutrition and hydration in a person who is permanently unconscious). In the case of artificial nutrition and hydration, opposition frequently is based on the false assumption that foregoing it is painful, although no exists evidence that this is the case, and there is substantial evidence that feeding by tube may cause discomfort in patients who are unable or unwilling or too weak to eat or drink. If a physician disagrees with a patient about any treatment, and both fully understand the burdens and benefits, it is the patient's own values that govern. A physician who disagrees with your wish to forego a particular treatment cannot force treatment on you. However, the physician is a moral agent, just as the patient is, and cannot be forced to participate in treatment that he or she finds morally unacceptable. In this situation, the physician would have the option of transfering your care to another physician.

Some people may feel that withholding life-sustaining treatment is permissible because it allows a person to die naturally, but withdrawing a treatment once started is taking a more active role and is equivalent to "killing." Nonetheless, among ethicists and under the law, withholding treatment and withdrawing treatment once it has begun are considered morally equivalent. Consider the case of a person who would not have wanted a particular treatment in the first place, but for some reason treatment was begun. Later, if it became ap-

Easing the Pain of Dying

When medicine can no longer fight off a life-threatening disease, and the physicians, family, and patient realize the futility of continuing such treatment, the nature of treatment must change. The emphasis must shift from cure to comfort, and the patient must be made as comfortable as possible by controlling pain and dispensing with the the intense atmosphere of high-tech medicine.

The role of family and friends also changes. They are no longer bystanders who play a secondary role to medical practitioners. Now, professionals move to the background and quietly provide the services and facilities for the patient, family, and close friends to share the time together until the patient's death. Then, when the patient does die, that professional support network will be there to help in the bereavement process for those left behind.

This continuum of support is best realized in the concept of modern hospice. Hospice services, depending upon the particular patient's needs, can be administered at home, at a hospital, or in a dedicated hospice facility. The services include equipment (for example, the rental of a hospital bed or oxygen equipment for the patient's home), spiritual counseling, in-home nursing (both for the patient's direct benefit and to relieve the family and friends acting as caregivers), needed medication for comfort, medical and psychological services, and physical therapy. Hospice is generally available to anyone whom a doctor certifies has six months or fewer to live and who wishes to stop trying to treat the terminal disease. Medicare has covered these benefits since 1982, but the program is still unknown by great numbers of people.

Unfortunately, even when patients and family elect to use hospice, referrals often wait until the very last stages of the terminal illness. A 1996 article in *The New England Journal of Medicine* reported that delay was so long that more than one in seven patients died within a week of enrolling in hospice. Confronted with a terminal disease, patients, families, and physicians need to consider hospice earlier.

parent that this was not what the patient would have wanted or that it was not working, it would be permissible to stop it. There is value in equating withholding and withdrawing. If someone were seriously ill, it offers the opportunity to try a treatment in the hope of providing a remission from illness, for example, by providing mechanical respiration through the use of a ventilator. If it were not permissible to later stop this treatment, physicians might be reluctant to start it, for fear that they might be consigning the patient to the respirator indefinitely.

Some doctors or family members might find it more difficult than others to decide to withdraw a treatment once started. Moreover, it is medically different to withdraw a respirator from a conscious patient than to have withheld it in the first place, because sudden cessation of treatment can produce air hunger and great discomfort. In this situation, the doctor must be prepared to administer sedating medication to ensure comfort before stopping mechanical ventilation, in which case the doctor needs to overcome any misgivings he or she may have about the possible "double effect" of the medication.

Whatever the specific circumstances, the patient and family should be able to be confident that the physician will be able to relieve pain and suffering, and that he or she is committed to answering their questions and working towards a death that can be peaceful and personally meaningful.

Pearl S. German, Sc.D., is Professor Emerita at Johns Hopkins University. During her long and varied career—caseworker for several service organizations and a metropolitan hospital, research analyst for the Social Security Administration, and teaching and health services research—she has had the benefit of exploring the dynamics of relationships between the elderly and their family and friends from several aspects. She has served as Director of the Interdepartmental Program in Gerontology in Public Health at Johns Hopkins, Chair and founding member of the Maryland Gerontological Association, Chair of the Gerontology Health Section of the the American Public Health Association, and Chair of the Baltimore Area Agency on Aging. Her many honors include the Key Award of the Gerontology Section of the American Public Health Association, the Stebbins Medal of Johns Hopkins University, and, particularly satisfying for a teacher, the Teaching Quality Recognition Reward of the Johns Hopkins Student Assembly. Today, partially retired, she feels she brings to her consulting work not only this professional experience, but the perspective of her own age. Though still busy, she finds the time to enjoy the inestimable pleasures of grandparenthood.

Relationships with Family and Friends

Pearl S. German

The importance of human relationships is celebrated everywhere. The crucial precept that "people tend to live in groups" affects research and theory in the humanities, sciences, and arts. In almost every society, the family serves as a living example of the strength and importance of human interaction and mutual support.

These important human bonds can take many different forms. For example, social relationships, in all their complex states, influence individual behavior and decision making. They often guide research in creating strategies designed to solve problems, thereby improving the lives of members of specific groups in the population. Although ongoing debate exists about how best to maintain and strengthen groups, the importance of interactions among individuals is unquestionably the basis of a functioning society and the source of support for the people in it.

The differences among people and their needs can be clearly understood by considering our own relationships with family members, friends, colleagues, community service personnel, and, even, local merchants. The need for these relationships and the ways in which people interact varies among people and over time. Observations of a broad array of groups reveal that not everyone interacts the same way, even with close individuals. Every individual's needs change as a result of age, circumstances, environment, and unpredictable occurrences. For example, an individual who is 65 and healthy has different needs and requires different support than does a person who is 85 and frail. Similarly, temporary injuries, limited physical pathology, and trauma may mean limited periods of dependency, but deteriorating dementia, terminal illness, and permanent disability mean an increasingly permanent need for intense help. To provide the appropriate type of help requires careful assessment, so that the caregiver understands what will be most supportive. Underlying all these scenarios, however, is the ongoing importance of human interaction. While many relationships are enduring, all are changing in some way. The one irrefutable conclusion is that relationships are important, necessary, positive, and play an important role in the lives of all people.

Thus, in planning to assist any individual in need, all available resources need to be evaluated. Appropriate social support, or the lack of it, has been associated with the course of disease, the ability to live independently, and the general quality of and satisfaction with life. In some cases, family members and close friends can provide the necessary care. An individual's complicated web of relations with family, friends, and other significant people is commonly referred to as *the social support network*; this type of support is called *informal support*. A study of the interactions between the network and the individual, particularly of how the network meets the needs of individual, can be used to profile an overall life situation. It can also be used to summarize the overall resources available to the older person. If this informal support proves inadequate, various community service institutions and/or health care systems can then combine with professional caregivers to totally or partially meet the individual's unfulfilled needs. This resource is known as a *formal support* network.

This chapter presents situations in which various kinds of relationships function to produce a positive effect on the lives of older individuals. In describing these relationships, the specific nature of social support will be discussed, along with the kinds of stresses—physical, social, and psychological—that people face as they age. Even when *formal* and *informal* relationships work successfully to meet the specific needs of older people, stress is created on all parties. These tensions need to be understood so that both the caregiver and receiver will be prepared for the normal push and pull involved in such relationships.

The Social Support Network of Older Individuals

Two forces influence the nature and strength of social support networks for older individuals. Older individuals have had the opportunity to develop many contacts through work (including homemaking), leisure activities, religious institutions, and/or community activities. In most cases, they have developed extensive friendships of varying degrees of intensity. Finally, most have two families—their childhood families and their own children. All of these are potential sources of support, although the strength, depth, and variety will vary from individual to individual and within any social network. For the individual, the role of the different members of this network vary. For example, access is an important consideration. Family members, particularly children and friends of long duration, may live far away; friends and family members may be ill or die; and the older individual may need to relocate for financial, social, or health reasons. Thus, even if older individuals may continue making new friends, they more often are confronted by a diminishing pool of individuals who are important to them.

This pool needs to be summarized when assessing an individual's support network. Clinical evaluation and planning for an older person includes methods for characterizing networks and the relationships that make up that support system. The first step is to assess the larger system of *informal* support; then, the appropriate *formal* support system can be created.

Informal support comprises all of the help given by family members, friends, neighbors, and anyone close to the individual. The help, which includes a broad array of activities, is usually given without remuneration and often on an "as needed," nonstructured basis.

Formal support comprises a variety of services given under the auspices of religious, public, and private community organizations, including health care service agencies. Although a cost may be involved, demonstrated need and lack of funds can sometimes result in no-cost or very low-cost services. The professionals who are associated with these supports provide direct service, supervise volunteers and others, and provide referrals to other sources of community services.

Support is not only divided into formal and informal; it is also characterized by type—emotional, social, physical, and financial. Often, more than one type of service is combined in the care given to an individual.

Emotional support covers psychological and caring expressions about people and their personal problems. We are all familiar with this kind of support, which is often given in situations that cannot be changed (for example, a loss through death) and in combination with other types of support that may engender particularly uncomfortable responses in the individual receiving care.

Social support includes activities that help a person become more involved with others or facilitates continuation of an existing relationship. This is a continuous process, but specific efforts may be required with older individuals. Examples of this support are invitations to events, transportation to events, and home visits.

Physical support assists individuals with all activities related to everyday living. As people age, they may be unable to carry out essential daily tasks or may be able to do so only with help. Such support includes regular and systematic assistance with medical care; daily personal care; housecleaning; cooking, and shopping.

Financial support involves the transfer of funds to the person in need. It can run from total support to supplementing of income to specific funds for special needs that arise.

These sources and types of support illustrate the range of services that networks offer and give examples of the number of ways in which family members, friends, and community services are essential. The need for social supports can be more fully appreciated after considering the problems, experiences, and challenges of growing older.

The Special Role of Support for the Aging Population

Throughout life, everyone needs a group of individuals with which to be close. Each age group has specific needs that require attention from and interaction with others. In infancy and childhood, for example, such nurturing groups are essential to the survival and well being of the young. Later, children learn new skills and the importance of social interaction through play groups and friends. This essential need continues during adolescence and young adulthood, but in a less urgent and life sustaining way. For the older person, however, this group of caring people can be essential, if sporadically required. The needs of older people, which are very specific to the aging process, can be remarkably different.

A good deal of attention and compelling anecdotal material has described the abandonment of older individuals by their families. Stories are told about demented elders left in a public place with a box of diapers and no identification; the widely publicized "warehousing" or dumping of elders in nursing homes with no ongoing and regular visiting or monitoring of their welfare; and the isolation of older people in dreary, substandard one-room residences eating dog food. These stories underscore the importance of continuing care on the part of family members and friends. As these scenarios, many of which are no doubt true, are examined, a number of facts need to be kept in mind.

First, not all old people need direct help to survive or to avoid dying earlier than they should. Rather, they need close relationships to enrich their lives, increase their satisfaction with life, and stay healthy.

Second, most systematic studies of older people living in communities as well as in institutions such as nursing homes and retirement communities do not substantiate charges of widespread abuse. True isolation is relatively rare among seniors and is difficult to define. In nursing homes, for example, most patients have visitors and the majority of families are known to the administrative and professional health staff because of discussions of inquiry and/or complaints. Additional evidence is provided by several studies of nursing home admissions. In these studies, the researchers required information from informed family members who had been expected to be reluctant participants. Instead, most families were very involved with the nursing home resident and were eager to describe the events leading up to placement. In many cases, the family had been reluctant to place the individual, felt guilty about having done so, and found that discussing the events helped them by demonstrating to society that they had no viable alternative. Most researchers concluded that in the vast majority of cases, families and friends remain actively concerned about an older person and institutionalization is selected because no other feasible option is available.

This is not to say that isolation does not exist either in the community or in institutional settings. In some instances, an older person will reject or refuse the comfort of family and friends. However, the more likely scenario is that the older person cannot recover from the loss felt over the death and/or alienation of close friends and family. In such situations, community resources with outreach programs may be more successful in meeting the needs of older individuals. Occasionally, there are rare individuals who do indeed prefer the solitary life. Recently, a strong-minded literary woman in her late seventies wrote a memoir describing her experiences during a snowed-in winter in Maine. She deliberately chose this experience following the death of a dear companion to test her survival ability and resources.

For most people, however, growing needs are met by support networks that consist of family members, friends, and organized community resources. The availability and proper use of such resources remains crucial in meeting the special needs that occur in later years. Although the informal support network has, of course, carried out this function for generations, the addition of the formal support network has helped to extend the individual's ability to live independently, avoid or limit the impact of disabilities, and recover from or contain a critical health problem. These findings are support by observation, research, and, in some cases, randomized clinical trials (RCTs). RCTs are undertaken to evaluate the effect of intervention by comparing groups that have had specific intervention with a those that have not. Intervention can take many forms. For example, it can mean testing the potency of a new drug or an old drug used in a new way against a disease or condition; testing the application of health care services, including certain relatively high-tech procedures, in the outcome of some condition; and investigating and assessing the impact of ancillary services, such as physical therapy, health education, and psychological counseling).

Studies that examine and evaluate the role of social supports on the problems of older people show that intervention is often a way of increasing or shoring up existing social networks by assisting family members and friends with the responsibilities of caring for an older person. When the formal network assists with some activities, family members and friends, who may be unable to provide all of the necessary care, feel more comfortable providing the personal support an individual needs. If an informal support network does not exist, then the formal network can try to supplant it. Thus, relationships among the various members of the social support network can be complicated and have very long histories. They need to be carefully evaluated in seeing that all of the needs of individuals are met.

As people age, significant changes take place in everyone. These changes create new needs that are best addressed by a network of concerned, interested, and able family members and friends. Many older people handle these changes gracefully, using associations with other people in their environments to assist. For social and psychological reasons, all of us require some degree of interaction with people important to us. In fact, this interaction is a sign of being part of society. What, then, are some of the factors that distinguish the older individual's use of a support network to meet different and more crucial needs.

Physical and Health Status

While aging does not mean long-term disease and disability, the evidence shows that the incidence of these conditions does increase as people age. Other changes affect body mass, the condition of skin and bone, and organ functions. These changes can often decrease one's ability to carry out daily activities and to maintain the same level of social and physical activities that had characterized earlier years. Yet, these activities are often the very ones that individuals wish to continue. The major concern, of course, is that the less one is able to perform the activities of daily living, the greater is the threat to independent living. The more an individual needs assistance with routine tasks, the more likely it is that the individual will have to accept confined living with others or will have to be placed in an institution.

For an older individual to continue to live independently, assistance can be provided in meeting the needs of daily living. Someone else can perform these functions or can assist the individual as much as necessary. The individuals who are most likely to make and implement such decisions are family members and close friends. The more this group is willing to provide the necessary support, the longer an older individual will be able to remain in the familiar surroundings of home.

However, other factors affect the ability of one's family members and friends to function as an informal support network. Over the generations, the nature of the family has changed. The increased movement of individuals and families has seen an end to the tight family community that existed at the beginning of the twentieth century. This is now a comparatively rare phenomenon found largely in rural areas — and even there, the flight of young people is evident. Much more common is a geographically far-flung network of family and friends. These factors have no doubt influenced the growth of community services, which visit and help make arrangements for older people with a geographically less accessible informal support network.

Adapting to Changes in Health Status and Function

For all older individuals, although at different paces and with different outcomes, the loss of the geographically close family is a life adjustment that often causes unhappiness and, at the very least, an upheaval in the rhythm of one's life. Somehow, everyone involved must adjust to this loss of geographically proximity. The social web created by family, friends, and acquaintances is the strongest source of help for older people. The existence of such a web enables the older person to move positively into the later years. Therefore when this group becomes less available, any loss of functioning poses a greater threat to independent living. These elderly must confront a decrease in physical strength with increasing medical problems and altered functioning.

The older person must cope with two major insults simultaneously: loss of strength and other signs of being old on the one hand and the need for assistance on the other. These factors may diminish an individual's view of him or herself as a functioning, able person. The need for assistance with routine tasks has a psychological impact on the older individual. In general, psychological problems are easier to resolve if the older individual has a close, positive, and long-standing association with the caregiver. The nature of this relationship will determine if close family members and friends can provide the proper structure for achieving the best results. If the relationships are difficult to begin with for either party, the psychological effects of the individual's growing physical needs may well go unheeded. In such cases, close kin and friends are better advised to supervise someone else who will deliver the direct care or even to seek community/professional services and step back while they are being delivered.

When an individual seems unable to adapt to changes, psychological counseling may provide part of the answer. There are geropsychiatrists, social workers, and psychologists expert in handling problems of aging. In addition, some home health caregivers are trained and, as a result of their experiences with the problems of the elderly, particularly sensitive to the needs of older people. The resolution of psychological problems is crucial, because they often impede the way in which an older person handles changes and adjusts to necessary help. The way older people respond to

Illness and Alienation

When illness requires hospitalization, it is quite common for both patient and family to feel alienated by the experience. For the patient, such alienation is an impediment to recovery. Many elder patients are particularly affected, but an understanding of the causes and some simple responses can do much to overcome this.

In the first place, despite recent changes in design and decoration, a hospital is not a good substitute for home—it is technological and antiseptic in both intent and appearance. Moreover, while the hospital's existence is due to the patient, the hospital's routine is organized to serve the staff. Much of the medical work (physicians' rounds, tests, physical training) takes place in the morning and so visitors are not allowed at that time. When family and friends do arrive to visit, it is only after the patient has had a long day filled with efficient strangers. And the visitors tend to arrive all at once and compete for chairs, attention, and expressions of good will. Young children may not be allowed to visit. The food, usually eaten alone, is wholesome and dietetically correct, but often not quite what the patient would really like.

A little planning and effort can make a big difference.

- A phone call or two in the late morning would probably be welcome. Find out if there is a morning snack or juice time and you can have a relaxed telephone coffee klatch.
- Try to have family and friends come at staggered times during the visiting hours and meet in smaller, more comfortable groups. Teenagers could come in the afternoon immediately after school.
- Bring some familiar items from the patient's home to personalize the room—some pictures, a scarf for a dresser, a chess set for a frequent player.
- Let a family member or two join the patient for dinner in the hospital. Check with the medical staff for the availability of guest meals or the possibility of bringing food from home.
- Above all, do all these things with the patient's consent. All will be wasted if he or she loses a greater sense of autonomy, by your just taking charge and imposing your program.

help directly affects their ability to continue to live independently.

Another approach is to make the best use of more intimate, informal caregivers by giving them support and help in dealing with the psychological problems that accompany increasing dependency. That there is stress for both caregiver and care receiver is a well-documented issue that will be discussed at a later point.

Dealing with Loss

Another psychological stress for older individuals is the loss of family and friends. The longer one lives, the greater these losses become. Unfortunately, these losses are often accompanied by increasing physical limitations. The most critical losses are of spouses, siblings, and life-long friends — people with whom the older individual had a meaningful relationship. Most of these losses occur because of death among people who in the older person's cohort (age group). This loss of a valued family member or friend means a loss of companionship that ushers in a period of mourning. In addition, it may increase anxiety by bringing on thoughts of one's own death. The occasion of the death of a younger person crucial to the older person is a particularly difficult loss, but fortunately, it is far less frequent than loss of one's cohorts. In general, these difficult events are, in most cases, best handled by other individuals close to the older person.

The older individual may also experience loss because of geographical relocation — either by the support person or the individual. If the older person is relocating, it is a double blow. The person must not only face leaving a familiar place, often at the cost of less independence or autonomy, but must also cope with the loss of those individuals who may have represented an important source of support.

A more subtle loss is the usually slow erosion of status and friends that results from retirement or leaving the workplace. When an individual retires, the status that work provided is retired as well. If the person is still strong and functioning, other activities, such as volunteer work and travel, may serve as substitutes. Although the status is not the same, these activities enable the individual to retain some identity through work and achievement. If the retirement occurs later or because of poor health, it is often viewed as a doubly unwanted occurrence that represents the loss of physical vigor and of the career/job status. This is another example of how an older person must often deal with multiple blows to his or her self-identity and status and to the type of life style that the previous status had bestowed.

Not all individuals find retirement onerous. Relief is often experienced if work had become burdensome and if symptoms and emerging medical conditions created demands beyond the resources of the individual. Although this is a more comfortable transition, there may be a certain amount of uneasiness at no longer doing "work." This uneasiness can be addressed by family members and friends. Friends, most likely to be in the cohort of the older person, can recount their own experiences and reassure the retiree. Family members can explain that such activities are no longer demanded of the older individual; indeed, they may possibly be detrimental. Retelling life experiences enables older people to review their lives and accomplishments, thereby helping them to accept their new life.

Clearly, growing older involves adapting to an incredible amount of change. To make this adjustment requires considerable support. It cannot be emphasized enough that close associations represent the most promising milieu within which to offer this support. If, however, such support is not always available or sufficient, community resources are available to assist both the older person and the individuals making up the support system. Both the older individual and those offering help need to know when outside, more formal, community resources are required either to supplement or to assume the task entirely.

The goal is always to ensure the highest level of independent functioning possible and the greatest satisfaction, as defined by elderly individuals for themselves. Younger individuals can have a very different perspective of what is a satisfactory—or acceptable—life for an older person. All of the problems discussed in this section must be addressed to achieve independent living and maintain an acceptable quality of life. A certain balance must be reached so that the older individual reaches a degree of acceptance and adaptation to a feasible level of function, even if all problems are not solved.

Stress of Both the Caregiver and the Older Person

The stressors to which older individuals are exposed can be found in the changes—physical, psychological, economic, and social—that accompany the progression of life. Examination of the many changes and increasing needs experienced by all people as they age includes looking at the nature of the stress these changes bring. For older people, this stress is centered within the individual and has its most direct effect on overall function. Although changes within older individuals are often dramatic, their ability to adapt depends on the environment in which they experience such changes and how others perceive and handle these changes. As noted, the vast differences among people make for very different reactions and degrees of strength in dealing with such change. As a result, the ultimate impact of the aging process is not the same for everyone. Some experience a very graceful, active, autonomous aging. For individuals in this category, the diseases and conditions associated with aging have often been, to their good fortune, moderate and manageable, resulting in a minimal need for help. Other individuals experience severe physical, mental, and social decrements resulting from a combination of disease and a rapid pace of bodily changes. These individuals need a great deal of support.

In addition, any new physical or mental change may be accompanied by stress that requires a new combination of support at different level of intensity. This can include direct help from others, as well as help from those who are organizing different resources keyed to the needs of the individual. Often, the helper may best supervise others in the community, who are more experienced in providing the needed care. The older person receiving help must approach that need in a positive way. Both the giver and the recipient are in a sensitive position. They need to recognize each other's feelings and understand the problems that can arise in this important relationship. This sensitivity to each other is necessary if the goals of caregiving are to be met. Major concerns center on the loss of status on the part of the older individual, particularly the need to take rather than give, and perhaps on economic issues. Recipients of care most certainly feel a loss of self-direction and autonomy. All of these common problems occur at different points and in varying degrees for different people. Thus, how the care is delivered and how the recipient feels is affected by whether the need for care is temporary or permanent, whether it includes personal care or household tasks, and who the caregiver is.

The other side of the coin reflects the feelings, status, and problems of the caregiver. If the caregiver is experiencing stress, it will be mirrored in the caregiver's behavior. If long-standing, unresolved problems still exist with friends and family members, the stress on both the giver and receiver will be intensified. A caregiver who is under stress must still be sensitive to the stress experienced by the older person. If this is not the case, the stress will increase for the older person regardless of whether the caregiver is part of the informal and formal support network.

The Function of Social Support Networks

Clearly, family members and friends play an essential role in the lives of older people, who can experience a variety of problems during the aging process that lead to a need for help. For help to be effective, both the giver and recipient need to understand each other's role and the goals of the help program. When necessary, the support offered by the informal network can be supplement or replaced by the services of appropriate community and national organizations.

Often family members and friends first become caregivers, either directly or indirectly, during a crisis, when there is little time to consider the what, who, when, and for how long care is required. However, once these crises become less intense, time exists to consider alternatives or to moderate the plan that had been set in motion to deal with the crisis. There is always a need to make arrangements that are more efficient, less costly, more enduring, and more acceptable to both friends and family, as well as to the older person. Other concerns that can now be investigated with somewhat less urgency include the adjustment required of both caregivers and the older person, particularly when the specific need is one that is unlikely to change. Almost all caregiving plans, even those aimed at conditions and accompanying needs that are not likely to improve, require flexibility and preparation for change. Because needs can increase or decrease, sometimes rapidly, it is wise to examine alternatives and take the time to evaluate the specific plan that has been put into place. The relative degree of satisfaction and acceptability for both the caregiver and recipient with any plan is not always apparent early in the specific situation.

Thus, family members and friends should follow some general guidelines before making choices and decisions about the older person's care. In providing emotional, social, physical, and financial support, remember the basic premise, "different strokes for different folks."

In most cases, an ongoing social interaction exists between older people and their friends, family members, and new acquaintances. This includes people they have met while participating in activities at the senior center or church, and while doing volunteer work in which other older people may have participated. These social networks provide an essential function by keeping older individuals in the larger social. They also often provide help by providing transportation and companionship for social, business, and health-related activities. Just by keeping in touch and being on hand, family members and friends play an important role.

However, some older individuals have more serious needs. Initially out of the ordinary, these needs may well become permanent and require constant attention. Such needs should be considered systematically, with careful attention to the issues and problems already discussed. Depending on the situation, the solution to these needs may be arrived at mutually, with the older person entering into the discussion with the caregiver or the person arranging for the care. If the older person is unable to participate, the responsible person may be required to make what is often a relatively fast decision. It is, of course, extremely important that the older person be involved as much as possible. Not only will this the resolution more workable, but it will take into account the growing ethical concern with the rights of patients in general and older patients in particular. A large body of literature now focuses on the issue of patient rights and self-direction. Most conclude that, wherever possible, the individual should have the greatest degree of freedom and self-direction. The problem usually arises in defining the term "wherever possible" and in dealing with situations in which serious differences arise between the desires of the individual and the feelings of the caregiver, particularly if the caregiver believes that the individual's welfare is at risk.

A series of steps can assist in the preparation of an initial plan, as well as in monitoring and adapting the plan by evaluating changes in the individual's situation. Appropriate planning helps both the older individual and the caregivers, whether the help is sporadic, temporary, or permanent. Because an individual's situation changes over time, the guidelines given below should be applied with all concerned individuals in mind, with a knowledge of the availability of resources, and with a careful assessment of whether the impact of the help on all participants can be tolerated.

The Role of the Support Network

As in most situations, it is not easy to clearly define a need and then identify the appropriate resource to meet it. The extreme situations — critical and extensive care or little or no need — are not so difficult to resolve, as the feasible options are few and self-evident. In these cases, the problems are limited to obtaining the required resources. Most situations, however, fall somewhere in the middle. The older person is required to help with the identification of the need and to cooperate with the decision maker. For example, does one party or both feel help should and can come from friends and family members, organized services, or both. Of course, joint decision making is impossible if the older person is too impaired to consider with members of the informal network the best solution to the needs that have arisen. More than any other sources, friends and family members are in the position to discern the existence of need and assess its nature. For example, if an older individual is not eating or bathing properly, this often first becomes apparent to those familiar with the individual. Informal networks are also a resource with which another member of the household—a spouse, friend, or sibling living in the same setting—may turn to share concerns. This applies to a caregiving spouse, who is becoming exhausted yet still feels guilty about not adequately meeting the partner's needs.

Once the need is identified, whether physical or mental (such as increasing depression or confusion), the depth of the need must be evaluated. This analysis should include some projection about the length of time help will be needed. Is the help to be permanent or temporary? Is some assistance required or is total take-over of most areas of functioning necessary? Without such a "diagnosis," energy and resources will be wasted and the result will be general frustration. Reaching an accurate assessment may involve collecting additional information. If an older person appears depressed and withdrawn, one needs to determine if this is a natural reaction to a loss or other occurrence. Some extra attention, such as outings of various kinds and visits, may lead to an improvement. This type of information assists in determining exactly what an individual needs and whether this situation requires professional attention or increased immediate social interaction with those closest to the individual. Whatever the process, which will vary from situation to situation, a working understanding of a person's needs is the strongest basis for the next step in the process of offering help.

Identifying the Appropriate Resources

Based on an appropriate assessment (even if only a working "diagnosis") of need, friends and family members are in the best position to determine what resources are necessary to meet that need. This will depend on the kind of person the older individual is, the nature of the informal social support network, and how both can work together. In addition, family members and friends will be able to appraise the existing resources in the home of the older individual. Outsiders would require more time to complete such an evaluation. One must also consider what resources are available in the community of the older person and how to gain access to them. Almost all communities have listings of directories from a referral system that has been established by Areas on Aging Agencies supported by Older Americans Act funds. This resource can provide information on community resources and how to reach these resources.

A second resource, probably equally important, is the medical caregiver, the physician or clinic where the older person receives general health care. If the emergency or sudden need is a health situation, the medical resource will have to be involved. The physician, nurse, and clinic staff will be able to assist in the identification of the individual's needs, as well as the extent, length, and intensity of the treatment.

These guidelines for determining and providing care may appear to involve many participants and much effort. However, note that each member of the team will become involved in different degrees and the processes of evaluation and decision making will require different degrees of effort depending on the situation.

Stresses on Caregivers and Care Receivers

The anticipated and unanticipated problems, discomforts, and disturbances that are an inevitable part of all human relationships, become heightened when care is given or received because of some dysfunction or crisis. At this point in the plan, awareness and knowledge of these issues can be a deciding factor in meeting the individual's needs. Individuals in need may not want the services at all or not in the way the givers feel they should be provided. Often the older individual wants more help than is needed or available. Either party may choose to continue the care beyond the point needed. Caregivers sometimes treat older people as if they were less capable than they are. This may be the result of concern, an overestimation of the risk involved, or a lack of continuous oversight that would highlight changes in the situation. By increasing stress and tension, all of these situations can make a care plan unworkable. These situations are fairly normal and can be worked through. Sometimes, however, less emotionally involved outside sources can better deal with these situations and reestablish the working relationships needed by older individuals.

At other times, the required amount and type of care is too arduous and burdensome for friends and family members to handle. This causes great physical and emotional stress for the caregiver, as well as the care receiver. The individual requiring care may feel guilt or resentment, while the caregiver is simply exhausted. Even if the caregiver does not resent the time required, his or her own live may begin to suffer from a lack of attention. Such situations require reevaluation, with the possibility of supplementing the caregiver's efforts or replacing them entirely. The care may even become inappropriate because of the demands made on the caregiver. Consultation with the medical care source and/or the appropriate national and community agencies may prove helpful in these circumstances. Some community sources not only offer such assistance, but also have programs developed just to give respite time to caregivers.

In other situations, the caregiver may determine that the older person can no longer be cared for in the home. Deciding when to institutionalize an individual in a nursing home or other establishment is difficult. If the older person is alert and aware of the decision, it becomes an even more painful step to take. Surveys show that the two greatest fears among older people are becoming demented and going into a nursing home. These two fears, of course, are highly correlated, but they do illustrate the understandable apprehension of older people. It would be hard to find an older person who would welcome placement in a nursing home or see it as anything but the last option. Although there are ways of working through such situations, they are not easy. Individuals who have no close network of family and friends often accept this decision with greater equanimity. There are, in fact, individuals who, once placed in an adequate facility, find the setting less distasteful than they had anticipated.

These potential types and sources of stress summarize the various situations that develop when family members and friends step in to help an older person. They remind us that, despite the best intentions and a strong informal support network, caregiving includes much discomfort, even when the bonds between older people and their supporters are strong and enduring. These relationships remain important and the positive effects are far more crucial than the disruption that some situations may create. Times of dysfunction, disagreement, or exhaustion during caregiving can be worked out; the positive effects can be retained even if the outcome is cessation of the support at home. Even when the older individual is in an institution or a new setting, continuation of the informal support network is critical.

Preventive Services and the Role of Close Relationships

Another important area associated with caregiving by a close circle of friends and family members is the consideration of preventive services. At first, the idea of prevention among older individuals may seem to be an oxymoron. We know that more than 80 percent of people 65 and older have at least one chronic disease that will always be with them and that the majority of this group actually has two or more such diseases. We also know that aging is associated with less vigor, with changes in organs and systems, and with a variety of other unwanted problems. If we think of prevention as a single kind of action, one designed to prevent or delay diseases and conditions from occurring for as long as possible, then it may be inappropriate in the discussion of growing older. However, epidemiologists identify several types of prevention other than the total avoidance of disease, which is referred to as *primary prevention*.

These other types, which are extremely important, offer an appropriate goal for older individuals: to remain as independent as possible for as long as possible and to experience an acceptable level of quality of life. This implies that pain and undesired effects of existing diseases can be avoided and/or controlled. Such prevention also includes early diagnosis and treatment. This goal of all screening, which increases the possibility for control and avoidance of serious secondary illnesses, is known as *secondary prevention*. A further step on the prevention ladder, *tertiary prevention*, includes rehabilitation for the aftermath of such occurrences as stroke and fractures, particularly fractures of the hip. Secondary and tertiary prevention can be effective in the prevention of disability, that is, the loss of function because of existing diseases.

The network of close friends and family members are in the best position to carry out the activities that fall into the categories of secondary and tertiary prevention. This is illustrated by the fact that older men who are married have a longer life expectancy. Although many factors contribute to these statistic, some of the hypotheses are that married men are more likely to receive better nutrition, are helped to better compliance with medication and other prescribed regimens, and seek and receive medical care on a regular basis. There are also psychological benefits from living in a relationship with a spouse. Isolation is avoided and social interaction is increased, creating a more satisfying life style. The presence of a spouse has been demonstrated to have an effect on the course of a disease and on other attitudes leading to behaviors associated with better physical condition in general.

Another benefit of continuing interactions with a close social network is that this group is more likely to note early symptoms, changes in behavior, and other signs that "something is wrong." Prompt attention to acute illness, deteriorating conditions, or new diseases can make a difference in the course of the disease or condition and shorten the recovery time. Prompt and good care can limit the effects of a condition or disease and possibly limit permanent impairment or disability. Older people, who have fewer reserves, can be helped to avoid an aftermath that involves loss of function and disability or to achieve a recovery to a previous state of function.

Summary

The close relationships with family members and friends that individuals develop throughout their lives have different meanings and impacts at different stages of life. Such relationships, which are critical through early childhood, remain extremely important into adulthood, even if their nature and function changes. For older individuals, who experience many kinds of changes, this social support network serves as a bolstering and sustaining group. If necessary for meeting the health and social needs of older people, this network can be supplemented or replaced by organized services within most communities. But whether supplemented or not, this network offers social as well as other essential services to older people. The individuals who make up this informal network can delivery services directly in the individual's home or plan and supervise outside help. They offer encouragement, contact with the world, and caring and love, all of which improve one's quality of life. In addition, such support has been associated with a better course of treatment for diseases that occur, increased morale, and behaviors that seem to have a positive influence on one's later years.

These situations create problems and stress for both the helping network and the person receiving the help. Differences of opinion on what is needed, how much support is desirable, and how much independence anyone can be allowed are a few of the areas in which disagreement can arise. The ethical issues of self-determination and autonomy remain difficult to solve in many cases. Caregivers may become exhausted and experience psychological problems as a result of the issues involved in giving care, including neglect of a caregiver's own health and family. At the same time, the older individual may have difficulty accepting such support, particularly if the caregiver is a child who was once dependent on the older person. Too many ongoing demands or the reverse, refusals of care, are often the outcome of this dilemma. Although these stresses can sometimes be managed by caregiver and care receiver through recognition and discussion, these situations sometimes benefit from readily available expertise.

Another important role for close friends and families is secondary and tertiary preventive medicine. Although disease prevention may be impossible in an older population, its members show promising potential for programs designed to avoid complications, minimize pain and suffering, and improve the prospects for rehabilitation. Thus, secondary and tertiary prevention is aimed at preventing a disability that will rob the older individual of whatever independence is possible. Individuals in close contact with the older person are best able to observe changes in existing conditions, the appearance of new conditions, and increasing pain and immobility. Attention to such situations increases the potential for improvement, for the relief of pain, and for a decrease of sensory loss.

A final role for friends and family members is to provide continuing contact with the world and ongoing support for older individuals who require institutionalization. Evidence shows that older persons adapt better to the widely feared and almost never voluntarily chosen option of removal to a nursing home or other facility with the help of friends and family members. Continuing contacts with important figures, help with adaptation, and an indirect but strong monitoring of the quality of care are essential for individuals who will be spending their remaining years in an institution.

There are occasional individuals who manage a Thoreau-like existence. But even Thoreau came to Walden with a network of individuals important to him, and he left Walden to return to a "social" life involving others. Even individuals who age gracefully (yes, it is possible) are more vulnerable than when they were younger for a variety of reasons. The social support web provided by long-standing friends and family members who care and love, as well as that of new friends, is essential to older people and probably constitutes the most important aspect of their lives.

For Further Information

This book is intended to serve as a practical overview of aging today. It encompasses the medical, psychological, legal, financial, residential, ethical, and social aspects of aging for those who are part of, or soon will be part of, a unique demographical and social phenomenon. The world has never experienced so rapid a rate of growth in the oldest segment of its population. This growth is occurring at a time of great technological, social, and economic transition. Everywhere, institutions thought immutable are being forced to undergo rapid change.

Consequently, this book cannot be expected to serve as the last word on the subject, nor can it completely cover everything to the depth that the reader might require. Our goal is to provide you with a good foundation on which to base your personal decisions. Of course, these decisions should be made in consultation with the professional help you already have—your doctor, lawyer, and religious counselor. The list below should allow you to explore the areas about which you seek further knowledge. We have restricted the list to readily accessible material. It is of several types: books available in your local bookstore or library; pamphlets or brochures that are obtainable at little or no cost; and material available through the Internet.

If you have no experience using the Internet, now is a good time to start. Over the past few years, the Internet has matured from a little-known network useful for academics and scientists to a vast, broad-based, user-friendly technology with something to offer everyone—including you. If you do not own a computer, a relative or friend who does might be happy to show you how it works. Alternatively, there is the library. The American Library Association reports that in 1997 60 percent of the nation's public library systems offered Internet access — more than twice as many as in 1996. A few minutes of instruction is all you will need to start using this technology. Although the Internet may be new, it still exposes you to the major problems of acquiring information you have always faced: distinguishing the worthwhile from the worthless and finding the time to read and to integrate what you have read. Just as with other media — television, radio, books — there is a lot of inaccurate and misleading "information" on the Internet. Unless you are researching an area with which you are knowledgeable, restrict your initial searches to sites run by organizations that have proved reliable elsewhere.

Preparing for Healthful Aging

As the contributors have made clear, the best prescription for a more healthful old age is to adopt a good diet that is high in nutrients and low in artery-clogging fats, make exercise part of your lifestyle, be moderate in your exposure to alcohol and sunshine, and do not smoke.

Katherine A. Albert. *Get a Good Night's Sleep.* New York: Simon and Schuster, 1996.

> A small but thorough guide to improving sleep patterns written by the director of the sleep laboratory at the NYU–Cornell Medical Center in New York City.

Melanie Barnard, Brooke Dojney, and C. Wayne Callaway. *The AMA Family Health Cookbook.* New York: Pocket Books, 1997.

> Even more than the healthful recipes, the book is useful for its 50-page overview on nutrition and the additional hints and tips for a good diet throughout the book.

Robert N. Butler and Myrna I. Lewis. *Love and Sex after 60.* New York: G.K. Hall, 1996.

> An informative look at sexuality in later years written by a Pultizer-prize winning geriatrician and his wife. It is a clearly written and authoritative book that debunks many myths while offering much advice and reassurance.

Walter H. Ettinger, Jr., Brenda S. Mitchell, and Steven S. Blair. *Fitness after 50: It's Never Too Late to Start!* Tucson, AZ: Fisher Books, 1996.

A well-written, clearly illustrated book to get you into the best condition since your teens (or maybe even better condition).

John W. Rowe and Robert L. Kahn. *Successful Aging.* New York: Pantheon, 1998.

This book, written by a physician who is president of Mount Sinai Medical Center in New York City and a professor emeritus of psychology and public health at the University of Michigan, is the result of research sponsored by the MacArthur Foundation among thousands of older Americans and Swedish twins. It carefully delineates the data that disprove a number of widespread myths about aging.

U.S. Pharmacopeia. *The USP Guide to Vitamins & Minerals.* New York: Avon Books, 1996.

A thorough, easy-to-read guide to dietary supplements for the general public that includes recommended allowances for different age groups, as well as appropriate warnings about possible side effects.

When Illness Strikes

Sooner or later, the healthiest of us falls victim to one or another illness. When that happens, we need to learn about our illnesses so that we can communicate with our doctors and take an active, informed role in selecting a course of treatment, following the program, and evaluating its effects. Given the extreme changes in the sociology of medicine in recent years (particularly the disturbance of the traditional physician–patient relationship by insurance companies and government), it is more important than ever that we be knowledgeable patients.

American Diabetes Association. *American Diabetes Association Complete Guide to Diabetes: The Ultimate Home Diabetes Reference.* Alexandria, VA: American Diabetes Association, 1996.

Causes and types of diabetes, treatment, nutrition, exercise, sex, possible complications—every aspect of the illness and its consequences can be found in this expertly written book.

Joanne Ardolf Decker. *Making the Moments Count: Leisure Activity for Caregiving Relationships.* Baltimore: Johns Hopkins Univ. Press, 1997.

A guide for caregivers to provide activities that engage the mind and spirit of the ill, aging, or even terminally ill patient. In addition to a number of basic examples of activities, guidelines are provided to adapt activities to differing abilities and interests.

Donald F. Klein and Paul H. Wender. *Understanding Depression: A Complete Guide to Its Diagnosis and Treatment.* New York: Oxford Univ. Press, 1993.

A terse approach to the biological basis of depression. The physician authors, widely known in their field, make a strong case for antidepressive medication as the first line of treatment for clinical depression.

Nancy L. Mace and Peter V. Rabins. *The 36-Hour Day: A Family Guide to Caring for Persons with Alzheimer's Disease, Related Dementing Illnesses, and Memory Loss in Later Life.* Baltimore: Johns Hopkins Univ. Press, 1994.

An essential guide for anyone who is caring for an Alzheimer's sufferer.

Michael D. McGoon. *The Mayo Clinic Heart Book.* New York: William Morrow, 1993.

Edited by the director of the Pulmonary Hypertension Clinic of the Mayo Clinic, with contributions from other Mayo staff, the book contains nearly everything the average person needs to know about the human heart. Risk factors, diagnoses, treatments, diet, and a host of other topics are clearly discussed and amply illustrated.

Medical Economics. *The PDR Pocket Guide to Prescription Drugs.* New York: Pocket Books, 1997.

Drawn from the standard medical reference book, *The Physician's Desk Reference*, but rewritten for the nonprofessional reader, this thick paperback provides information (such as common dosages, family of drug, possible side effects, and common interactions) on more than 1000 prescription medications.

William Styron. *Darkness Visible.* New York: Random House, 1990.

This small book is a memoir of a gifted writer's personal struggle with depression. No book more clearly portrays the inner turmoil of the afflicted.

U.S. Pharmacopeia. *The USP Guide to Medicines.* New York: Avon Books, 1996.

Similar to the *PDR Guide* above, this book covers some 2600 medications. For most purposes, the difference in the books is one of style.

Patrick C. Walsh and Janet Farrar Worthington. *The Prostate: A Guide for Men and the Women Who Love Them.* Baltimore: Johns Hopkins Univ. Press, 1995.

A thorough but easy-to-read book about the prostate, with charts and tables that explains problems and treatment options. The books primary author is a Johns Hopkins surgeon who developed a new and now widely used technique in prostate surgery.

Barry L. Zaret, Peter Jatlow, and Lee D. Katz, eds. *The Patient's Guide to Medical Tests.* Boston: Houghton Mifflin, 1997.

The text, written by three physicians, explains hundreds of the most frequently performed medical tests in clear text aided by a generous number of simple illustrations.

A Place to Live

One of the foundations of our everyday lives is where we live — the location and type of home we have. Since most of us will grow old in an existing home, making modifications that better accommodate aging — making it safer and easier to maintain — makes sense. Getting as many suggestions and examples as possible is a good start. It is also a good idea to learn about the alternatives to aging in place.

American Occupational Therapy Foundation. *Changing Needs, Changing Homes: Adapting Your Home to Fit You.* 18 min. Bethesda, MD: American Occupational Therapy Foundation, 1996. Videocassette.

The video focuses on the process of making home modifications to fit real needs using the cases of six older people.

Rosemary Bakker. *Elder Design: Designing and Furnishing a Home for Your Later Years.* New York: Penguin, 1997.

A well-organized guide to adapting a home to make it safer and easier to maintain as one ages. It covers every room in the house and the entrances and grounds in a thorough fashion with checklists, dozens of ideas, and a resource guide to useful products.

Linda D. Cirano. *On Your Own Terms: The Senior's Guide to an Independent Life.* New York: G.K. Hall, 1996.

> A guide to living on one's own in the later years. It is particularly useful for its suggestions on room design and affordable products.

Hometime. *Building and Remodeling for Accessibility.* 35 min. Chaska, MN: Hometime, 1993. Videocassette.

> A do-it-yourself approach to modifying home entrances, bathrooms, and kitchens for accessibility.

ITT/Hartford and Modern Talking Picture Services. *For the Rest of Your Life: The Hartford House.* 24 min. Southington, CT: ITT/Hartford.

> The Hartford House was designed and built by the ITT/Hartford Insurance Group as a demonstration home to encourage public awareness of the benefits of home modification for the aging. The video is a tour and demonstration of the house's features.

Paying for It All

Next to watching your health, watching your finances is key to enjoying your later years. First learn the basics, then frequently review your anticipated needs, your plans, and potential new opportunities.

Kenneth M. Morris and Alan M. Siegal. *The Wall Street Journal Guide to Understanding Money & Investing.* New York: Simon & Schuster, 1994.

> With an easy-to-follow illustrated approach, this small book manages to cover the history of money, stocks, bonds, mutual funds, and options. A good book for the beginner.

National Association of Insurance Commissioners. *A Shopper's Guide to Long-Term Care Insurance.* Kansas City, MO: NAIC, 1996. Available at: *http://www.ltcfs.com/shoppers.html*

> A clear guide to the selection of an important, but to many, a difficult insurance purchase. It was written as a booklet under the auspices of the NAIC, the nation's oldest association of state government officials, the chief insurance regulators of every state.

Suze Orman. *The 9 Steps to Financial Freedom.* New York: Crown Publishers, 1997.

A guide by a popular financial commentator with more than 20 years of retirement planning experience.

Jane Bryant Quinn. *Making the Most of Your Money.* New York: Simon & Schuster, 1997.

An updated version of a best-selling primer on investment that is well organized and user friendly.

Mary Rowland. *A Commonsense Guide to Mutual Funds.* Princeton, NJ: Bloomberg Press, 1996.

A good overview of mutual funds—the types, how they work, various risks, helpful hints for investment, and more.

C. Frederic Wiegold, ed. *The Wall Street Journal Lifetime Guide to Money: Everything You Need to Know about Managing Your Finances—For Every Stage of Life.* New York: Hyperion, 1997.

A good, easy-to-follow guide in a field that has many, but distinguished by adapting each suggestion to three different age groups: those in their 20s and 30s, those in their 40s and 50s, and those who are older. Information abounds on investing, insurance purchasing, taxes, scams, debt management, and retirement planning.

Making Tough Decisions

Medical technology has developed the means to sustain bodily functions in ways that were inconceivable two generations ago. A host of institutional and legal changes (e.g., hospice and living wills) have been made in response. Where once patient and family were powerless to affect the end-of-life process, there are now choices. The line between life and death, once so clear, sometimes becomes fuzzy. Often there are no clear-cut decisions that present themselves. The law outlines some boundaries, but much is left to one's own understanding and preference. Whether in making plans for ourselves, helping family members to make their own decisions, carrying out a surrogate's duties, or trying to come to terms with a loved one's personal decision, some knowledge of the technology and the law is useful. There is also a significant body of literature in the field of bioethics requiring no specialized knowledge that might be of assistance.

Choice In Dying, Inc. *Artificial Nutrition and Hydration and End-of-Life Decisionmaking.* New York: Choice In Dying, Inc.

> Among the most generally misunderstood aspects of end-of-life decisionmaking are questions surrounding hydration and nutrition. This booklet lays out in a clear way for the general public the medical facts and ethical considerations.

Choice In Dying, Inc. *Dying at Home.* New York: Choice In Dying, Inc.

> A booklet that discusses the medical, legal, and psychological questions that a family needs to examine when a terminally ill member wishes to die at home.

Karolinska Institutet. *Ethics in Biomedicine.* Stockholm, 1998. A web metasite. Available at: *http://www.mic.ki.se/Diseases/k1.316.html*

> The Karolinska Institutet is Sweden's prestigious medical school and research center that is also responsible for selecting the winners of the Nobel Prize in Medicine or Physiology. Of interest to you, if you are interested in pursuing some more reading in ethics, the Institutet has prepared (in English) an extensive metasite, the Internet's equivalent of a bibliography, of pointers to notable websites all over the world that deal with various issues of bioethics.

National Council on the Aging. *How to Get the Most from a Family Meeting.* 1997. Factsheet. Available at: *www.ncoa.org/caregiving/familymeeting.htm*

> A loved one's mental or physical condition sometimes requires a meeting to plan the family's response. This brief guide can help ensure that such a meeting is productive.

National Council on the Aging. *Organizing Paperwork.* 1997. Factsheet. Available at: *www.ncoa.org/caregiving/paperwork.htm*

> This contains a very convenient checklist for all the important documents to which caregivers or next of kin might need access.

National Public Radio. *The End of Life: Exploring Death in America*, occasional series on *All Things Considered.* 1997– . Available at: *http://www.npr.org/programs/death*

> A series of programs each dealing with a particular aspect of death, including grief and bereavement, palliative

medicine, the rule of double effect, funeral homes, and doctors and death. The website includes both transcripts and audio versions of the individual shows, an extensive bibliography, and some resources.

David C. Thomasma and Thomasine Kushner, eds. *Birth to Death: Science and Bioethics.* Cambridge: Cambridge Univ. Press, 1996.

Each subject area (for example, the extension of life, care for the dying, or physician-assisted suicide) is presented from several perspectives: first, a contributor presents an overview from a scientific or historical viewpoint of the available technology and what it can achieve, and then other contributors discuss the ethical implications that arise as a result.

Organizations

In the future it is inevitable that personal situations, government policy and law, medical understanding and treatment, the economy, and social conditions will change, and you will need to gather new information and make new plans for your later years. As we have suggested elsewhere, it is a good idea to start with the professionals whom you already know — your doctor, lawyer, and religious counselor. But beyond them, additional help is available. The general organizations listed below have consistently been found to be reliable sources of help to the public on aging-related information, programs, and referrals. They can provide information, publications, and lists of resources, and can lead you to additional organizations that deal with specialized problems and needs.

Alzheimer's Association, 919 N. Michigan Avenue, Suite 1000, Chicago, IL 60611-1676 **ph:** (800) 272-3900 or (312) 335-8700/9602 **fax:** (312) 335-1110 **web:** *http://www.alz.org*

> A not-for-profit organization with more than 200 chapters and 1800 support groups throughout the United States. It maintains a 24-hour information and referral line and produces brochures, a newsletter, and books on the disease, research, and ways of coping.

Alzheimer's Disease Education and Referral Center, National Institute on Aging, P.O. Box 8250, Silver Spring, MD 20907-8250 **ph:** (800) 438-4380 or (301) 495-3311 **fax:** (301) 495-3334 **web:** *http://www.alzheimers.org* **e-mail:** *adear@alzheimers.org*

An arm of the NIH's National Institute on Aging, this governmental center distributes information on the disease and current research, and provides a referral service for treatment centers and support groups for both both patients and family caregivers.

American Association of Retired Persons (AARP), 601 E Street NW, Washington, DC 20049   **ph:** (800) 424-3410 or (202) 434-2230   **web:** *http://www.aarp.org*   **e-mail:** *member@aarp.org*

The largest not-for-profit organization devoted to the issues of aging, the AARP combines education programs, advocacy, member benefits, and community services on a wide spectrum of aging-related matters, such as insurance, nursing homes, managed care, exercise and diet, and caregiving. It produces useful reports and brochures and a monthly members' magazine, *Modern Maturity.*

American Heart Association, National Center, 7272 Greenville Avenue, Dallas, TX 75231   **ph:** (800) AHA-USA1
web: *http://www.americanheart.org*

The organization offers a great deal of information on maintaining the heart, good nutrition, exercise, and quitting smoking. Much of it is available as free brochures or on the website.

American Medical Association, 515 North State Street, Chicago, IL 60610   **ph:** (312) 464-5000   **web:** *http://www.ama-assn.org*

The nation's largest professional group for physicians, the AMA provides a great deal of useful information for the consumer on general health and fitness. The website includes a physician finder, an interactive personal physical training planner, an atlas of the human body with descriptions of functions, nutritional information, and a host of healthful recipes.

Asociacion Nacional por Personas Mayores, National Association for Hispanic Elderly, 3325 Wilshire Boulevard, Suite 800, Los Angeles, CA 90010-1724   **ph:** (213) 487-1922 or (800) 953-8553 (in CA only)   **fax:** (213) 385-8553

A national, not-for-profit organization focusing on the needs of aging Hispanics. The group offers help with obtaining employment, assistance in filing income tax and Social Security forms, and a number of classes in such subjects as English as a second language, nutrition, and consumer education. ANPPM produces bilingual brochures on a variety of topics and a quarterly newletter. A telephone help line with bilingual operators provides referrals to appropriate agencies and organizations.

Children of Aging Parents, 1609 Woodbourne Road, Suite 302-A, Levittown, PA 19057-1511   **ph:** (800) 227-7294 or (215) 945-6900   **fax:** (215) 945-8720

> A not-for-profit organization that provides referrals to a wide variety of services including nursing homes, elder law attorneys, daycare centers, respite centers, retirement communities, and government organizations.

Elderhostel, 75 Federal Street, Boston, MA 02110-1941,   **ph:** (617) 426-8056   **web:** *http://www.elderhostel.org*

> A not-for-profit organization offering educational vacation trips all over the world for adults aged 55 and older. The reasonably priced programs, which normally last 5 to 7 days, are all-inclusive, providing full room and board, 3 to 4 hours of classes daily, field trips, and extracurricular activities.

Health Care Financing Administration, 200 Independence Avenue SW, Room 403-B, Washington, DC 20201   **ph:** (202) 690-6145   **fax:** (202) 690-7159   **web:** *http://www.hcfa.gov*   **e-mail:** *question@hcfa.gov*

> This government body is responsible for the management of Medicare and Medicaid. It publishes a broad range of materials for the consumer that describe the benefits and rules for eligibility of these two programs.

Healthfinder   **web:** *http://www.healthfinder.gov*

> This government website is one of the best places to start in researching any aspect of health, whether it be nutrition, disease, treatments, benefits, or new findings.

The National Council on the Aging, Inc., 409 3rd Street, SW, Suite 200, Washington, DC 20024   **ph:** (202) 479-6653 or (202) 479-6654   **fax:** (202) 479-0735   **web:** *http://www.ncoa.org*

> A not-for-profit organization that serves as both an information gathering point and advocate for the aged. While directed to addressing the professional community, it does have a few good resources for the general public.

National Hospice Organization (NHO), 1901 North Moore Street, Suite 901, Arlington, VA 22209   **ph:** (800) 658-8898 or (703) 243-5900   **fax:** (703) 525-5762   **web:** *http://www.nho.org*

This organization is devoted to promoting the concept of hospice. It provides information about hospice services, publishes an annual directory of hospices and offers a hospice finder service for terminally ill patients and their families.

National Institute on Aging Information Center, National Institute on Aging, PO Box 8057, Gaithersburg, MD 20898-8057 **ph:** (800) 222-2225 or (301) 496-1752 **fax:** (301) 589-3014 **web:** *http://www.nih.gov/nia* **e-mail:** *niainfo@access.digex.net*

Part of the National Institutes of Health, the NIA conducts and supports research in a variety of disciplines that relate to the aging process. The Institute also produces some material for the general public, including the Age Page, a series of brief handouts on several aspects of aging, most but not all relating to physical or medical conditions.

Social Security Administration, W. High Rise Bldg., 6401 Security Boulevard, Room 4200, Baltimore, MD 21235 **ph:** (800) 772-1213 or (410) 965-1720 **web:** *http://www.ssa.gov*

There is a lot to know about Social Security and the Administration makes it all available to you in many convenient forms, from handouts to handbooks.

U.S. Administration on Aging, U.S. Department of Health and, Human Services, 330 Independence Avenue, S.W., Washington, DC 20201, **ph:** (202) 619 0724 **fax:** (202) 260-1012 **web:** *http://www.aoa.dhhs.gov* **e-mail:** *aoa_esec@ban-gate.aoa.dhhs.gov*

This government body works with state and area agencies on aging and with service providers to develop and coordinate community services to help older people achieve personal independence. It maintains the Eldercare Locator, a toll-free national directory assistance-service administered by the National Association of Area Agencies on Aging and the National Association of State Units on Aging, designed to help older persons and caregivers locate support and resources.

Index